C000295483

The Costumes of Burlesque

The Costumes of Burlesque: 1866–2018 is the first volume to inclusively document burlesque costume from its birth in the 1860s through the global burlesque movement in 2018. This lushly illustrated book presents the history and development of this American art form by documenting the origins, influencers, and genuine articles that created its aesthetic. Showcases of legendary performers, including Lydia Thompson, Gypsy Rose Lee, Sally Rand, Bettie Page, Kitten Natividad, and Dita Von Teese and many more, demonstrate costume styles through the years.

This guide gives readers a clear view of how burlesque costume looked and why, and teaches collectors, burlesque performers, and fans alike to recognize vintage pieces for what they are and to build their own costumes with inspiration from the originals. With detailed costume documentation, over 400 images, and interviews with prominent costume designers such as Catherine D'Lish and Garo Sparo, *The Costumes of Burlesque* brings 150 years of burlesque history to life.

Coleen Scott is a costume designer with an MFA in Costume Design from Boston University, where she received the Kahn Award upon graduation. She has worked for nearly 20 years in theater, opera, film, and television including projects with designers Stephanie Maslansky, Tina Nigro and Academy Award winner Ann Roth. Coleen taught Costume Production and Makeup for Stage and Studio at Saint Ann's School in Brooklyn, New York, from 2005 to 2018. She works with her creative partner, photographer Ben Trivett, doing makeup and styling for fine art portrait photography and accepts commissions for lectures, workshops and creative design projects.

The Costumes of Burlesque

1866–2018

Coleen Scott

Routledge
Taylor & Francis Group

NEW YORK AND LONDON

First published 2019
by Routledge
52 Vanderbilt Avenue, New York, NY 10017

and by Routledge
2 Park Square, Milton Park, Abingdon, Oxon, OX14 4RN

Routledge is an imprint of the Taylor & Francis Group, an informa business

© 2019 Taylor & Francis

The right of Coleen Scott to be identified as author of this work has been
asserted by her in accordance with sections 77 and 78 of the Copyright,
Designs and Patents Act 1988.

All rights reserved. No part of this book may be reprinted or reproduced
or utilised in any form or by any electronic, mechanical, or other means, now
known or hereafter invented, including photocopying and recording, or in any
information storage or retrieval system, without permission in writing from
the publishers.

Trademark notice: Product or corporate names may be trademarks or
registered trademarks, and are used only for identification and explanation
without intent to infringe.

Library of Congress Cataloging-in-Publication Data
A catalog record for this title has been requested

ISBN: 978-1-138-74225-3 (hbk)
ISBN: 978-1-138-74226-0 (pbk)
ISBN: 978-1-315-17858-5 (ebk)

Typeset by Alex Lazarou

To my parents and husband for their constant support and love.

To all the burlesque legends, living and gone, who paved the way for this new wave of performers choosing to take their clothes off on stage as a means of artistic self-expression.

CONTENTS

FOREWORD

The Costumes of Burlesque is a lushly illustrated book. The book delves into the rich history of burlesque and the theatrical costuming of stripping. Yes, before the strippers strip they are oftentimes costumed in elaborate gowns, painstakingly sewed in dressing rooms across America. Embroidered, rhinestoned, and feathered the costumes are an important part of our American entertainment culture and Scott starts at the beginning and takes the reader up to the burgeoning neo-burlesque movement.

The costumes and history in the book start with Adah Isaacs Menken and her scandalous "nude" horse ride across the stage. Soon after, Lydia Thompson and her "British Blondes" arrive; a troupe of stocking-clad women who scandalized New York when they first appeared in 1868. Over the decades burlesque—a misconstrued art form—morphed and the costumes grew more elaborate; think of Gypsy Rose Lee, who removed her clothes that were held together with straight pins to Blaze Starr who spent six months sewing crystals onto a dress that in the end was so heavy, she could barely walk in it. "I couldn't wait to get it off," she told me.

Burlesque and its costumes take their influence, as highlighted by Scott, from Broadway, the Ziegfeld girls, Victorian acrobats, the can-can dancers of the Folies Bergerè and more.

By examining the "obscenity and nudity legislation" that shaped burlesque, the author delves into how burlesque, namely the strippers, shaped much of entertainment and society's precarious relationship with the theatres and clubs that packed them in during burlesque's heyday.

In a rare twist of burlesque histories, *Burlesque Costume History* connects the costumes from the "death of burlesque" in the 1960s, says Scott, through their transitions and rarely explored relationship to the 1970s, 80s and 90s strip club and pornography-dominated decades that gave way to the current, global, neo-burlesque movement and aesthetic.

In her research and photo documentation of modern burlesque costuming, Scott underlines the strippers' power and control in what they present of themselves on stage especially in their choice of costume. She makes a point that it is the performers' self-empowerment and love of the medium that drives them to commit to burlesque—an art form I believe shaped much of American entertainment and remains an important part of our popular culture, though clearly still stigmatized and misunderstood.

Leslie Zemeckis
Bestselling author of *Behind the Burly Q* &
Goddess of Love Incarnate

PROLOGUE

Whenever sex and sexuality are included in the discussion of artistic merit, neutrality is not. A person tends to choose a side when it comes to sexual display, performance, preference, and what should be public or private. **Burlesque** will always be on the "sensuality and nudity are positive stage conventions" side of that argument. Conservative members of society and academia think first of strippers or stripping and its surrounding morality or suspected values before they venture to consider burlesque's historical importance and artistic integrity. Burlesque did not begin as an art form that centered around female flesh. In the 1860s productions called **burlesques** were narrative shows that included humor, parody, and political statements, especially as all-female casts sprung up late in the decade. The costuming of these women-centric casts was always a point of attraction for audiences, because they were scandalously revealing compared to every day female dress. Since the 1890s, the reveal of flesh (or what was assumed to be flesh), be it the abdomen, legs, or the entire body, has been a focus of burlesque performance even before it transitioned into the art of striptease. There are many ways to phrase it, but the art of the **ecdysiast** is the art of clothing removal and the presentation of nudity or the illusion of nudity on stage. It is this stripping that helped shape the obscenity and nudity legislation in our country, and it is this art form that set examples contrary to societal beliefs of how a woman should look and behave. Although it wasn't the only element in a burlesque show, by the 1920s flashing or stripping was the central action of a burlesque performance, and through the twenty-first century it is the stripping (and the teasing) that makes it burlesque.

Women-centric theatrical burlesques transformed, guided by businessmen who were running them, into more sex-centric performances, focused on striptease. Still, throughout the history of burlesque, women traditionally prevented from autonomy outside of the family unit, were making their own money, travelling the globe, and living a seemingly glamorous lifestyle that many everyday women were intrigued by and even envious of despite the negative cultural opinions about burlesque performers that were prevalent. The negative opinion of a woman doing burlesque did not begin with striptease.

Burlesquers like Lydia Thompson were judged as loose women simply for having a career on a stage where social norms were challenged. Even when the speaking voice of the woman onstage disappeared and burlesque became body focused, a woman who performs burlesque, both then and now, embodies a level of confidence not only to put herself on display, but also to understand that she is in control of her presentation. In the sexualized performance of burlesque it is this control that burlesque dancers own—control over their body, control over the audience, and control over career, finances and life—that make burlesque inherently feminist art.

A multitude of performance and dance styles have influenced the look of burlesque costume, but it has its own set of rules making the clothing a most significant part of a successful performance. The intrinsic requirements of burlesque costume make its study imperative from a costume history standpoint. This is an entire category of costume dedicated to easy removal, magical reveals, and, in many cases, ultimate glamor. For over 100 years, highly paid women hired master artisans to create their costumes. Surviving and well-preserved pieces demonstrate the best craftsmanship, decoration, and imaginative assemblage of any theatrical costuming at the time. Extravagant fabrics and trims, generous *embellishment*, and the latest technology exemplify the costume of a feature burlesque performer. Another aspect of burlesque costume, both vintage and modern, is the DIY nature of certain pieces of an ensemble. Dancers then and now regularly make their own pasties and **g-strings**, and add extra enhancement to costumes. The visual history of pieces mended or altered time and time again because the overall value was too high to replace them demonstrates aspects of burlesque costuming that carry through today. The development of signature acts and their costume evolution over time can be another fascinating way to view changing costume trends. The politics of burlesque as a career choice and the combination of extravagant and self-made art-specific costuming make the scholarship of burlesque costume history a study in both women's history and masterful and inventive costuming.

INTRODUCTION

How to Navigate this Book and Research Further

The Costumes of Burlesque documents the origins, influences and genuine articles of burlesque costume between 1866 and 2018. The focus is primarily on the United States, with early additions from the United Kingdom and France. This book visually tells the story of burlesque costume and how it developed, transformed, and reinvented itself over its 150-year history through the inclusion of historic photos of performers in costume, case studies, and photographic documentation of costumes. The content of this book is organized historically, but not always chronologically, from early burlesque through the modern burlesque revival.

Photos are relied upon to give the broadest view of costume variety over this expanse of time. For more detailed information, imagery is further described in captions. Almost every image will lead the viewer on a separate path of study, so it is recommended that one take the time to read captions for any imagery that sparks interest. Case studies appear either as a visual and written showcase of an individual, which could include promotional imagery or portraits, or as an interview. In the first half of the book the reader will find more descriptive and visual case studies as performers are long- deceased. The second half of the book includes interviews with legends and performers alive to tell their personal stories and share photos directly. Close-ups of burlesque costume ensembles collected during travels across the Unites States and England directly document construction, convention, and ornamentation, providing not only an insider's viewing experience, but also one as close to hands-on as possible. The ability to see closures, structure, fabric and embellishment in color and high resolution is of the highest importance when studying historic costume for reasons related to replication and innovation.

For quick reference and further scholarship, the book includes a glossary of key words, endnotes and a bibliography. Key words, which you will see written in **bold text**, are interspersed throughout the chapter. You can find definitions for all key words in the Glossary, though sometimes they will be defined alongside the word within the text or illustrated with a nearby image. Endnotes are identified with a number and are listed at the end of each chapter.

Every topic covered is rich and worthy of individual research. Most are topics of countless books, many of which are included in the Bibliography. Including every detail of history, clothing, performance, and all those who participated in burlesque is impossible in a survey of 150 years, but the goal is to provide an overview that is comprehensive, inclusive, academically stimulating, and costume forward.

INCLUSIVE

American culture has a history of racism and homophobia, and burlesque is not immune to these cultural negatives. The appropriation of cultural dress is used in costume designs throughout burlesque history, also seen in the history of mainstream theater, film, and other popular entertainment. Examples of misappropriation in costume are included in this book to show what was done and should not be repeated. Photographic examples of performers of color who broke through barriers or sometimes even upheld stereotypes in the name of a job in the theater are featured as well. Racism kept headlining performers of color separate from White counter parts, grouping them under the "Exotic" category, which included Asian, Latina, and Black dancers. Very few

Black performers were booked in clubs that had a primarily White audience, therefore venues were segregated. There was burlesque for Black audiences presenting a range of dance styles, many of which were adapted by White dancers in watered-down or racist, over-exaggerated versions. The key point here is that women of color were performing, making a living, and breaking the boundaries of what it meant to be a woman in American society, but they have been swept even further under the cultural rug because of the color of their skin with no regard for their talent or impact on burlesque history. Additionally, through much of this history, gay and trans performers (and those in general society) remained closeted to avoid persecution, yet they, too, were present. A wholehearted attempt has been made to represent the diverse groups of performers on the burlesque stage from its inception, and to call attention to the misnomers and boundaries in place that caused separation and inequality in this industry that permeated American culture.

ACADEMICALLY STIMULATING

Burlesque was a female-centric performance art that dominated popular culture and entertainment for over a century in the United States, and it once again has a massive resurgence that has generated scholarly interest. The academic world has delved into topics related to burlesque such as *Salomania*, and the popularity of the "Streets of Cairo" exhibit at the *Great Columbian Exhibition* and later The World's Fair, but very few scholars have looked directly at burlesque and its significance in America after the 1950s. The first of its kind, this book delves into the costumes and world of burlesque as it transitioned into the go-go and strip club scenes of the 1960s–1990s, leading to the currently thriving global burlesque landscape.

Thanks to Robert C. Allen and Rachel Schteir, early nineteenth and twentieth century burlesque history has gotten some time in the scholarly spotlight. Cultural anthropology scholars like Judith Lynne Hanna have shed light on sensuality in international dance and culture, and have argued in favor of the artistic merit of stripping and its protection under the First Amendment in the 1990s and 2000s. The Smithsonian Museum in Washington DC has begun archiving the collections and costumes of burlesque performers and researchers with its acquisition of Ricki Corvette's scrapbooks and ensembles. The New York Public Library and the Museum of the City of New York have fantastic archives of early twentieth-century burlesque. The Burlesque Hall of Fame Museum in Las Vegas, formerly Exotic World, was started in the 1980s by performer Jennie Lee and then expanded by her friend Dixie Evans. It has since developed into an exceptional resource with a growing collection of costumes and countless of photos of burlesque performers. Perhaps Charles McCaghy has made one of the biggest contributions to the preservation of later burlesque history and the significance of striptease in America. His collection of research and memorabilia from burlesque to clubs is housed in the Jerome and Robert E. Lee Theater Research Institute at The Ohio State University. The Smithsonian, The Burlesque Hall of Fame Museum in Las Vegas, and The McCaghy collection are all open doors to scholars looking to delve further into this rich history whether it is from a cultural, historical, or costume point of view.

With the help of all of these institutions and others, including The Metropolitan Museum, The Museum at F.I.T. and The Victoria and Albert Museum, as well as private collectors like Neil "Nez" Kendall, Miss Vicky Butterfly, and Janelle Smith, this book provides a look at never-before-seen garments, imagery, and information direct from the mouths of the performers who were keeping burlesque alive with the times. The decades after burlesque's last heyday in the 1950s did host a transition in costumes, dance styles, laws and clubs that turned *burlesque* into *stripping*. This book illustrates that even after the art of burlesque was considered dead by the generation who enjoyed its glamour in the 1950s, elements of burlesque remained in the world of entertainment. Burlesque costumes influenced designs in strip clubs, Las Vegas, and on film and television without pause because it had so deeply penetrated American popular culture.

COSTUME FORWARD

Documenting burlesque costumes is the top priority in the design of this book. It is imperative to show the designer, draper, collector, performer and student the broadest variety of design and detailed attention to construction. In some cases, dance, theater, and circus costumes have been studied to demonstrate fabrication that was popular in certain time periods. This book demonstrates as many examples of real costume ensembles as possible with a focus on popular or classic styles, thus providing the reader with an idea of what burlesque *looked like* for each of the periods represented. Burlesque is an art form, and like any of its counterparts there are multitudes of variation. I encourage you to use this book as a springboard and discover them for yourself.

The Costumes of Burlesque will inform and inspire the continued expansion of research on this topic. The exponential growth of the global burlesque community is mirroring demand in the academic world for more information about burlesque costuming and history. International schools of burlesque and BurlyCon, the annual burlesque education conference in Seattle, are creating educational programming centered around learning everything there is to know about burlesque. A multitude of performers are presenting their art on stage and simultaneously participating in graduate and PhD programs of study focused on burlesque; Dr. Lucky PhD, Miss Alyssa Kitt, and Rita N. Wink are just a few. Burlesque costumes are a vehicle for examination of historical and modern construction techniques, design and materials; but their study also highlights a broader range of topics including performance studies, women's studies, and the history of American popular culture.

Figure 1.1 Courier Company. Women Wearing Brief Costumes, Holding Veils, With Feathers in Her Hair, ca. 1899.
(Courier Litho. Company, from the United States Library of Congress. www.loc.gov/item/2014635681/)

CHAPTER 1

THE BIRTH OF BURLESQUE
1866 – 19 TEENS

INTRODUCTION

Burlesque[1] pokes fun at society. It holds a mirror to the ridiculous—be it politics, interpersonal relationships, or passing trends. Much like any other form of theater or performance art, burlesque provides an escape or a catharsis that cannot easily be achieved while one is engaged in the difficulties of everyday reality. The burlesque of the period highlighted in this chapter, 1866 through the 19-teens, was popularized just after the abolition of slavery in the United States.[2] Societally, we encountered a complete divide in the belief systems of US citizens, while simultaneously experiencing hasty growth of urban industrial and cultural centers where those seeking more opportunity flocked.

It was these growing cities that clamored for affordable pastimes accessible to their new residents. Crowded tenement apartments were not a retreat after long days in hot workrooms. The wealthy attended "refined" performance art in the form of theater, opera, and ballet, but the swiftly expanding middle class demanded distraction from horrific working and living conditions, and as combatant to boredom. The occasional traveling circus was such a distraction, but because it was not a permanent respite, other diversions developed. The **museum**, **vaudeville**, and burlesque grew up together, with one proceeding the other. They took inspiration from the **high-brow** art forms, and added their own structure and styles. After the turn of the twentieth century, early film was viewed at **nickelodeons**, and the themes there ranged from the respectable to the lascivious.

The costumes of burlesque borrowed from all popular entertainment of the time. Opera, theater, and dance were influenced by favorite stories, influential people, and newly discovered cultures. Burlesque did not exist as its own original art form at this time—it was simply known that when one attended a burlesque, one witnessed some combination of storytelling, music, dancing, and costumes that supported the production. Before the birth of this art form, the mishmash of theater for the people in the United States created an environment and audience ready to accept burlesque on its own, and a generous population opposed to it.

Before burlesque, Adah Isaacs Menken caused a stir on the **legitimate theater** stage by appearing "nude" tied to a galloping horse in the play *Mazeppa*.[3] She was not nude, in fact, but was wearing a nude **bodysuit** that was convincing enough in her fast dash. Previous to her portrayal, a rubber dummy would be tied to a horse and led across the stage. Unafraid to play a male role, Menken demonstrated her beliefs that continually defied conventional gender roles. She was very aware of her public image, and cunningly promoted herself with the press. She did not declare her mixed Creole race publicly because at the time it would not have been accepted positively, so she made up different stories about her origin, making her seem mysterious and protecting her from racial attack. In addition to her marketing prowess, Menken was a prolific poet and writer, with over one hundred poems and numerous articles published. She wrote on literature and, more

1

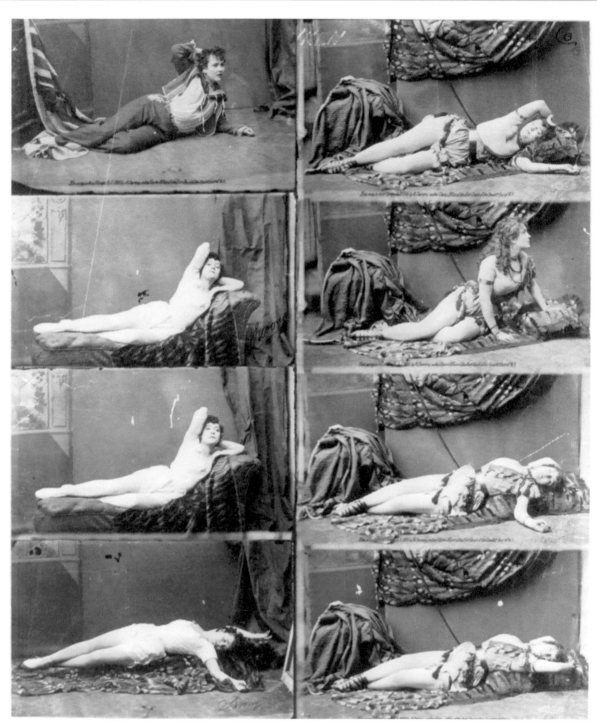

Figure 1.2 Adah Isaacs Menken poses provocatively on a chaise lounge in several states of dress. Menken would use photography for self-promotion in a very modern way—choosing photos expressing whatever personality she wanted to convey to the public at the time as exemplified by this group of 1866 images by N. Sarony. (Retrieved from the Library of Congress, www.loc.gov/item/2005683729/)

Figure 1.3 A ballerina in a white costume with flowers in a dance pose, 1890.
(Copyright: 1890 by the Calvert Litho. Co., Detroit, Mich, Library of Congress: https://www.loc.gov/item/2014636779/)

Figure 1.4 A woman dressed as a ballerina flirts with the camera making the viewer wonder, "What's under that skirt?" (1902). Copyright by Fitz W. Guerin, St. Louis.
(Library of Congress www.loc.gov/item/96506056/)

interestingly, on politics, which was not common at the time, seeing as women did not win the right to vote for another 60 years. Tartar in *Mazeppa* would be her last major role. Adah Isaacs Menken died at 33, but her outspoken nature, her hidden culture, her writing, and her nude costume, would be her legacy.

The nude bodysuit worn by Adah Isaacs Menken was not a new invention for her role. In fact, the knitting technique employed in its creation was seen in multiple garments, namely the tights and later leotards of ballet dancers, the statuesque costumes for tableaux vivants, and the stockings of both can-can dancers and fashionable ladies. Ballet became a popular performing art in the latter half of the 1800s, but as French dancers brought new costume styles to the performance, the sight of a dancer's entire leg or even the silhouette of their lower half beneath calf-length sheer skirts was enough to cause a stir. The newest incarnation of the costume in the late 1800s kept the bodice and skirt silhouette from earlier, but the skirt became much shorter. The silhouettes you see in the pictures in Figure 1.3 and 1.4 reveal the legs from the knee down. The

second image of a pseudo ballet dancer in Figure 1.4 has a playful and sensual feel, purposely enticing the viewer to think about what might be seen from behind the lifted skirt.

The first ballet costumes of the mid-nineteenth century were structured, in that the bodice was boned or a corset was worn under a dress with a bodice and full skirt. This style of ballet costume is still used today in some classical ballet. The use of knit leotards with tights in dance came in with male ballet dancers like Vaslav Nijinski in the early twentieth century. These leotards are excellent examples of the silk knit weave and garment shape used in dance and theater. The weave was previously made in wool and cotton. This fabric and weave is used in the flesh tone bodysuits of actors in tableaux vivants. The Victoria and Albert Museum Cloth Workers Centre houses a Nijinsky costume from *Spirit of the Rose* (1911) and the following pages show the garment in detail.

Figure 1.5 *Vaslav Nijinsky wearing the full Spirit of the Rose costume designed by Leon Baskt, including the leotard featured in Figure 1.6 to 1.9 (1911).*
(Billy Rose Theatre Division, The New York Public Library for the Performing Arts)

Figure 1.6 Hand-painted silk knit leotard with hand painted silk organza petals and metallic soutache trim. Worn by Vaslav Nijinsky in The Spirit of the Rose, 1911. Designed by Leon Baskt. (Copyright: The Victoria and Albert Museum)

Figure 1.7 Close-up of the fabric painting and metallic soutache trim that has been hand sewn on the leotard to create line work and the painted organza petals on the leotard. Each petal is individually attached by hand. (Copyright: The Victoria and Albert Museum)

Figure 1.8 The crotch of this leotard has been altered over time as evidenced by the purple elastic seen in the image. Though there may have been a longer rise of silk knit or bias here when the leotard was first made, it most likely deteriorated. The fact that newer elastic is part of this leotard speaks to the fact that dance and theater costumes in the past were kept as part of the theater stock, and were repurposed for other productions repeatedly, until they were no longer functional and got discarded or used for scrap material. This is why costumes in good condition from the 18th and 19th centuries are hard to come by. (Copyright: The Victoria and Albert Museum)

*Figure 1.9 Close-up of the bias binding on the leotard's leg opening in **self fabric**. Notice that this has been machine sewn. Sewing machines were readily available to the costumer and home sewer from the late 1800s. (Copyright: The Victoria and Albert Museum)*

The idea of a lifted skirt and a flash of leg as a **tease** was seen in ballet, but the visuals of a high kicking leg amid endless layers of ruffles will always be attributed to the **can-can** girls of The Folies Bergère in France of the second half of the nineteenth century. The can-can high-kicking style of dance, along with its frilly costumes, made its way to the United States and was a popular part of burlesque shows and **music hall** entertainment. Costumes for this exuberant dance are signature—including mid-length to long ruffle-lined skirts over circular ruffled **petticoats**. There are often feathered headdresses or hats included in the ensemble, and black or striped stockings, which more easily displayed the separation between the top of the stocking and the flash of **bloomers**. The enticement for the audience was not just the beauty of a sea of ruffles and legs and colors moving on the stage at once, but the possibility that something other than a leg might show from beneath the skirts. In the following decades a trend for contrast **embellishment** and shorter bloomers started, which helped the audience see more than just petticoats.

Figure 1.10 Can-can dancer painting by Henri de Toulouse Lautrec, late nineteenth century. (Henri de Toulouse Lautrec)

Figure 1.11 A can-can dancer from the Moulin Rouge, 1910s. (The Everett Collection)

Figure 1.12 This image of Saharet from 1905 shows just how high dancers were kicking up their skirts. The lace ruffled petticoats shown here demonstrate volume in this costume style. Later versions show contrast color or multi-colored ruffles of taffeta lining the top skirt, and lace petticoats are removed, which reveals the whole leg of the dancer. The rustling sound of this crisp fabric has become synonymous with the can-can. **Leg shows** that featured chorus lines of these dancers were a part of popular entertainment, but by nature they were not innocent. This dance form was sensual and flirtatious, it was meant to tease and arouse. It could be said that the can-can is the first to employ the **reveal**, and like burlesque, this reveal is inherent to any recognizable or credible performance of the dance. (Georg Gerlach, 1905)

Figure 1.13 A poster advertising the Rentz Santley Novelty and Burlesque Company's dance performance showcasing "Gay Life in Paris" with the Jardine Mabille Dance Troupe, 1890.
(Courier Lithorgraph Co. Buffalo, NY, 1890. Retrieved from the Library of Congress)

The practice of repurposing costumes that are part of a theater's collection is expected and, for collectors and vendors of historical costume, can add or detract value to a piece. Sometimes fun can come in a purchase of something that is thought to be from one era, but discovering its provenance is much earlier upon looking under layers of embellishment and repair. Bridget's Closet is a London-based vendor that specializes in theatrical costume from the French folies, opera, and theater. She has collected and sold legendary costumes that are part of performing arts history, and she was gracious enough to share some of her discoveries with this author.

Figures 1.14 to 1.18 are a document of an original Folies Bergère can-can dress that has been sold to a private collector. Bridget acquired over a half dozen of these dresses in different color schemes, which were later purchased by a museum. This dress is a beautiful example of the taffeta ruffled skirts in later designs. Though it is not as old as the turn of the twentieth century, it can give the costume maker, performer, or collector a good idea of a construction technique and *embellishment* details.

Figure 1.14 A can-can costume from the Folies Bergère in Paris (1920s–1940s) The bodice is flesh toned and embellished with organza and beading to resemble a corset and necklace. There is a built-in shrug with ruffled sleeves in iridescent organza. The skirt is split in the center front to reveal built-in dance panties covered in ruffles to match the gold tone ruffles of the skirt canter. The skirt shape looks to be a full circle with ruffles that change in color from golden yellow to orange, to pink to red. This is just one color scheme for this style of dress—they come in every color, but the silhouettes are consistent, with variations on sleeve and how many separates there are.
(Bridget's Cabinet, London)

Figure 1.15 View of the Folies Bergère can-can dress from the back. There is a zipper closure with a large bow covering the center back zipper closure that extends into the skirt. The outer layer of the skirt is made of red taffeta with orange iridescent organza on top. The black trim appears to be velvet ribbon and rosettes.

Figure 1.16 The zipper shown here dates the dress so that the viewer knows it is either not original to the dress, or not a dress from the turn of the twentieth century, as it is a more modern style and size. In looking at construction, we see that the zipper runs through the center back of the built-in underwear, not down the back of the skirt. Instead, the visible red seen in the bottom right of the image is a placket opening in the back of the skirt. The organza bow on the outside of the skirt covers this opening and visible zipper. The ruffles on the underwear are not only decorative, but act as an additional layer of volume around the hips of the dancer.

Figure 1.17 A front view from under the skirt. Though faded, one can see that the base layer of the underwear is a bright yellow, which matches the lining of the ruffled skirt, but would be extra eye-catching against the bright ruffles of the outer edges of the skirt. It is also notable that the ruffles closest to the body on both the skirt and underwear are neutral flesh tones, giving the illusion of skin in frenzied movement.

Figure 1.18 A close examination of the ruffle application shows the tiers of color in these ruffles made of **taffeta** and **organza**. The ruffles are applied in two layers, one shorter and one longer, for each color. The ruffle edge finishing looks like a **zig-zag stitch rolled hem**, possibly over a cord or with a heavier thread to create a firmer edge.
(All images of this garment are courtesy of Bridget's Cabinet, London)

Figure 1.19 A page from the 1902 Sears catalog showing "Ladies Fancy Hosiery." (Sears Catalog, 1902, page 971)

Shows that included can-can numbers were called leg shows for obvious reasons. What was on the leg was of great importance to the overall aesthetic of the dancing girls. Just as the nude body suits and tights were made of a cotton or silk rib knit, so were the stockings. It was common for a dancer to wear nude tights with knee-length stockings of color or stripes over them tied with a ribbon to keep them up at the knee, which were the earliest **garters**. The stocking industry was not just one note, they were able to embellish with florals, swirling designs and novelty prints. **Stockings** were not just for the stage, of course. The fashionable lady's ensemble was not complete without a beautiful pair, usually in black, that would cover the leg if the slightest of ankle might show during daily activities. The French stockings from 1900 shown in Figures 1.21 to 1.23 are in the collection of the Museum at the Fashion Institute of Technology in New York City.

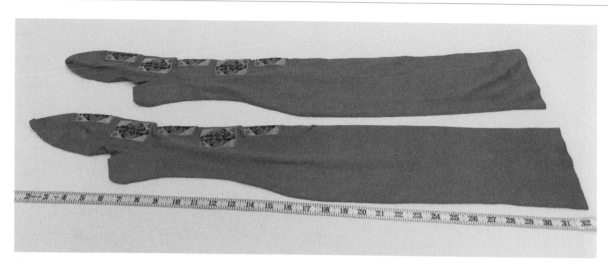

Figure 1.20 These red silk stockings are embellished with playing cards that look like a queen of hearts. Novelty stockings like these demonstrate a lively wearer and a sense of humor in fashion. They would not likely be seen on a conservative member of society.

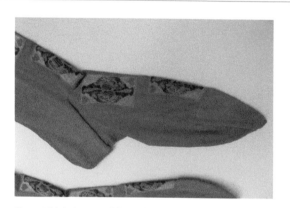

Figure 1.21 A close-up of the stocking foot shows the variation in knit at the toe, and the seam along the heel and center back, hinting at the method of construction and shape of the knitted piece before it was joined into a tubular shape.

Figure 1.22 The close-up view of the playing card design shows that the stocking might have been knit first, and the cards embroidered into the knit afterwards. The author was not able to look inside the stocking during the viewing. If this embroidery was hand-done (and it most likely was), it is painstakingly small and evenly stitched.

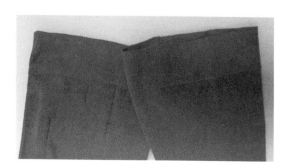

Figure 1.23 The top of the red silk stockings is a double layer of the fine rib knit. Their place of manufacture, Paris, is woven into the knit of the socks. This weave looks different from the embroidery look of the playing cards on the lower portion of the stocking. Several small snags can be seen on the stocking to the left, but for the most part, these look unworn.
(All images on this page by Coleen Scott, with permission from The Museum at The Fashion Institute of Technology, New York City, 2017)

Figure 1.24 Two Women in Day Dresses: Preparatory drawing for a fashion plate from Le Moniteur de la Mode by Artist Jules David. October 19, 1886. Accession number 53.664.21. (The Elisha Whittelsey Collection, The Elisha Whittelsey Fund, 1953. Metropolitan Museum of Art, New York)

Figure 1.25 "Studies in expression. The author and the soubrette." Charles Dana Gibson was known for his lifelike illustrations. This image captures several typical women's ensembles as well as that of a "soubrette" or showgirl, 1902.
(Library of Congress)

Figure 1.26 "Three Women in Tights" 1899.
(Courier Lithorgraph Company, Buffalo, NY 1899. Retrieved from the Library of Congress)

Everyday clothing for a "respectable" American woman in the late nineteenth century was conservative in its coverage of the female body with fabric from neck to wrist to floor, although the fashionable **silhouette** had many variations over the nearly 50 years covered here. The 1860s woman would wear a full skirt of layered **crinolines** and wide-bottomed sleeves whereas the 1880s woman would be wearing a **bustle** with all fullness to the back of her ensemble, along with slimmer and more diminutive sleeves. The late 1800s lead into the turn of the twentieth century and the Victorian silhouettes of **leg-o-mutton sleeves** and gored skirts, and the sleeve caps diminish to a more natural fit with the new **S-curve corsets** supporting a **pigeon-breasted** silhouette. The later Edwardian years bring a less extreme silhouette with a higher waistline and straight skirts. These fashion trends contrast highly to the short bodices, **trunks** and tights worn by female performers in costume. It is no wonder that women in the performing arts were judged by "upstanding" women as being loose or frivolous, and frequently condemned as prostitutes. Women on the stage were not following the prescribed societal roles common in US society at the time. The silhouette of the female performer is not modest, but think how ridiculous it would be for a woman to perform acrobatic routines, stunts, or difficult ballet moves in a full ensemble like Figures 1.24 and 1.25!

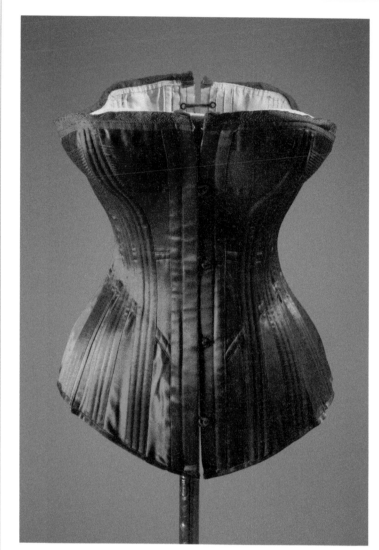

*Figure 1.27 A red satin corset from 1890 with a steel **busk** and steel grommets. Silk outer and cotton twill lining.*
(The Museum at The Fashion Institute of Technology)

Both performers and everyday women wore stockings and corsets. **Corsets** are tightly laced undergarments covering the chest, torso, and high hip made rigid with thin vertical strips of whalebone or steel. In the late 1800s and into the early twentieth century, the corset usually remained under the costume with some outfits showing the silhouette and structure underneath more readily like those in tableaux vivants (see page 23). In the following pages, we will examine a standard corset from 1890, and an acrobat costume from around the same time that resembles those worn over a corseted body. Circus shows were some of the earliest forms of leisure

entertainment for the working class in the United States, so while the upper crust might have first seen slim or sheer costumes at the ballet, the everyday citizen would have seen this costume style when the circus came to town. The female audience member viewing a circus act or a ballet performance could much more logically accept the costumes of lady performers when their physicality demanded less cumbersome clothing. It was the burlesque and stage shows creating situations other than physical activity for their costuming choices that became a source of outrage for morality groups and conservative audiences.

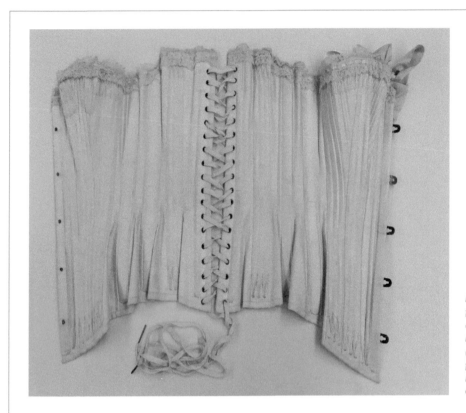

Figure 1.28 The outside of a corset from 1890. Notice the embroidery and trim, steel busk, grommets and lace tips, and gussets at hips. (Coleen Scott, with permission from The Museum at The Fashion Institute of Technology, New York City, 2017)

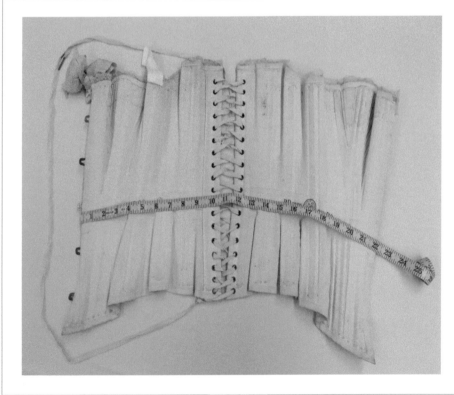

Figure 1.29 The inside of the corset, showing an approximate waist measurement of 22□, which is on the average to larger side for the time. (Coleen Scott, with permission from The Museum at The Fashion Institute of Technology, New York City, 2017)

Figure 1.30 Close-up on the bust area of the 1890 corset. The hand embroidery, lace and ribbon detail are beautiful, and the minute stitching on the bone channels is notable, as is the direction of the channeling at the bust to accommodate curves.
(Coleen Scott, with permission from The Museum at The Fashion Institute of Technology, New York City, 2017)

Figure 1.31 The inside label notes that this corset was made in Belgium.
(Coleen Scott, with permission from The Museum at The Fashion Institute of Technology, New York City, 2017)

Figure 1.32 A close-up of the embroidery on the bottom front of the corset and steel tips on the corset lace.
(Coleen Scott, with permission from The Museum at The Fashion Institute of Technology, New York City, 2017)

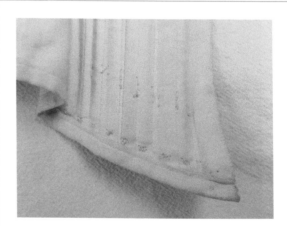

Figure 1.33 The backside of the embroidery shows that it was applied after the corset was constructed.
(Coleen Scott, with permission from The Museum at The Fashion Institute of Technology, New York City, 2017)

Figure 1.34 The well-known acrobat and strongwoman Charmion, 1897.
(F.W. Glasier. From The Wisconsin Center for Film and Theater Research. Image ID: 71533)

Charmion, also known as Charmaine, was a French acrobat and **strongwoman** who became famous for her "trapeze disrobing act." (See: Figure 1.35) Her death-defying striptease was captured on **kinetoscope** film by Thomas Edison in 1901. The act was not new, but the audience that the film reached was wider than live traveling shows. The influence of film on burlesque costume and vice versa is evident through its entire history, including these early years. Thomas Edison played an important role in making more than one **mother** **of burlesque** famous. In the trapeze disrobing act, Charmion does not start in a typical circus jumper like the one featured in Figures 1.36 to 1.40. She begins in an everyday **shirtwaist**, skirt and hat, and undresses while changing position and demonstrating her strength on the trapeze. Her final look, however, is bloomers, tights, a corset and a **corset cover**, which bears a striking resemblance both to circus costumes, and to the popular **carte de viste** images of women undressing.

Figure 1.35 A still frame from Thomas Edison's "Trapeze Disrobing Act" film for the kinetoscope, 1901.

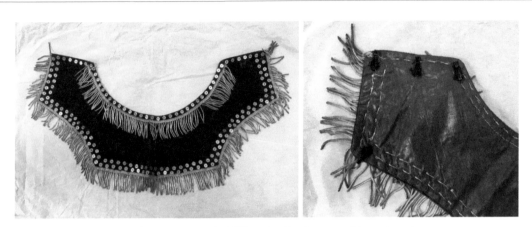

Figure 1.36 Men's Victorian acrobat costume from the 1890s made with velvet, cotton lining, and metal **sequins** and fringe. The collar was hooked onto a bodysuit. Closures can be seen in the closeup to the right. (Mark Schmitt. Used with permission from Illinois State University's Special Collections, Milner Library)

Figure 1.37 Matching velvet trunks with center front hook closure. (Mark Schmitt. Used with permission from Illinois State University Special Collections, Milner Library)

Figure 1.38 Matching wrist gauntlet for the acrobat costume. Metal hooks would attach to the bodysuit. (Mark Schmitt. Used with permission from Illinois State University Special Collections, Milner Library)

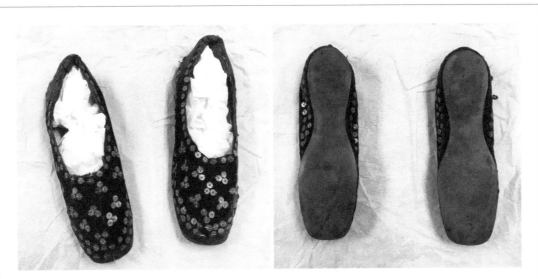

Figure 1.39 The matching velvet slippers are decorated with metal sequins and have a leather sole.
(Mark Schmitt. Used with permission from Illinois State University Special Collections, Milner Library)

Figure 1.40 Two images of Victorian acrobats. The men on the left, Chester Parons and F.F. Welsh, are wearing
the costume featured in the previous pages, and the second is Mademoiselle Theola, a female performer in a
similar trunk style with fringes.
(Used with permission from Illinois State University Special Collections, Milner Library)

Figure 1.41 Female Acrobats on Trapezes at Circus, *ca. 1890. www.loc.gov/item/93500071/.*
(Library of Congress)

The traveling circus showcased animal acts, clowns, acrobats and trapeze, but they were frequently accompanied by sideshows showcasing human oddities or people from faraway lands with foreign cultures and physicality. Early sideshows were marketed as museums, with education in mind, and were considered respectable sources of entertainment. Both storefront and traveling museum exhibits could be viewed apart from the circus, with one of most famous early museums started by P.T. Barnum in New York City in 1841. Aside from the displays of scientific anomalies and anthropological exhibits on view for the cost of admission, more theatrical entertainment became part of the museum's offerings, usually at an additional cost, and usually in a separate room. Some of the first of these performances were advertised as tableaux vivants. These "living pictures" were put on initially by churches demonstrating well-known religious stories or works of art. In the museums, the tableaux took on other artworks and sculpture that might feature figures in the nude. To keep the demonstration

"respectable" and within the rules of morality groups, the illusion of nudity could be shown IF the figures remained still while on view. This likened the performance to a viewing of a statue or painting, the act of which was considered artful and culturally enriching.

Performers' costumes for tableaux vivants resembled classical art of Greek and Roman statues, which involved fabric draped conspicuously over the body for coverage, with or without full nude bodysuits like the one used by Adah Isaacs Menken for her theatrical role in *Mazeppa*. As a showman and entrepreneur, Barnum knew that people were coming in to the museum to be educated not only on science and anthropology, but also for a peek of anatomy that they might rarely see in daily life. Other museums and traveling shows picked up this form of entertainment, and offered comparable back room shows that more often than not, showed a glimpse of skin. To get around the regulations regarding nudity and movement on stage, the curtain would close between costume changes

Figure 1.42 Ida Florence, "The California Prize Beauty," late nineteenth century, wearing a full nude bodysuit over a corset and a long veil in a statuesque pose complete with a pedestal. (Houseworth's Celebrities, San Francisco. From the Charles H. McCaghy Collection at The Ohio State University)

Figure 1.43 Example of a tableaux vivant, with three women posed in the style of Greek or Roman sculpture. Costumes in this scene are composed of draped fabric and braided trim. Image: Reconciliation by Randall, Ann Arbor, MI. 1891. (Library of Congress)

Figure 1.44 "Birth of the Pearl," 1903. This tryptic demonstrates the use of tableaux and reveal. With each curtain opening, more of the "nude" lady is shown. It is clear, even from these grainy images, that she is wearing a nude bodysuit. (Library of Congress)

and more skin would be revealed with each reopening. This technique was also seen in music halls frequented by the middle and working class.

These back room productions led to the disreputable public opinion of many traveling museums and circuses. Those entities who survived the shift either chose the direction of the formal, strictly anthropological or art-centric museum of cultural respect, or the direction of the **low-brow**, working man's traveling entertainment machine. The separation of class with regard to popular entertainments in America at this time resonates deeply with the development of burlesque and its repeatedly forced separation from the "respectable entertainment" of high society.

Figure 1.45 An illustration of scenes from The Black Crook, 1879. Women are seen playing nymphs, fairies, and goddesses, all of whom are wearing revealing costumes for the time.
(N.Y.: H.A. Thomas Lith. Studio. 1879. Library of Congress)

The popular entertainments of museums, the circus, and nickelodeons boomed at the turn of the century, but the theater was going strong from the start. The theater world, like the dance world, has a divide between the low-brow and the high-brow performance styles within the genre. In many cases, the two separate categories are also associated with the economics of the audience. As we continue to look at the history and costumes of burlesque, it will become evident that socio-economics of an audience are, in fact, an even bigger factor for social acceptance than the quality of performance or performer featured. In addition to the economics, theater that

deviates or challenges the social norm is also sequestered from the mainstream and forcibly categorized as "lesser."

When an art form that is considered "low brow" gains popularity and infiltrates the popular culture, it has a voice, and that voice is usually allowed to speak after times of great struggle or repression in a society. With the abolition of slavery in the United States in 1865, came a wave of social change that paved a way and gave a voice to many who were segregated, underrepresented, and discriminated against. Seeing that former slaves could now own a business, property and have a vote, women began to speak out politically for their own rights.

Figure 1.46 Belle Howitt in The Black Crook. *Her costume reveals a lot of leg and arm, though it is clear from this image she is wearing a full bodysuit under her top layer.*
(Flickr commons. From page 82 of Theatrical and Circus Life*)*

Figure 1.47 Chorus ladies from The Black Crook.
(Culver Pictures)

The theater is a place where artists can shine a light on society, and play the roles they want to see reflected in the real world. In addition, it is a place of fantasy and escape, where audiences come to see a thing more beautiful than the realities they have to face at home. One groundbreaking production that influenced burlesque was **The Black Crook** in 1866. A spectacle of enticing beauty, with choruses of dancers, singers and mythical beings, it is considered the first American musical theater production, and was a smash hit in New York with sold out shows for months. The minimal costumes of the chorus girls were commented on by reviewers, but there was acceptance of their attire because they could be categorized as "otherworldly" and therefore not subject to the rules of modern society. The scale of the production added to the acceptance of the designs for overall aesthetic value.

The popularity of *The Black Crook* paved the way for other large-scale productions featuring choruses of women playing disparate roles in revealing costumes, but a bigger change came with the visitation of Lydia Thompson and her troupe of **British Blondes** from England in 1868.

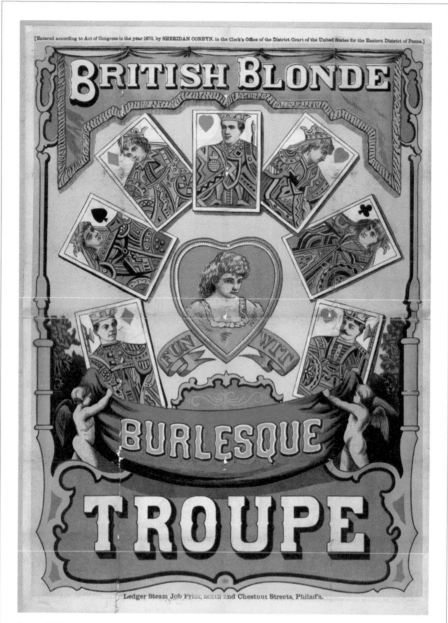

Figure 1.48 A poster for British Blonde Burlesque, 1870.
(Library of Congress/Public domain)

Lydia Thompson and her all-women troupe would rewrite popular plays and insert current political commentary and comedy into the plots. They would also play ALL of the roles. In the days of Shakespeare, men played all roles on stage, and their gender swapping was an accepted part of the theater going experience. In the 1860s it was new to an American audience (the troupe had been performing burlesques in England prior to their US debut) that Miss Thompson and her female cast would play men in stories with male lead characters, and dress the part. At the same time as she gained fame for her portrayal of male roles, Lydia Thompson was ridiculed for her ability to play masculine characters convincingly. As a male character with a female physique and costumes that revealed it, she was an object of the male gaze, but when men could not reconcile their arousal with the fact that her character was male, written critiques of her moral reputation appeared in lieu of critiques of her performance.

Figure 1.49 Lydia Thompson in costume for three different male roles.

Figure 1.50 Lydia Thompson in costume for her first famed role in Ixion and in another favorite, Robinson Crusoe.

Figure 1.51 Bessie Clayton is advertised as "The World's Greatest Dancer" in Joe Weber's production of The Merry Widow. Her ruffled petticoats and slippers display costuming influenced by ballet and can-can, making her familiar to a wide audience. (Strobridge Litho.Co., c1908. Library of Congress)

The Thompson troupe's popularity enticed American copycat troupes to follow suit and produce their own all-female burlesques. Mabel Santley, a female troupe co-owner, put on productions of the leg-show variety. Joe Weber staged operetta productions such as the revealing Merry Widow in Figure 1.51. Productions like this included speaking and singing roles, and the songs became part of the popular music vernacular. Operettas are the relatives of musical theater, and productions like Weber's were accessible and attractive to a broad audience as opposed to opera, which was strictly associated with a monied viewership.

Figure 1.52 Poster for the Bon-Ton Burlesquers, 1898. Notice the woman on the front in a music hall style costume manipulating the well-dressed men. This poster mocks their audience, but by the looks of the men in the poster, the audience doesn't seem to mind.
(H.C. Miner Litho. Co. 1898, Retrieved from the Library of Congress)

Up until this point, burlesques involved plots where women spoke their roles just like any actor would, with a little timely humor or political commentary peppered in, and family audiences in attendance. The can-can style chorus lines of the Folies Bergère brought in the dance and live music element to popular American entertainment combined with other variety

Figure 1.53 Maud D'Orby, a French music hall soubrette, wears a risqué gown. Late 1800s/early 1900s.
(Personal collection of Neil "Nez" Kendall)

Figure 1.54 Millie De Leon was a music hall performer who caused an uproar when she tossed her garter into the audience.[4]
(Image from "A Pictorial History of Burlesque" by Bernard Sobel, 1956, page 116. Printed with permission from The Crown Publishing Group and Penguin and Random House Publishers)

acts. In later years this catered to a wealthy male audience. Operettas staged in full scale were not within the budget of smaller venues and poorer audiences looking for a fun evening out. The music hall brought together all of the elements of popular stories, music, and lively dance, for a lower cost and a touch more bawdiness. They were the nightclubs and variety shows of the Victorian era. For a fraction of the cost of going to the theater, one could see and hear a beautiful **soubrette** sing favorite songs from popular operettas, have a few laughs and enjoy a chorus of ladies dancing.

The costume of a soubrette consisted of a spectacular dress. The term soubrette comes from the role type of the same name in operettas. The soubrette characters are often the cunning or flirtatious maid or servant, an inherently seductive figure. Though song stylings would vary based on the vocal role of the singer, the music hall soubrette was meant to captivate the audience as a solo entertainer. To describe it visually, we see a woman in a beautiful and usually risqué gown, entertaining the audience with a song and maybe dancing too. Figures 1.56 and 1.57 document the gown of a music hall singer named May Moore Duprez from 1910. It is part of the collection at the Victoria and Albert Museum in London. The dress is a perfect example of the flashiness and sex appeal that these singers were allowed to demonstrate on stage.

Figure 1.55 Another fine example of a music hall performer's costume.
(Image from "A Pictorial History of Burlesque" by Bernard Sobel, 1956, page 95. Printed with permission from The Crown Publishing Group and Penguin and Random House Publishers.)

Figure 1.56 Front view of a sequin dress worn by music hall singer May Moore Duprez. Fabric is embellished by hand and the neckline is accented with a ruffle of red chiffon bound in red satin. A corset would have been worn underneath to create the proper silhouette.
(Copyright: The Victoria and Albert Museum)

Figure 1.57 *Back view of May Moore Duprez's Dress. Closure was probably hook and bar originally,*
but this has been replaced by snaps.
(Copyright: The Victoria and Albert Museum)

Figure 1.58 An image of the "Streets of Cairo" stage and performers. From the original image caption: "The young woman in the centre of the stage, who is represented in books of travel as an Eastern houri, is about to render the celebrated danse du ventre, and it will be seen that practice in the movement of her body rather than her feet has greatly developed her abdominal region. We are to understand that this development has increased her beauty in the Oriental imagination, as it has certainly lessened I according to Western cannons of taste … Stamping her foot forward, the dancer will move her shoulders up and down, increasing the contortions of her body, striking the castanets she carries, whirling sometimes, but more often stamping forward, each time to a posture nearer the floor, until, as she seems to expire in the excitement of the rapid music and cries of the musicians, other houris rise from their couch and take her place, or join her, waving long strips of illusion or lace in a graceful and rhythmic manner. No ordinary Western woman looked on these performances with anything but horror …"
(The Dream City, A Portfolio of Photographic Views of the World's Columbian Exhibition, 1893. Author's collection)

If music hall singers were an example of purposeful sex appeal at this time, then the ***hoochie-coochie*** dancers at the Great Columbian Exhibition and The World's Fair in 1893 were an example of accidental sex appeal. As mentioned before, many Americans had frequented museums or circus sideshows and had some acquaintance with people of cultures different from their own, but this contact was very limited, and in the interest of showmanship, information that was given to audiences was not necessarily true, or was exaggerated.

The 1893 World's Fair in Chicago, also known as the Great Columbian Exhibition, was a massive display of human invention, culture and entertainment that was visited by thousands of people. Americans were curious about other cultures because of anthropological studies and museum exhibits that reminded them they are not the only people on the planet, and they were certainly not the first. To this end there were entire villages and environments constructed and groups of people from all over the world enlisted (some against their will or under false

Figure 1.59 A dancer from the "Streets of Cairo" exhibit. Her traditional costume became the basis for **cooch tent** dancers in circus sideshows and traveling museums. An excerpt from the original caption for this image: "A PERFORMER OF THE DANCE DU VENTRE: We have here a close and trying study of a posture-dancer of the theatre in the Street of Cairo. The Western eye was but a moment in determining, at the World's Fair, that time has wrought as great a change in the dance as in the alphabet … whereas, dancing began by movements of the body rather than the lower limbs, it has now developed into the Western performance. When Western officials came to gaze on her rendition of the act by which John the Baptist lost his head, they were sorely perplexed. This dance was undoubtedly the style in Cairo, where our own Western Black Crook amazons would be instantly suppressed. Notwithstanding the indignation of the Board of Lady Managers, the danse du ventre proceeded, and though thousands went to see it, they did not go often, for the music was too irritating. Described in brief, the woman moved her shoulders and body rhythmically to the sharp beats of the tambour." (The Dream City, A Portfolio of Photographic Views of the World's Columbian Exhibition, 1893. Author's collection)

pretenses) to be a part of the exhibition. The "Streets of Cairo" exhibit included a theater that claimed to showcase both the music and the dance of Egypt. As is the case with generalized presentations of an entire culture, the **"Dance of the Seven Veils"** in this particular exhibit was a popular attraction, and the traditional costumes and movement of these dancers became synonymous with the overall impression of Egyptian entertainment and aesthetic. The costumes, which revealed the mid-section, were thought to be obscene, as were the dance moves, which involved slow undulations of the lower half of the body and torso. The harsh reviews and commentary of this exhibit had attendees flocking to see it for themselves. This is the first large-scale presentation of what came to be known as **bellydancing** in the United States.

LITTLE EGYPT

Newsboy

327

NEW YORK.

Figure 1.60 Ashea Wabe, also known as "Little Egypt," from a still by Thomas Edison. (Billy Rose Theatre Division, The New York Public Library for the Performing Arts)

The result of this hoochie-coochie dance demonstration was that audiences around the country who missed The Great Columbian Exhibition were a market waiting to be tapped by the entrepreneurial showman. Traveling circuses showcased their own versions of the hoochie-coochie dancers and the "dance of the seven veils" in sideshow tents, and though some may have tried to be authentic, the real audience draw was seeing a woman dance in scanty clothing.[5]

Little Egypt was a character name used by multiple dancers. It is said that one of the dancers from The Great Columbian Exhibition, Fahreda Mazar Spyropoulos, who originally performed in Arizona as Fatima, went by that name, but the images of the dancers from the exhibition catalog do not divulge this specific information.

Ashea Wabe was a hoochie-coochie dancer who became famous because, like the acrobat Charmion, she was filmed for Thomas Edison's kinetoscope. Though she is not the original

Figure 1.61 A woman dressed in a Salome-style costume dances with a snake.
(From the personal collection of Neil "Nez" Kendall)

*Figure 1.62 Mata Hari in a metal **breastplate bra** and belt made in the style of Salome costumes.*

"Little Egypt," the imagery of her is the most recognizable. Little Egypt was imitated by so many, the name and bellydancing became tantamount.

The "Dance of the Seven Veils" was not new to any American who was familiar with the Bible, or anyone well read in Hebrew scripture. The story of the dance predates the Bible, but the most popular story is that of Salome, who dances for Herod, and after distracting, and in some tellings, seducing him, requests that he behead John the Baptist. In both books,

Salome is associated with deadly seduction, and her veil dance has acquired the same association. She is the first femme fatale. Culturally Westerners, and especially Americans, have integrated this idea of the foreign seductress into their romanticized version of Orientalism.

The character of Salome, her sensual dance and her Biblical story, were turned into a popular (but repeatedly banned) play by Oscar Wilde in 1892, and an opera by Strauss in 1905. Mata Hari was one entertainer who embodied the aesthetic of the

Figure 1.63 *Gertrude Hoffman in costume for the role of Salome in the Oscar Wilde play, 1911.*
(Jerome Robbins Dance Division, The New York Public Library for the Performing Arts)

Salome-style femme fatale. The Dutch dancer and courtesan posed for nude or partially nude photos while wearing this costume style. Her real-life work as a German spy during World War I found her dramatically executed by a firing squad in France.

The risqué costumes designed for the character of Salome at this time included a metal headdress and a circular metal bra top, held together by strings of pearls or chains. The metal plates were embellished with stones or covered in pearls. The midriff was visible, though covered with a nude bodysuit or underdress, and the lower half of the body is wrapped in fabric with an embellished waistband, belt or scarf. The costume style was adopted by belly dancers and other "Little Egypts" performing their own "Dances of the Seven Veils." This ensemble is not too far removed from those traditional costumes seen at The World's Fair, but it is distant enough that Western audiences became enamored of this sanitized ornamented ensemble and forgot about the real culture it was adapted from.

Figure 1.64 *Opera singer Marta Witkowska wears a Salome-inspired bra, belt and headdress, early twentieth century. The top closely resembles the costume piece in Figures 1.65 to 1.67.*
(Wallach Division Picture Collection, The New York Public Library)

The costume pieces in Figures 1.65 to 1.74 are part of the personal collection of Vicki Butterfly, a London burlesque performer and collector of antique costumes. She was kind enough to share her collection of metal opera bras, belts and headdresses for documentation.

Figure 1.65 A metal bra used as an opera costume, late 1800s, early 1900s. Brass with glass rhinestones.
(Photo by Coleen Scott with permission from Vicki Butterfly)

Figure 1.66 Underside of the bra cup. The fabrication of these pieces involved pressing the metal into a mold and then joining the separate components together with solder.
(Photo by Coleen Scott with permission from Vicki Butterfly)

Figure 1.67 Side and back of metal bra strap. The loop at the end connects to a metal hook welded onto the other side. The rhinestones in this piece are crystal.
(Photo by Coleen Scott with permission from Vicki Butterfly)

Figure 1.68 A second Salome-style opera bra from the personal collection of Vicki Butterfly. Late 1800s, early 1900s. Glass stones and faux pearls. Red bead straps and accents around cups are a later addition to the piece.
(Photo by Coleen Scott with permission from Vicki Butterfly.)

Figure 1.69 This brass and crystal belt matches the bra in Figures 1.65 to 1.67. A very similar style is worn in Figure 1.64.
(Photo by Coleen Scott with permission from Vicki Butterfly)

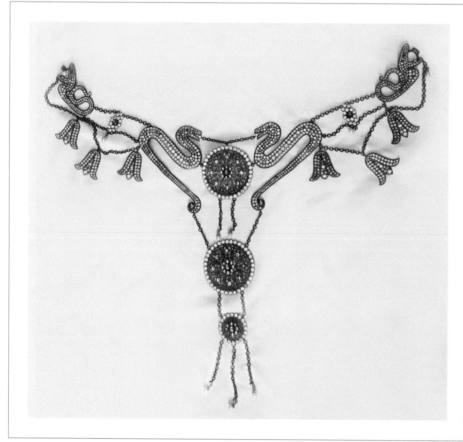

Figure 1.70 A snake-themed metal and rhinestone Salome belt. From the personal collection of Vicki Butterfly.
(Photo by Coleen Scott with permission from Vicki Butterfly)

Figure 1.71 *A metal headdress with turquoise and clear stones. This headdress might have been a bra in a previous incarnation. From the personal collection of Vicki Butterfly.*
(Photo by Coleen Scott with permission from Vicki Butterfly)

Figure 1.72 *Close-up of the underside of this headdress piece. The unused loop on the top left might be further evidence that this used to be a breastplate bra.*
(Photo by Coleen Scott with permission from Vicki Butterfly)

Figure 1.73 *Mata Hari wears a rhinestone peacock headpiece, 1910.*
(Wiki commons)

Figure 1.74 *A rhinestone peacock similar to that on Mata Hari at the left. In modern application, this piece has been used as a belt centerpiece, and has had stones replaced. From the personal collection of Vicki Butterfly.*
(Photo by Coleen Scott with permission from Vicki Butterfly)

Figure 1.75 A poster advertising Loie Fuller in the Folies Bergère, 1890s. (Everett Collection)

Vicki Butterfly is not only a collector of antique costume, she is a practitioner of the Serpentine dance; a predecessor of burlesque, a completely original style of dance dependent on costume, and the subtlest of teases. The Serpentine dance was made familiar by the early modern dancer, inventor and theatrical innovator Loïe Fuller.

Loïe Fuller invented the mechanics of the serpentine costume, and in 1894, to thwart imitators, she patented it. She also held a patent for a rotating platform on stage that enhanced her signature dance. The costume itself is a voluminous tent-like garment that is made of more than one full circle of fabric split at the center front and joined at

the neck. Rods with rounded ends are held in the hands to extend the diameter of reach. The rods aid in moving the fabric edges and keeping its momentum, similar to the way a ribbon dancer works a single piece on a rod. The resulting dance and movement is mesmerizing, and for the viewer looking to catch a glimpse of the seemingly bare body under the moving fabric, it would only happen if the dancer comes to a halt and opens the garment from the front.

Loïe was another innovative performer who was captured on film, but not by Thomas Edison. The *Serpentine Dance* film by Lumierè in 1896 shows her performance style that inspired modern dance techniques. Despite her attempts to stop them,

Figure 1.76 Loie Fuller in a serpentine dance, 1890s.
(Everett Collection)

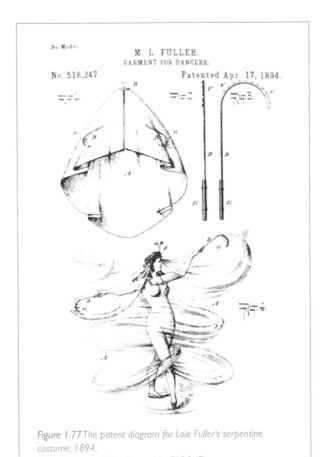

Figure 1.77 The patent diagram for Loïe Fuller's serpentine costume. 1894.
(The US Patent Office, Patent No. 518,347)

Figure 1.78 Loie Fuller does the serpentine dance, 1890s.
(Everett Collection)

imitators appeared near and far. In 1894 Edison made a film of Annabelle doing a less dramatic and clumsier version of the serpentine dance. In 1895, Edison films captured Annabelle in a serpentine costume strikingly similar to Fuller's, but her movements were again not as fluid. Loïe is the source for the most beautiful version of the serpentine dance. Although she was not specifically a burlesque performer, her costume and the (possibly) unintentional tease of her dancing in it, is a part of burlesque costume history.

Theatrical and plot-driven burlesques became sexualized burlesque when the common thread of audience arousal through revealing clothing transitioned to clothing removal to reveal something else, or, something more. The marketing of women's sexuality as a commodity in the theater at the turn of the twentieth century was an unfortunate transition away from the platform for women's voices to be heard that Lydia Thompson and burlesque troupes like hers established. When Michael B. Leavitt opened his first burlesque show in the late 1800s, he took a cue from vaudeville for show structure, and combined it with a popular burlesque as the finale, a choice that led to the demise of the burlesque as a theatrical storytelling convention.

Almost all of the influential theater and costume history presented in this chapter came before Abe Minsky or Florence Ziegfeld opened their first shows in 1908 and 1907 respectively. Ziegfeld tried to keep his shows respectable—the high ticket prices and elaborate costumes helped.

Figure 1.79 The Ziegfeld Revue Follies of 1907 was the first production of The Ziegfeld Follies. This image shows the chorus girls. (Billy Rose Theatre Division, The New York Public Library for the Performing Arts)

Figure 1.80 A group number from The Winter Garden theater, New York City, 1917.
("Minsky's Burlesque" Figure 6. Arbor House Publishers, 1986)

Figure 1.81 Chorus from the 1907 Ziegfeld Follies.
(Photo by White Studio Copyright Bill Rose Theater Division, The New York Public Library for the Performing Arts)

Figure 1.82 Lucy Weston in the Ziegfeld Follies, 1908.
(Museum of the City of New York)

The Minsky brothers and other businessmen like them who catered to the working class were the makers of burlesque as striptease in America. It all seemed to culminate on a fateful day in 1917, when a performer named Mae Dix started to remove her collar before she was off stage, and the audience went wild. Abe Minsky asked her to do it again every show from that point on. Voila! Accidental striptease, and the birth of a new performance art.

Notes

1   Burlesque etymology: mid-seventeenth century: from French, from Italian *burlesco*, from *burla* "mockery," of unknown origin. First definition: (Webster's) an absurd or comically exaggerated imitation of something, especially in a literary or dramatic work; a parody.

2   Slavery was abolished in 1865.

3   *Mazeppa*, 1866, New York City.

4   Anne Fliotsos, "Gotta Get a Gimmick: The Burlesque Career of Millie De Leon," *Journal of American Culture*, Volume 21, Issue 4: 1–8, Winter 1998.

5   The cooch tent in later years of sideshow and traveling circus history is synonymous with striptease.

Figure 2.1 Josephine Baker dancing, 1930s.
(Billy Rose Theatre Division, The New York Public Library for the Performing Arts.
https://digitalcollections.nypl.org/items/23f94090-2ae3-0131-934c-58d385a7b928)

CHAPTER 2

FLAPPERS AND PASTIES AND FOLLIES, OH MY! 1920S AND 30S

Just as the performing arts can be a projection of a Utopian society or an inciting reflection of the problems that need to change, they can perpetuate stereotypes in a terribly compelling way, infiltrating the core beliefs of a culture. The costume of Salome became a generic visual representation of Middle Eastern dress and female characterization. This type of stereotypical dress is found throughout burlesque costume history. An iconic example of a beloved and talented performer who built a career from her ***"Danse Sauvage"*** is Josephine Baker. Baker, like many Black Americans during the First World War, moved to Paris stating she felt freer from the everyday racism and segregation that limited her performance career and her daily life in the US. The image of Miss Baker in her iconic banana skirt costume is likely one of first things one recalls when thinking of her. The image and costume is also a reminder that some black performers became successful performing for White audiences by playing into the "savage" and "native" stereotypes of them still associated from the days of slavery in America and colonial European nations because it was a viable option to break into the entertainment industry.

Later in her career, after achieving worldwide fame, Josephine Baker was one of the top advocates for Black civil rights in America. She was so prominent that after the assassination of Martin Luther King Jr., she was offered the spokesperson position for the movement, but declined it. Baker's community leadership and long career make for a tale of supreme success during a time when the Black American community was fighting for their daily human rights. Because of this history and Baker's iconography, her banana dance costume remains one of the most significant articles in burlesque costume history. The following images of one of Josephine Baker's famous banana skirts were shared by Bridget's Cabinet in London.

Figure 2.2 Josephine Baker wears her famous "Danse Sauvage" banana costume, 1920s.
(Used with permission from CMG Worldwide)

Figure 2.3 One of Josephine Baker's banana skirts, 1920s. The construction is shimmy-belt style, with faux bananas hand stitched onto a silk ribbon belt. The construction of the bananas looks to be soft or foam-like in texture, with a painted shell coating—possibly ***papier mâché***, acrylic paint or glue. From the personal collection of Bridget's Cabinet, London. (Bridget's Cabinet, London)

Figure 2.4 A close-up of the bananas hand-sewn to the ribbon waistband. It looks like the "shell" of the bananas was pliable enough to push a needle through, and strong enough that they did not break off. (Bridget's Cabinet, London)

Figure 2.5 A banana close-up from a different angle. Notice the crinkled look of the banana on the right—a clue to the soft texture of the faux fruit. (Bridget's Cabinet, London)

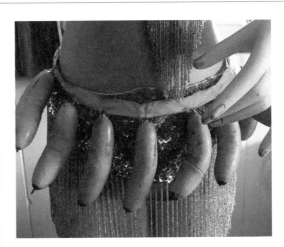

Figure 2.6 A photo of Josephine Baker's banana skirt on a mannequin, over an unrelated beaded costume. (Bridget's Cabinet, London)

Figure 2.7 *A 1920s beaded evening gown with extravagant hat worn by a flapper. This slim silhouette, bare arms, and corset-free fashion was a far cry from the rigid and modest styles just ten years prior.*
(From the personal collection of Neil "Nez" Kendall, Chester, England)

Figure 2.8 *A portrait of boisterous burlesque and vaudeville singer Sophie Tucker in a traditional 1920s ensemble. Miss Tucker gained fame in the early twentieth century. She was a full-figured woman who made fun of her size as part of her act. Sophie sang proudly about her Jewish heritage and loved jazz music. She was one of the first performers to bring it to White vaudeville audiences. She was fondly known as "The Last of the Red Hot Mamas."[1]*
(Butler Photo Studio, 1926. Collection of The Museum of the City of New York)

The 1920s arrived during the height of the first wave of feminists who were finally granted voting rights in 1920 with the passing of the 19th Amendment. American women experienced great liberation through **suffrage**, and this rebirth was reflected in the dramatic change in fashion that occurred in the 1920s. The silhouette of an everyday woman became very straight, eliminating the need for the curve-producing corset. Hemlines rose, waistlines dropped to the hips and women's previously cumbersome layers of **underpinnings** gave way to more freedom of movement for women who were encouraged to be more active and independent. This was the first era of sportswear development for both men and women, encouraging a shorter more streamline silhouette for activities

such as tennis and bicycle riding. Vulcanized rubber was invented, which applied to car tires and sneakers. Rubber production changed women's lingerie in the form of garters and elastics with encased rubber. Improvements in fine silk knits led to the creation of nude-colored silk stockings. 1920s eveningwear remained simple in silhouette, but the embellishment of silk gowns covered in glass hand beading are a stunning demonstration of the **Art Deco** aesthetic. The freedom for women in daily life translated to even more raucous behavior at night with the beginning of jazz music, **speakeasies**, and dance clubs.

Figure 2.9 A bra from the 1920s. The construction entails a layer of silk, silk straps and a band of decorative lace. There is no formal structure or boning in stark contrast to the corset from less than a decade earlier.
(The Metropolitan Museum of Art Digital Archives, New York)

Figure 2.10 The back of the bra. Notice the two channels along the closure in the center back.
(The Metropolitan Museum of Art Digital Archives, New York)

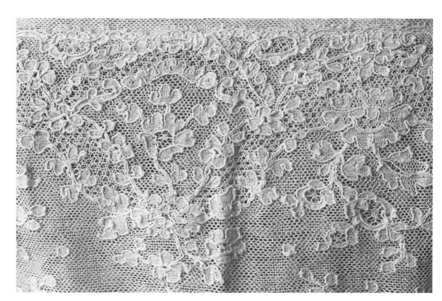

Figure 2.11 A close-up of the beautiful lace detail on the bra.
(The Metropolitan Museum of Art Digital Archives, New York)

Figure 2.12 Early and late career images of Carrie Finnell, 1920s and 1950s.

A trend of topless **chorus girls** and dancers in clubs manifested regulations requiring coverage of the nipple area, which led to the creation of **pasties**, a costume piece that is original to burlesque. The pastie, so called because it is an accessory that is literally pasted onto the center of the breast, is a symbol of early censorship that not only continues on in burlesque today, but also represents this part of burlesque history. Ziegfeld girl Carrie Finnell may have invented the first pair of pasties. In an early design, the pastie was a disc of buckram covered with skin-tone fabric and a bead in the center to replicate a nipple. This creation was clearly an act of protest—not only was it an accessory that covered as little skin as possible to obey **obscenity regulations**, but it is a deliberately designed costume piece that might still fool the audience into believing a dancer was nude. The censors did not appreciate this design and wrote a regulation to require that the pastie must be visible from the back of the theater. Carrie then became the first to add a tassel, which makes sense based on her act. She was able to make her breasts jump in and out of her dress with little movement. Her career spanned 45 years during which her "mammary manipulations" and comedy made her famous.

The pasties opposite and below are just one example of a 1930s style. These pasties were individually adhered to the breasts. By the 1930s there were new adhesives available in the form of Band-Aid style adhesive tape and eyelash glue for false lashes made popular for everyday wear by the film industry.

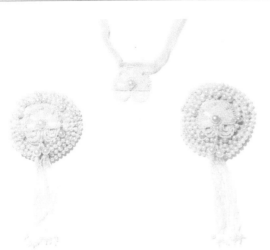

Figure 2.13 A pair of pasties from the 1920s. Materials are buckram, silk and pearl beading. The accessory at the top of the image is made of gauze, and is the remnant of a halter strap that attached the two pasties together. The pasties are over three inches in diameter. In some photos of 1920s dancers, large pasties like this were attached to strings and made into bras, much like the breastplate bra of a Salome style costume. Part of the reason for this is that cosmetic adhesive options were limited to early **spirit gum**. *Spirit gum was made of a resin and ether mixture, and would have been an irritant to the sensitive skin of the breast, especially if repeated wear was a factor.*
(Photo by Ben Trivett, 2016. Pasties from author's personal collection, and featured in The Pastie Project, *2017)*

Figure 2.14 Back view of 1920s pasties.
(Photo by Ben Trivett, 2016. Pasties from author's personal collection, and featured in The Pastie Project, *2017)*

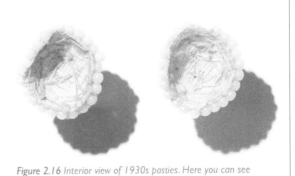

Figure 2.15 1930s pasties made of buckram, faux pearl beads, and thick thread, possibly dental floss. These pasties are only 1 1/2 inches in diameter and were adhered to the nipple area.
(Photo by Ben Trivett, 2017. Pasties from the author's collection, featured in The Pastie Project *2017)*

Figure 2.16 Interior view of 1930s pasties. Here you can see the thick thread used to attach the beads to the base. Dental floss was a popular material for beading because it was less likely to tear on the edges of glass beads.
(Photo by Ben Trivett, 2017. Pasties from the author's collection, featured in The Pastie Project *2017)*

Figure 2.17 The stage picture with a chorus of "butterflies" and a central "peacock" in the Ziegfeld Follies, 1920s. (The Ziegfeld Club)

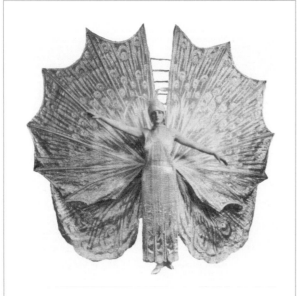

Figure 2.18 "Dolores in her peacock costume." (The Ziegfeld Club)

Early burlesque and its development into a sex-centric industry led to some of the first obscenity legislation related to popular entertainment in America. Before these regulations were made into laws, morality groups and "obscenity police" were forced to define what was considered obscene in order to regulate it. Literal definitions were required because visible boundaries had to be placed in order for censors to determine if a show was abiding by the rules or not. The creation of pasties was a direct result of these regulations. The differentiation between high-brow and low-brow theater was another factor that affected the strictness of enforcement regarding what could be displayed on the stage and, as previously discussed, this partially related to the economic class of the audience. The Ziegfeld Follies was not as harshly scrutinized by censors in part because of the wealth of their audience. The Follies' choruses of women in extravagant costumes were not performing **striptease**, their action on stage was more of a **parade and pose**. The costumes, though ornate, could be very revealing—more so than those in the over-regulated burlesque theaters.

As seen with the crowd-drawing performance of the hoochie-coochie dance at the turn of the century, **Follies**, burlesque and vaudeville variety style shows were imitated by countless theater groups hoping to make a profit. By the turn of the century, burlesque had created its own touring wheels, similar to those travelled by circuses and vaudeville groups. With censors aching to shut down the burlesque houses in big cities, especially New York, The Columbia, Mutual, Municipal and raunchier Independent Wheels were bringing burlesque to the rest of the country.

Figure 2.19 Four ornate costumes from the Ziegfeld Follies, 1920s.
(The Ziegfeld Club)

Figure 2.20 Follies dancer Emma Duval was the mother of the
1940s and 1950s burlesque dancer Tirza. Notice the amount
of skin showing in this 1920s look.
(From the personal collection of Neil "Nez" Kendall)

Figure 2.21 Dancer Mary Higgins from Club Anatole, 1920s.
This costume represents a traditional showgirl look of the
1920s, reminiscent of Erte's extravagant costume designs.
(Jerome Robbins Dance Division, The New York Public Library
for the Performing Arts)

Figure 2.22 *Fashion icon Erte's costumes for George White's Scandals, 1926. Press photo, private collection.*
(Private collection)

Figure 2.23 *A Ziegfeld imitator, this chorus of ladies from Jack Garrison and the Broadway Scandals is representative of a smaller-scale production that was part of a burlesque wheel.*
(Charles McCaghy collection of Exotic Dance to Clubs, The Ohio State University Special Collections)

Figure 2.24 *A postcard from a 1920s production celebrating the "Gay 90's" and featuring The Beefstock Girls, known for their full figures.*
(Personal collection of Janelle Smith)

SISTER ACTS

Figure 2.25 *The Adair Twins with ostrich fans, late teens, early 20s. The Adair Twins are representative of the trend for duos and "sisters" as an act in vaudeville and burlesque. Other popular pairs of the 1920s and 1930s were the Dolly Sisters and the Dodge Sisters.*
(Jerome Robbins Dance Division, The New York Public Library for the Performing Arts)

Figure 2.26 *The Dolly Sisters in the Ziegfeld Follies, 1920s.*
(Personal collection of Janelle Smith)

Figure 2.27 *The Dodge Sisters in dramatic late 1920s/early 1930s looks.*
(Personal collection of Janelle Smith)

The costume featured in Figures 2.28 to 2.33 is from the personal collection of Vicki Butterfly. This 1920s costume is an excellent example of a chorus girl's outfit for a themed group number. This particular ensemble is French, but it provides good insight to silhouette, construction and decoration seen in American performance imagery of the same era.

Figure 2.28 *1920s chorus girl costume and single fingerless glove or gauntlet. Body is nude mesh with silk used to cover the chest and trunk area. Accented with metallic **soutache**-style trim, **paillettes** and sequins. Gauntlet is made of black knit and heavily ornamented with sequins in two sizes and colors. From the private collection of Vicki Butterfly.*
(Photo by Coleen Scott with permission from Vicki Butterfly)

Figure 2.29 *Back view of 1920s chorus girl costume. The zipper is not original. The original closures were most likely hook and eye. Zippers were not commonly used in women's clothing until the 1930s. From the private collection of Vicki Butterfly.*
(Photo by Coleen Scott with permission from Vicki Butterfly)

Figure 2.30 *Close-ups of the embellishment on the trunks and **gauntlet** of the 1920s chorus girl costume. The small gold sequins on the trunks are not original, as one can see they are a different material than the others.*
(Photos by Coleen Scott with permission from Vicki Butterfly)

Figure 2.31 *Close-up of the center front decoration. The paillettes may not be original.*
(Photo by Coleen Scott with permission from Vicki Butterfly)

Figure 2.32 *View from the backside of the neckline. From this angle the bust darting and edge finishing can be seen.*
(Photo by Coleen Scott with permission from Vicki Butterfly)

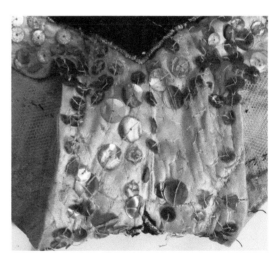

Figure 2.33 *View of the bodysuit **rise**, which shows the finishing at the leg opening and the sequin application that must be somewhat uncomfortable for the wearer.*
(Photo by Coleen Scott with permission from Vicki Butterfly)

GIRL REVUE FRONT. Brown & Dyer Shows early 1920's. Doc Cann with mustache is in ticket box to your left. Courtesy L. Harvey Doc Cann.

*Figure 2.34 Dancers in the **sideshow** burlesque tent pose outside with the **barkers** including Doc Carr, 1920s. Notice the show's marketing of an "Oriental Fantasy."*
(History of the American Carnival, part IV, page 100)

The circus had been travelling caravan for years, but now, the burlesque circuits were booking individual performers for tours, hitting one town after another, and every spoke of the wheel. Not everyone could be a headliner, however, and the circus sideshow was another option for burlesque dancers. A role in the cooch tent put dancers in front of a male audience, strictly for the purpose of titillating and teasing them in a sexy show. These displays began as belly dance-style performances as early as the 1890s, but became burlesque and strip shows by the 1930s with movement influenced by Black dance styles including the shimmy and the **quiver2**. In places where poverty was high during the Great Depression, the cooch tent could be a way out for some women, in hopes that they might move on to bigger and better shows, or in the least, a better life.

*Figure 2.35 Hinda Wausau claimed to be the first striptease artist when her solo **shimmy dance** in 1928 led to her costume accidentally "shimmying" off.*
(Personal collection of Janelle Smith)

Figure 2.36 Circus Artist, Düren, Germany, 1930–1932, by August Sander. The costume this artist is wearing
resembles that of the cooch tent and "oriental" themed girl shows popular in the US at the same time.
(The J. Paul Getty Museum, Los Angeles. Photo by August Sander [Circus Artist, Düren (Zirkusartistin)], about
1930–1932, Gelatin Silver Print, 11 3/8 x 8 11/16 in)

Figures 2.37 to 2.42 feature a 1920s **cooch dancer**
costume from the personal collection of Neil "Nez" Kendall and
The Striptease Museum, Chester, England.

Figure 2.37 A hand-beaded, fringed bra with halter strap, 1920s. Bugle bead fringe is attached across the top of the bra cups, with a second layer going across the bra through the center of the cups, and a third layer attached only to the lower half of both cups, but free in the center. Originally, this may have been attached center front.
(Photo by Coleen Scott. Costume from the personal collection of Neil "Nez" Kendal and The Striptease Museum, Chester, England)

Figure 2.38 The interior of the bra shows the hand stitching from the beaded trim. The bra cups have some stiffness and are built with a lower demi cup and a smaller top cup with a pronounced curve in the center. There is no underwire, nor would there be at this time. The outer edges and center seam are bound, and the construction creates a stiff, molded cup. The author presumes that this cup shape was creating the look of larger breasts, and might have been concealing a sizeable pastie that helped to fill in the shape.
(Photo by Coleen Scott. Costume from the personal collection of Neil "Nez" Kendal and The Striptease Museum, Chester, England)

Figure 2.39 A closer look at the inside structure of the bra cup. This angle gives a better view of the cup construction. The extremity of the top cup angle could be from age and warp in storage.
(Photo by Coleen Scott. Costume from the personal collection of Neil "Nez" Kendal and The Striptease Museum, Chester, England)

Figure 2.40 Matching **shimmy belt** for the cooch dancer costume. Made of a silky fabric with hand-made bugle bead fringe and individual sequin and seed bead trim at the waist.
(Photo by Coleen Scott. Costume from the personal collection of Neil "Nez" Kendal and The Striptease Museum, Chester, England)

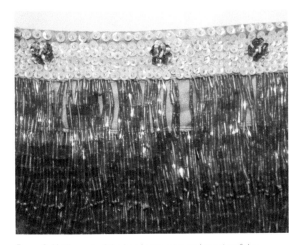

Figure 2.41 Close-up of the hand-sewn trim at the waist of the shimmy belt.
(Photo by Coleen Scott. Costume from the personal collection of Neil "Nez" Kendal and The Striptease Museum, Chester, England)

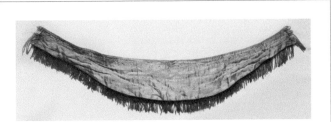

Figure 2.42 Underside of the shimmy belt. Visible hand stitching is seen where trim is attached. The belt closure is a double hook and eye.
(Photo by Coleen Scott. Costume from the personal collection of Neil "Nez" Kendal and
The Striptease Museum, Chester, England)

HULA

The shape and function of the shimmy belt hearkens back to the undulating movements of the lower half of the body in bellydance. In the costumes of the "Streets of Cairo" dancers, there is a sash or scarf tied at the hips that may relate to the cooch dancer's garment. The other relative of the shimmy belt is the **hula skirt**. The movement of fringe that is usually attached to the belt has the same visual vocabulary as a flowing grass skirt, and the movements of the **hula** also emphasize hip movement. Well-travelled Americans were familiar with the hula by the late 1800s, because steamship travel allowed for tourism in Hawaii. Although Hawaii went through periods of western colonial dominance where they were forced to stifle their ancient traditions, the people struggled to retain their culture.

Figure 2.43 Momi Kalama, Kansas City, 1921. According to the photo details from the New York Public Library, Momi Kalama was a hula dancer known as "The Pavlova of Hawaii." She performed in a show called Barney Gerard's "Girls De Looks" in 1921. What is not known for sure is if Momi was actually Hawaiian—this image is the only one we have found. It would not be extraordinary in the least if her tagline and name were just for marketing, but there is not enough information to be sure at this time.
(Photo by Bert Koch. Jerome Robbins Dance Division, The New York Public Library for the Performing Arts)

Figure 2.44 Hula dancers in The Edison Follies, 1920s. Like belly dancing, the hula was appropriated by chorus girls from Ziegfeld to Minsky. In most cases it was just another excuse for immodest costuming.
(Jerome Robbins Dance Division, The New York Public Library for the Performing Arts)

Figure 2.45
A 1930s duo dances the hula in trendy cellophane versions of the grass skirt and accessories.
(Personal collection of Neil "Nez" Kendall)

EXOTICS

Bellydance and hula both fell under the umbrella of **exotic dance** styles, which came to mean that they were from non-Western cultures, and were therefore "other." The term "exotic" was not only used to describe dance styles, but also performers from minority groups including Asians, Latinas, and Black Americans. Labeling a dancer as **exotic** in the burlesque scene translated into less work and lower pay than White dancers. The word exotic in the modern term exotic dance derives from this same discriminating use applied to dancers of color. Exotic in this context is not a connotation of race, but sensuality. To put it in a puritanical societal context: exotic things were desirable because of their supposed uninhibited nature, but they were to be avoided because indulging in sensuality was a sin. Whether the dance style or the people were judged as exotic, in the first half of the twentieth century the term forced performers of color into stereotypical roles projected by the White paying audiences, or kept them segregated.

Figure 2.46 *A trio of Asian chorus girls, 1930s. The stereotyped sensuality of Asian women was fetishized like many things in puritanical or religious society that are touted as sinful. (Photo by Bloom Chicago. Personal collection of Janelle Smith)*

Figure 2.47 *Princess White Deer in Ziegfeld Follies of 1922. The use of Native American ceremonial dress homogenized the American's picture of what Native Americans were. The thousands of tribes and people living on reservations were forgotten when this costume style was used to represent an entire population. The look recalls times past, allowing audiences to forget that Native Americans are not characters of yore, but living, present, native people who are still fighting to keep the land they have left. This costume is visually effective on stage and, because of its beauty, it was appropriated time and time again in burlesque performance.*

(Museum of the City of New York with permission from the New York Public Library)

Figure 2.48 Program cover from The Cotton Club, 1939.
(New York Public Library)

The Cotton Club was a famous Harlem burlesque club that was open from 1923 until 1935. It was a Whites-only club that featured some of the best Black performers of the time. The marketing reflects the club's target audience; program covers advertise a land of naked brown tribal people, but the inside of the program looks almost identical to the presentation for a Ziegfeld or Earl Carroll show, with Black women coiffed in fashionable White hairstyles, furs, and draped fabric. Like any live theater venue at the time, The Cotton Club was a business out to make money. One major difference was, that it created jobs for performers of color.

Figure 2.49 Maude Russel and her Ebony Steppers 1929 Cotton Club show "Just a Minute."
(Photographs and Prints Division, Schomburg Center for Research in Black Culture, The New York Public Library)

Figure 2.50 The inside page of a 1939 Cotton Club program advertising the performers.
(Private collection)

Figure 2.51 1938 Cotton Club revue dancers in Buenos Aires, Bertye Lou Wood (far left).
(©Toots Crackin/courtesy Everett Collection)

As burlesque popularity boomed in the 1930s with New York theaters right alongside *legitimate* Broadway houses,[3] some of the biggest names in burlesque history shared the stage including Sally Rand, Ann Corio, and Gypsy Rose Lee. Burlesque had separated itself from the nearly dead vaudeville and other mainstream theater and became centered in the art of the striptease. Burlesque shows were not *all* strip, however, and productions were well rounded with classic comic sketches and impressive group numbers interspersed in an afternoon or evening's entertainment. The censors were not far behind, and by 1937 New York City Mayor Fiorello La Guardia succeeded in his goal along with license commissioner Paul Moss in shutting down all but three downtown burlesque theaters by denying license renewal. Despite long-term political attempts to eliminate it, burlesque was not dead. Travelling circuits were booming all over the country, and New York shows found homes a little further uptown. Not to mention, the women performing

*Figure 2.52 Sally Rand promotes her **bubble dance**, 1930s. In this promotional photo, Rand looks to be completely nude, but when it came to stage performance and various local regulations, she presented the illusion of nudity with a barely there mesh bodysuit.*
(Photo by Maurice Seymour. Used with permission of Ronald Seymour. Billy Rose Theatre Division, The New York Public Library for the Performing Arts)

left individual legacies that penetrated the core of American cultural history.

Sally Rand became one of the most famous burlesque performers in America primarily for her acts performing "nude" with feather fans or a giant bubble. Rand was not the first or only **fan dancer**, but she had a major rivalry with former Earl Carroll[4] and Ziegfeld dancer Faith Bacon about who was first. This battle went on for years, and exploded in the press when both women were scheduled to perform

at the 1933 Chicago Word's Fair. Bacon sued Rand in 1938 and tried to have her banned from doing the fan dance. Sally responded by saying "The fan idea is as old as Cleopatra, and so what? She can't sue me for that." She cited Bacon's jealousy over Rand's success and added: "the public already has decided which of us it likes best."[5] The facts are that Faith Bacon danced with fans before Sally, but Rand took the spotlight and became more beloved. Rand's career outlasted Bacon's by 30-plus years.

Figure 2.53 Sally Rand with her famous oversized ostrich feather fans, 1930s. (Billy Rose Theatre Division, The New York Public Library for the Performing Arts)

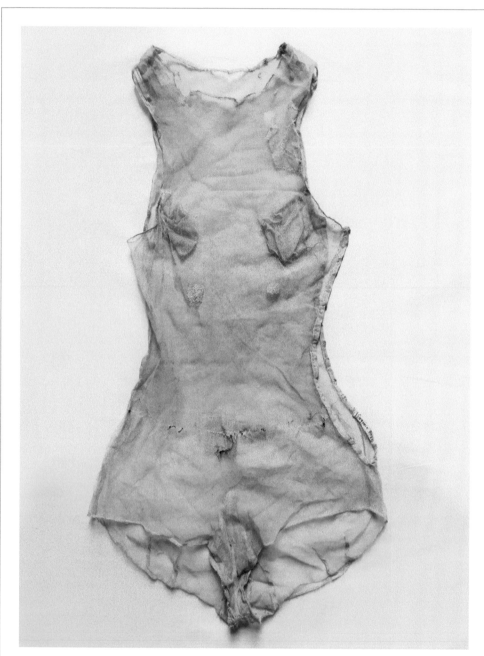

Figure 2.54 A 1930s mesh bodysuit with hook-and-bar and snap side closure, hook and bar left shoulder closure, and circular built-in pasties or nipple covers made of the same mesh. The suit has many areas of repair, and a label with a more recent performer's name—"Virginia Ray." *(Photo by Coleen Scott. Bodysuit from the personal collection of Neil "Nez" Kendall)*

The mesh bodysuit featured in Figures 2.54 to 2.58 once belonged to Sally Rand. It has been repaired and repurposed for other dancers, but is original to Rand, according to its owner–collector, proprietor of the travelling Striptease Museum, and Burlesque Hall of Fame Board Member, Neil "Nez" Kendall. This style of bodysuit was used by burlesque performers to give the illusion of nudity, but is more often seen embellished at the breasts and crotch areas to look like the performer is wearing pasties and a ***merkin*** or g-string.

Figure 2.55 This close-up of the neckline shows the hook and bar closure at the left shoulder (five sets), some rips and repairs, and the turned edge of the neckline, which looks to be sewn by machine. The mesh is a single layer. It is not very stretchy, closer to a tulle, and is made in the shape and measurements of the body it fits, which explains the darting and closures.
(Photo by Coleen Scott. Bodysuit from the personal collection of Neil "Nez" Kendall)

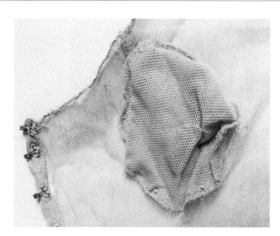

Figure 2.56 The pastie is made of multiple layers (at least three) of the same mesh with a machine stitch around the edge. For attachment, it is only tacked along the bust dart and as invisibly as possible in several places on the single layer of the bodysuit.
(Photo by Coleen Scott. Bodysuit from the personal collection of Neil "Nez" Kendall)

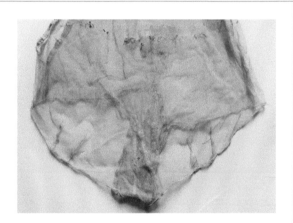

Figure 2.57 The bottom half of the bodysuit shows damage where a waistband or accent was attached to the bodysuit. The back of the leg openings have two small darts on each side for shaping around curves of the buttocks, and the crotch is reinforced with two triangular gussets center front and back made of the same mesh and a center seam, which probably provided a better fit anatomically.
(Photo by Coleen Scott. Bodysuit from the personal collection of Neil "Nez" Kendall)

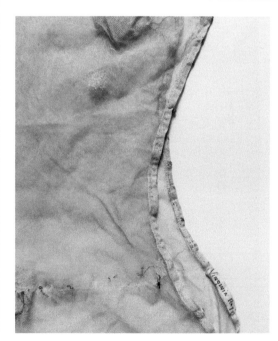

Figure 2.58 The side closure shows a reinforced edge for attaching the hooks, bars and snaps. The hooks and bars here are the same ones found at the left shoulder. This style of closure was seen on bias gowns of the time as well, but was not intended to open easily. This makes sense for a nude bodysuit in burlesque, because it would be the final layer of a performer's costume, and would not be removed on stage.
(Photo by Coleen Scott. Bodysuit from the personal collection of Neil "Nez" Kendall)

Figure 2.59 Ann Corio feature, Stage Magazine, page 43, 1935. Ann wears a slightly different and more decorated version of the bodysuit featured on the previous pages. (Photos by Alfredo Valente)

When the term "burlesque queen" is used, people are referring to someone like Ann Corio or Gypsy Rose Lee. The two women are arguably the most influential burlesque performers of all time because of their career longevity and their American household recognition. Ann began performing in 1925 with Minsky's and became a B movie star in the 1940s.

In the interest of preserving the fading art of burlesque, she produced and directed a nostalgic Off-Broadway show in 1962 called *This Was Burlesque*, which she took on the road and made into a book. Ann's burlesque style was classic 1930s, and Figures 2.59 and 2.60 show her posing and performing in a perfect example of a 1930s gown and fur ensemble.

Figure 2.60 Ann Corio wears a stunning sequined gown, gloves and fur wrap. Photo by Murray Korman, 1930s. (From the personal collection of Janelle Smith)

Figure 2.61 Gypsy Rose Lee, 1931. Gypsy is wearing a nude leotard covered in leaves.
(Billy Rose Theatre Division, The New York Public Library for the Performing Arts. With
permission from Erik Preminger)

If Ann Corio was an example of classic burlesque, Gypsy Rose Lee was an example of original burlesque. She was known as the "intellectual stripper" because in her famous routine "The Psychology of a Stripteaser" she talked about literature and the arts onstage while casually removing her clothes and revealing very little. Lee's background in vaudeville from childhood made her a performer who knew how to carry herself onstage and command an audience. In her early years, she designed and built costumes for herself and some of her chorus, and used fishnet bodysuits as a base to add strategically placed decoration. Lee was Minsky's biggest star attraction for several years before she left to do several fruitless films and the Broadway show *Star and Garter*.

Figure 2.62 *Gypsy Rose Lee in her "Psychology of a Stripteaser" costume. 1931 at Minsky's.*
(Billy Rose Theatre Division, The New York Public Library for the Performing Arts. With permission from Erik Preminger)

Figure 2.63 Alla Nazimova stars in Charles Bryant's silent film Salome, 1923. It is a retelling of Oscar Wilde's play of the same name. Nazimova was a queer filmmaker, producer, and actress. The costume she wears in this image, and others throughout the film, are a beautiful representation of the Art Deco aesthetic. (Everett Collection)

*Figure 2.64 Mae West co-wrote the script for the film Go West Young Man. She started her career in vaudeville and burlesque theaters and became a playwright, published author and film star. This mermaid-style silhouette paired with a wrap or fur to create enlarged shoulders was a signature look in 1930s eveningwear and influenced burlesque wear. Gowns were cut on the **bias** to achieve a body-hugging silhouette. (Everett Collection)*

FILM

New York City was the center of culture and entertainment in the 1920s, and it was also the hub of the film industry. Things started to change in the 1930s with the burlesque theater shutdowns, and film's move to Hollywood. The glamorous influence of film on popular culture grew even deeper with *talkies* and the movie industry dominating the world of spectator entertainment because of its affordability. Like burlesque, the romance of the movies helped people to escape the despair of The Great Depression or boredom with everyday life, and the allure of the silver screen found its way to the everyday person. The film business boosted the beauty industries with silent film stars setting trends for makeup, hair, and fashion. Talkies caused a shift in the film industry, requiring actors who could deliver a line as opposed to the dependence on pantomime and facial expression of silent films. Hollywood looked to the stage for its new batch of starlets, which included the shameless straight talker Mae West, and *femme fatale* Marlene Dietrich.

Figure 2.65 Marlene Dietrich in The Blue Angel, *1930. Costume designer: Tihamer Varady. Dietrich was a German-born actress who started her career as a chorus girl. The Blue Angel was her first major film role, and, in it, she played a burlesque performer. This image shows her in a burlesque costume for a stage performance within the film. After moving to the United States, she worked with the same director Josef von Sternberg on six Paramount pictures. The characters she portrayed in the films* Morocco, Dishonored, Shanghai Express, Blonde Venus, *and* The Devil is a Woman *solidified her legacy as a femme fatale.*
(The Everett Collection)

Figure 2.66 *More 1920s and 1930s burlesque stars. Clockwise from top left: Georgia Sothern; Flo Ash in cellophane; Fanny Brice (and Bob Hope) in the Ziegfeld Follies 1936; Evelyn Keller; Mary Jane Halsey and Estelle Etterre. (2 and 5 From the collection of Janelle Smith, 3 from the Everett Collection, 4 Billy Rose Theater Division, New York Public Library)*

Burlesque became an original performance art form during the 1920s and 1930s in America. It permeated American society, and became intertwined in the theater, music, film, dance, and colloquial humor that America had to offer. In the coming decades, burlesque would solidify itself as the first completely American-made art form, with costumes that were particular to its very specific needs.

Notes

1 www.loc.gov/item/today-in-history/january-13 Library of Congress retrieved January 18, 2018.

2 For more information on Black dance history and its influence on popular dance in America read *Black Dance in America: A History Through Its People* by James Haskins. 1990. Harper Collins.

3 The New York Theater scene was inspired by burlesque's popularity and vice versa. On Broadway in 1927 a play called *Burlesque* was put on in the "legitimate" Plymouth theater with Barbara Stanwyck as the lead.

4 Earl Carroll's Vanities was another popular Ziegfeld competitor with female choruses and solo dancers. It reached a height of popularity in the 1940s and will be featured in the following chapter.

5 "Sally Defies Foe to Fight 'Like a Man,'" *The Pittsburgh Press*, October 13, 1938.

Figure 3.1 Gypsy Rose Lee on the road in a Rolls-Royce with Show Girls 1957. Gypsy wears her costume
from the film Screaming Mimi.
(Billy Rose Theater Division, New York Public Library with permission from Erik Preminger)

CHAPTER 3

"THE GOLDEN AGE"
1940S–1950S

INTRODUCTION

When burlesque was completely pushed out of the theater district on Broadway in the early 1940s, it didn't disappear, it just moved uptown. The regional **burlesque circuits** were a booming business that continued in the 1940s and 1950s. In this chapter, the term "The Golden Age" of burlesque corresponds to the "Golden Age of Hollywood" and the relationship between the two, especially as burlesque refined the art of striptease and then declined in popularity in the 1960s. In the 1950s burlesque show structure was not just a series of ecdysiasts[1] removing their clothing, it was a production, complete with group numbers, chorus girls, and familiar, unchanging, comedy sketches. Burlesque shows were recognized in the mainstream as a couples' activity for a night out, and acknowledged in Hollywood as a popular art form. Evidence of burlesque's influence presents itself in the popular, now classic 1940s and 1950s films *Ziegfeld Girl* with Hedy Lamarr, Judy Garland, and Lana Turner, *Ziegfeld Follies* starring Lucille Ball Fred Astaire, and Lena Horne, *Salome* with Rita Hayworth, *Lady of Burlesque* with Barbara Stanwyck (based on Gypsy Rose Lee's novel *The G-String Murders*), and scenes like *Singin' in the Rain*'s theater montage, and *White Christmas'* "Sisters" number to name a few. A number of Marilyn Monroe's films showcased her as a showgirl or burlesque performer, and all of her costumes designed by William Travilla are exquisite. Burlesque's influence did not stop with film, it infiltrated the plots and casts of legitimate Broadway shows as well like *Star and Garter* starring Gypsy Rose Lee, Carrie Finnell, and Georgia Sothern. With opportunities on stage and screen, as well as the growth of celebrity tabloid and cheesecake magazines, burlesque dancers had a larger media platform upon which to gain superstardom.

Figure 3.2 Gypsy Rose Lee in the Broadway show Star and Garter, 1942. Costume design by Irene Sharaff. © New York Public Library. (Billy Rose Theater Division, New York Public Library. Used with permission from Erik Preminger)

Figure 3.3 A promotional lithograph of Rita Hayworth in Salome, 1953.
(Author's collection)

Figure 3.4 Ziegfeld Girl, from left, Hedy Lamarr, Judy Garland, Lana Turner, in showgirl costumes by Adrian, 1941.
(Everett Collection)

Figure 3.5 Ziegfeld Follies, Lucille Ball, 1946.
(Everett Collection)

Figure 3.6 Lady of Burlesque, Barbara Stanwyck, 1943.
(Everett Collection)

Figure 3.7 There's No Business Like Show Business, *Marilyn Monroe, 1954. Costume designed by William Travilla.*
(©20th Century-Fox Film Corporation, TM & Copyright/courtesy Everett Collection)

Sherri Britton is one of the biggest burlesque stars of the 1940s. She performed through the 1930s as well and was a feature in residence and Leon and Eddie's nightclub on 52nd Street in New York City for seven years. She was known for having elegant costumes, but a risqué dancing style. Britton was stripping in nightclubs well into the late 1950s, but she also acted in numerous plays and performed as a cabaret singer. Some of the most recognizable burlesque images of her have her wearing a net or heavily decorated bra and a **panel skirt** as seen in Figure 3.8.

Figure 3.8 Sherri Britton in a more intricate top and panel skirt, designed in a Salome influenced style. For Leon and Eddie's, New York City, 1940s. (James Kollar. From the personal collection of Janelle Smith)

Figure 3.9 A collection of Sherri Britton's pasties. Leslie Zemeckis' personal collection. (Leslie Zemeckis)

The silk bra and panel skirt in Figures 3.10 to 3.13 from the 1940s is a perfect example of the panel skirts worn by Sherri Britton and numerous other burlesque dancers.

Figure 3.10 Green sequin triangle bra. The bra is fairly rigid with the sequin trim, satin base, and net lining. There is no underwire, just a tunnel for the elastic around the ribcage. There is a hook attached to one side of the elastic and the other part of the closure is missing. Another popular material for a softer bra structure was a double layer of tulle. (Photo by Coleen Scott from the personal collection of Neil "Nez" Kendall)

Figure 3.11 View of the inside of the bra cup. (Photo by Coleen Scott from the personal collection of Neil "Nez" Kendall)

Figure 3.12 Green silk panel skirt with triangular front waistband covered in sequins. The back waistband is straight across. There is a hook and bar closure on the left side. Panels are not removable on this skirt, but were rigged with snaps in other examples of this style.
(Photo by Coleen Scott from the personal collection of Neil "Nez" Kendall)

Figure 3.13 Inside of the panel skirt belt. The label reads "House of Ellwood" LaVonne Creations, Chicago, Illinois. The rolled hem on the side of the panel is visible here, as is the silk lining of the belt and the meandering machine stitching from the sequin application.
(Photo by Coleen Scott from the personal collection of Neil "Nez" Kendall)

Figure 3.14 The beautiful burlesque queen
Betty Rowland in a 1940s look.
(Photo by John E. Reed)

Burlesque costumes, like Hollywood glamour in the 1940s, flaunted excess and allowed for a viewer's escape from war rationing and worry. Earl Carroll's shows competed with the Ziegfeld Follies for their dinner show presentations of elegantly or thematically dressed showgirls. Gowns, gauntlets, negligees, beads, fur and feathers, especially those ensembles designed by Rex Huntington, distracted and enticed the audience, and were truly the stuff dreams were made of. One of the best examples of a glamorous escape where dreams might come true was Las Vegas. The El Rancho hotel's opening in 1941 and later the Flamingo and Sahara hotels created another home base for both burlesque and showgirls that continued to top itself in the 1950s.

Figure 3.15 A program
back for Earl Carroll's
dinner show, 1940s.
(Author's collection)

The birth of Las Vegas as a travel destination fit right in with the stylings of burlesque shows, and the mafia ties to the performance art. In Las Vegas, New York, and other major US cities like Chicago, the mafia has always been associated with **nightclubs** and gambling. The stories of so many burlesque performers involve relationships, partnerships, and terrifying entrapment of Mafioso-controlled clubs. This threatening environment doesn't translate in magazines and media of the time, where burlesque performers are seen basking in the glamour of lavish gifts including fur and jewelry, luxury apartments, and a general money-is-no-concern lifestyle. Still, the burlesque business was a lucrative career, and in the 1940s and 1950s when women still did not have many options for career paths, the glamour of the stage and travel drew many away from abusive home lives, poverty, and boredom.

Figure 3.16 Las Vegas Show Sheet from the 1950s with a showgirl in a feather and rhinestone costume as the featured image. (Author's collection)

Figure 3.17 Postcard for the Stardust Hotel, 1950s. Showgirl costumes in Vegas take a cue from the giant burlesque ensembles of the Folies Bergère and Ziegfeld. (Author's collection)

Figure 3.18 A 1950s showgirl-style costume in green satin with pink sequin accents, fringe, and matching
fingerless gauntlets
(Photo by Coleen Scott. Costume from the personal collection of Neil "Nez" Kendall)

Figure 3.19 *Back view of the 1950s showgirl costume and gauntlets.*
(Photo by Coleen Scott. Costume from the personal collection of Neil "Nez" Kendall)

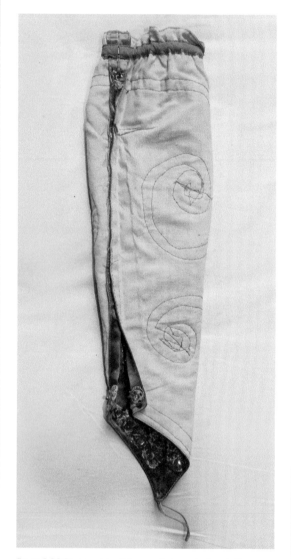

Figure 3.20 *Reverse side of the gauntlet reveals the stitching of the sequins, a tunnel for elastic at the top of the glove and a placket with snap at the wrist for easy removal.*
(Photo by Coleen Scott. Costume from the personal collection of Neil "Nez" Kendall)

Figure 3.21 *A view of the inside of the showgirl costume showing* **pinked seams**, *stitching, and zipper placement. Snaps on the back suggest that additional accouterments were attached, most likely a* **bustle**, *skirt or feather accessory.*
(Photo by Coleen Scott. Costume from the personal collection of Neil "Nez" Kendall)

Conjoined twins Violet and Daisey Hilton were the **showgirls** of the sideshow. They were joined at the hips and buttocks, and shared no limbs or vital organs. They were brought up in an abusive home that purchased them as babies to be moneymakers. The sisters were trained in dance and music, and taken on tours where they performed but never received any of their earnings. They were able to free themselves from their abusers in 1931 and performed in vaudeville and later burlesque. The sisters were featured in the film *Freaks* in 1932 and

Chained for Life in 1952. Their later career consisted of making appearances at screenings of their films. The sisters worked with famed burlesque costume designer Rex Huntington for some of their ensembles. The following pages show Huntington's 1942 and 1957 designs for two burlesque costumes belonging to Daisey and Violet, along with pattern pieces and payment ledgers. The notes and sketches shown in Figures 3.24–3.29 are a wonderful record of thoughtful costume design and construction for clients with very special needs due to physicality.

Figure 3.22 Cover of a promotional program for the Hilton Sisters, 1950s. (Personal collection of Neil "Nez" Kendall)

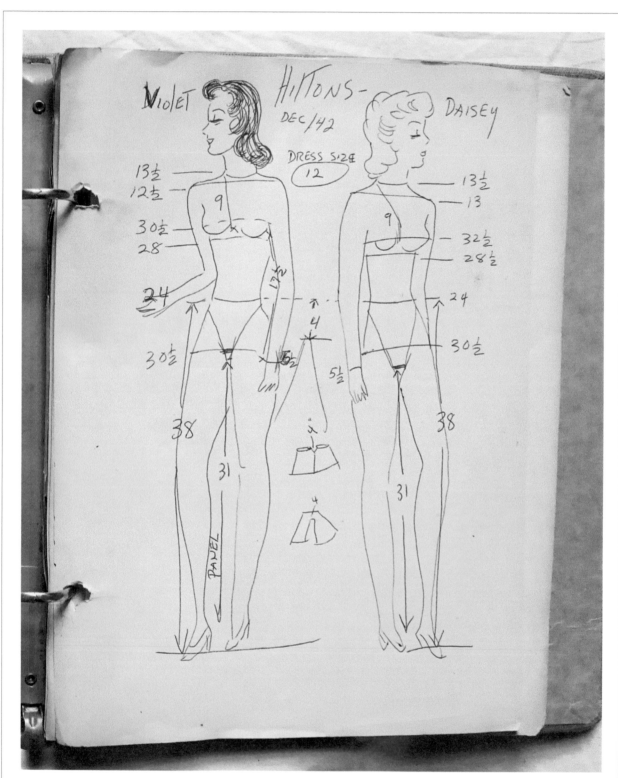

Figure 3.23 A binder containing Rex Huntington's measurements and designs for Daisey and Violet Hilton. These measurements are dated December 1942. The measurements in the center between the torsos represent the area where the sisters were conjoined.
(Photo by Coleen Scott. From the personal collection of Neil "Nez" Kendall)

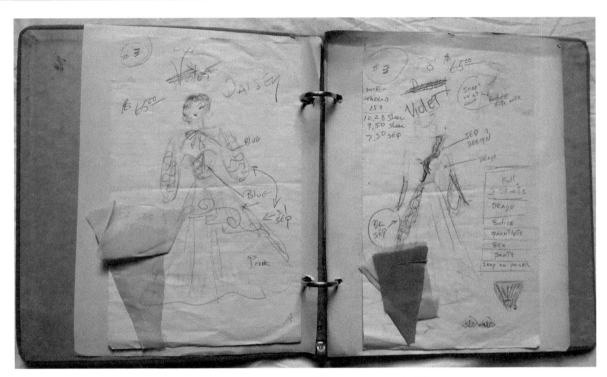

*Figure 3.24 Sketches for individual burlesque costumes for the sisters with **chiffon** swatches attached. When the sisters became adults Daisey went blonde and Violet stayed brunette, and their costumes no longer matched. Harrington's sketches respectfully represent the sisters as individuals with separate tastes.*
(Photo by Coleen Scott. From the personal collection of Neil "Nez" Kendall)

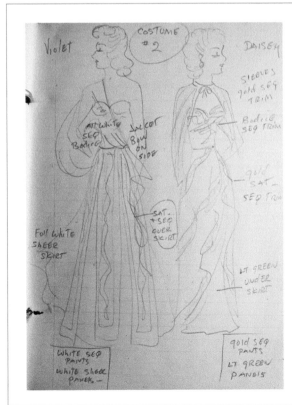

Figure 3.25
Rex Huntington sketches of two gowns for the sisters in 1956.
(Photo by Coleen Scott. From the personal collection of Neil "Nez" Kendall)

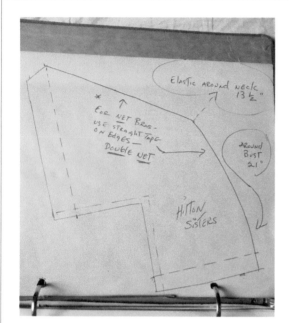

Figure 3.26 Pattern for a triangle bra used for the Hilton Sisters with very helpful notes on construction and measurements. (Photo by Coleen Scott. From the personal collection of Neil "Nez" Kendall)

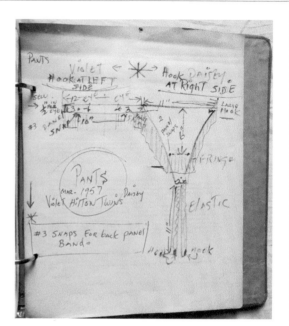

Figure 3.27 Sketch for removable panties for Violet and Daisey with special notes about alternating sides for closures, 1957. (Photo by Coleen Scott. From the personal collection of Neil "Nez" Kendall)

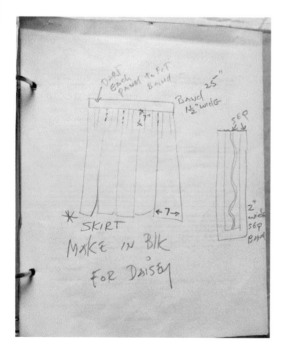

Figure 3.28 Panel skirt design for Violet and Daisey. (Photo by Coleen Scott. From the personal collection of Neil "Nez" Kendall)

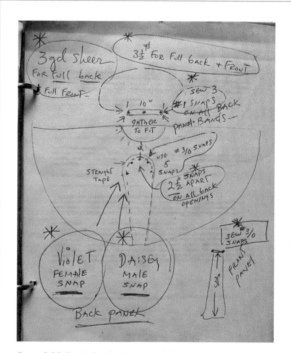

Figure 3.29 Sketch for the back panel skirt with special snap construction for the conjoined sisters. (Photo by Coleen Scott. From the personal collection of Neil "Nez" Kendall)

Figure 3.30 This red 1940s burlesque gown is credited to Rex Huntington. It is made in a popular silhouette, but its most special feature is the lining, which is made from flour sacks.
(Photo by Fatema Gharzai, costume from the personal collection of Janelle Smith)

Figure 3.31 A close-up look of the "flour sack" lining of the red Rex Huntington dress.
(Photo by Fatema Gharzai, costume from the personal collection of Janelle Smith)

In fashion, the silhouette of the 1940s carried over from the 1930s fitted garments. A curvaceous body was desired, but hemlines rose, partially due to supply rationing during the war. Clothing was designed with as little additional length or fullness possible in daywear. Accents in tailoring techniques became the de rigueur detailing. Extra seams did not add more fabric, but demonstrated complexity. After World War II, fashion changed drastically. **The New Look** from Dior exhibited everything the restrictive 1940s silhouette was not. Full skirts, nipped waists and curvaceous heels with matching accessories were the order of the day for those with means. Evening wear could reflect this volume with full skirts, but open necklines and slim fitting gowns with beautiful accents or mermaid flounce skirts decorated the figures of the elegant woman as well. **Negligees** and **dusters** made of yards of lace or chiffon embodied luxury for the burlesque performer or the leisurely woman at home.

Lingerie experienced stylistic changes in the 1950s with the shape of bra cups reaching their peak conical shape. Shapewear was a must under clothing for the perfect hourglass silhouette. Although lingerie was functional in creating the desired body shape under the everyday woman's clothes, it was also visible on the bodies of fetish and pinup models like Bettie Page in popular **cheesecake** magazines. This **fetish** for lingerie including stockings and garters translated well on the burlesque stage of the 1950s.

Figure 3.32 Bettie Page and Tempest Storm were famous for their duo fetish modeling in lingerie, stockings and garters, 1950s. (Irving and Paula Klaw, Everett Collection)

Figure 3.33 *1950s black lace and stretch bustier by Marie Rose Lebigot for Lily of France. From the collection at the Museum at FIT, New York City.*
(The Museum at FIT)

*Figure 3.34 A view of the inside of the bustier from the back. Here you can see the **underwires**, the woven interior that keeps the front of the body smooth and flat and the elastic black panels in the sides and center back hug and stretch around curves. From the collection of the Museum at FIT, New York City. (Photo by Coleen Scott)*

Figure 3.35 A close-up view of the outer bustier cup. Notice the top-stitched seams on the cup and the lace and ribbon accents. (Photo by Coleen Scott)

Figure 3.36 A close-up of the hook and eye tape. The hooks are sewn flush to the right side of the center back opening. Notice in Figure 3.34 that the closures do not extend to the bottom of the corset. (Photo by Coleen Scott)

*Figure 3.37 One **garter clip** at the bottom of the bustier. The clip is hidden under the black ribbon and all is attached to the bustier with black lingerie elastic. There are two clips on the front and two on the back of the garment. (Photo by Coleen Scott)*

Bettie Page is one of the most recognizable **pin-up** and **fetish models** of the 1950s. Page modeled for Irving Klaw's sister, Paula Klaw,[2] for many of her most famous bondage images. She was also a well-known burlesque performer primarily because of films like *Varietease* in 1954. Her dance style was **bump and grind**, and she conveyed a wild and mischievous persona both on film and in photos. The fetishizing of lingerie in the 1950s contrasts the conservative values of the country at the time. The concept of the **nuclear family** encouraged women to take care of the home, and not be too

sexually overt, similar to the social construct of the conventional Victorian era. This creates a situation where people who do not follow the social norms are considered outsiders because they are "deviant". Strippers have always been **deviants,** and certainly posing in lingerie or partially nude in submissive or dominating postures, Bettie Page was a prime example of deviance. Her popularity in magazines and in burlesque films speaks to the fact that a large audience desired deviance they were not allowed in daily life.

Figure 3.38 A still frame of Bettie Page from a striptease film, 1950s.
(Everett Collection)

Figure 3.39 A promotional poster for Varietease starring Bettie Page and Tempest Storm, 1954.
(Public domain)

The 5 Minute Change

1. Tempest leans forward to receive accolades from the crowd. Tempest always raises a "Storm" of applause.

Tempest Storm, the sultry-eyed specialty dancer who rocks 'em and socks 'em at Oakland and Las Vegas theaters, says "They ain't seen everything yet," after her first act. Said her manager, it takes about 3 changes before the audience "sees her at her peak." Here's one of Tempest's 5-minute changes, though nothing can change the architecture of this marvelously molded maiden.

16

Figure 3.40 Tempest Storm in a GALA magazine feature, May 1953, Vol. 4, No. 1.

Bettie Page and Tempest Storm were featured together in fetish photos and in the film *Varietease*. Tempest Storm was a regular feature dancer at the El Rey club in Oakland, California, and was known for her amazing figure, her signature bumps and grinds, and her brief relationship with Elvis Presley. Tempest's classic numbers included a wrap or fur, a gown, gloves, a net bra, a panel skirt, a panty, G-string and pasties. These garments constitute the standard set of necessities for a burlesque dancer of the 1950s. The typical burlesque act at this time could run as long as 30 minutes, creating a need for multiple garments to extend the tease. The 1953 *GALA* magazine feature in Figure 3.40 shows Tempest as she goes through the motions of an act and mentions "it takes about 3 changes" before the audience "sees her at her peak."

Figure 3.41
A burlesque poster for the
film Striporama starring
Lili St. Cyr, 1953
(Wiki Commons)

Classism has always been a factor within the history of
burlesque. Lydia Thompson and her troupe's audiences were
mixed in class, and the wealthy, couples, and families came to
see burlesques. In the 1920s and 1930s burlesque became a
working class entertainment with primarily male audiences. In
this next era, as frequenting luxury nightclubs was a popular
"date night," burlesque was once again an entertainment that
appealed to a more monied crowd. Couples would come to
dine and drink the night away with a little risqué and glamorous
entertainment. Famous biographies of burlesquers are filled
with their stories of movie stars and royalty who came to visit
their shows and became love interests. Lili St. Cyr is famous
for her publicized romances and for her ornately furnished,
elevated burlesque performances which exemplify the glamour

and refinement frequently part of the entertainment at the best
clubs.

Lili St. Cyr was not happy to just bump and grind, she liked
a narrative, and her signature acts each tell a different story.
She bought massive pieces of furniture to make elaborate
sets for her boudoir and bath acts. Not only did Lili have
creative costuming and props for her act, but she also spared
no expense, and put much of her income back into her
work. Some of Lili's most well-known acts are: The Bath, The
Homecoming, Spanish Dancer, Toreador, Salome, Leda and the
Swan, and a strip with a live trained parrot. Lili knew how to tell
a story with her movement, and with her costumes. Her dream
was to become a movie star, and though she did several films,
burlesque remained her claim to fame.

Figure 3.42 Lili St. Cyr featured in Modern Man, August 1956, wearing her "Wedding in Monaco" costume. Lili was featured in magazines as much for her beauty and burlesque as for her tumultuous love life. (Modern Man, August 1956. Author's collection)

Figure 3.43 Lili St. Cyr in her Salome costume, 1950s. (Author's collection)

Figure 3.44 Lili as Leda and the Swan, 1950s. The visual of this costume is similar to that of Sally Rand and her Swan act, but the costume details, like her feathered sandals, are what set St. Cyr apart from other performers. (John E. Reed. Author's collection)

Figure 3.45 Two pairs of Lili St. Cyr's pasties. Materials: buckram, sequins, beads, plastic wrap. Late 1950s. (Butch Wax Vintage)

It is important for the reader to consider what it meant to do a burlesque act in the 1950s when striptease was the central action. 1920s and 30s acts were built around the performer singing, or parades of girls on the theater runway, which took time while still being entertaining. In the 1950s, the tease was the thing. A long act meant a long, drawn-out striptease. It was common for a dancer to get down to her bra and underwear and then put on a large negligee or duster to start the tease all over again before the final reveals. There was still live music

being played in most theaters and clubs, so in the wait between garments coming off, if the dance wasn't enough, you could enjoy the band. Lili St. Cyr's narrative acts in burlesque set a scene for changes in what burlesque could be.

La Savona was a Czech 1950s and 1960s performer with very creative costuming that tells a story. Her "space witch" costume portrays a visitor from outer space, and a more practical story of a costume that takes time to remove.

LA SAVONA

A TOUCH OF SPACE MAGIC

Figure 3.46 La Savona in her cape and smallest costume pieces for the "Touch of Space Magic" act. Space themed acts were common in the 1950s, a time of early space exploration, with prevalent movies, books and television questioning whether there was life on other planets. (Personal collection of Neil "Nez" Kendall and a gift from La Savona)

Figure 3.47 The tulle cape for La Savona's "space witch" costume, 1950s.
(Photo by Coleen Scott. Personal collection of Neil "Nez" Kendall and a gift from La Savona)

Figure 3.48 A close-up of the cape collar shape and embellishment, as well as the armhole openings and center front edges, both lined with sequin trim.
(Photo by Coleen Scott. Personal collection of Neil "Nez" Kendall and a gift from La Savona)

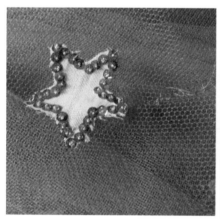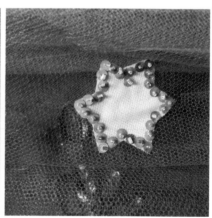

Figure 3.49 Three details of the hand-appliqued decoration on the cape. The left image shows some repair to the tulle.
(Photo by Coleen Scott. Personal collection of Neil "Nez" Kendall and a gift from La Savona)

Figure 3.50 The headband in blue lame shows rhinestone and "cat ear" accents.
(Photo by Coleen Scott. Personal collection of Neil "Nez" Kendall and a gift from La Savona)

Figure 3.51 La Savona's mask is actually two masquerade-shaped masks layered with a feather accent in the center. All is attached to a black pair of sunglasses, and the top of the mask shape is supported with a wire to keep its width.
(Photo by Coleen Scott. Personal collection of Neil "Nez" Kendall and a gift from La Savona)

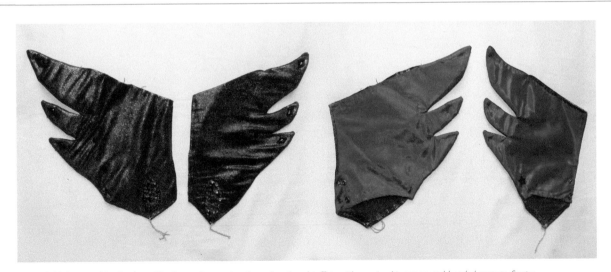

Figure 3.52 Front and back views of La Savona's gauntlet gloves. Lamé and taffeta with sequin, rhinestone and beaded accents. Snaps (more complete on the left back) help with fit at the wrist. Finger loops are damaged, but would hook around middle finger.
(Photo by Coleen Scott. Personal collection of Neil "Nez" Kendall and a gift from La Savona)

Figure 3.53 The festive strapless bra for La Savona's "Space Witch" costume. It is a store-bought bra that has been dyed, covered in fabric and decorated. Many dancers had sewing skills and made their own costumes. Adding extra embellishment and beads to their own costumes during downtime backstage between their three or more daily shows was a common pastime.
(Photo by Coleen Scott. Personal collection of Neil "Nez" Kendall and a gift from La Savona)

Figure 3.54 A close-up view of the **fishnet** tights worn for the act. The fishnet looks like it has been dyed a mossy green color. The stocking seams and elastic waistband are made of a home-dye-resistant fiber as they retain their flesh tone color.
(Photo by Coleen Scott. Personal collection of Neil "Nez" Kendall and a gift from La Savona)

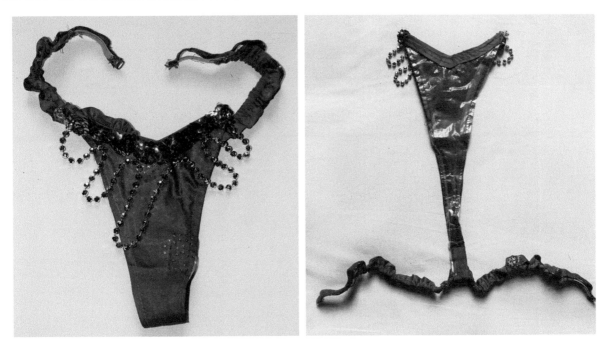

Figure 3.55 A quick-release thong worn over the G-string. The plastic lining on the interior of the thong is a regular finding in undergarment sets of this time.
(Photo by Coleen Scott. Personal collection of Neil "Nez" Kendall and a gift from La Savona)

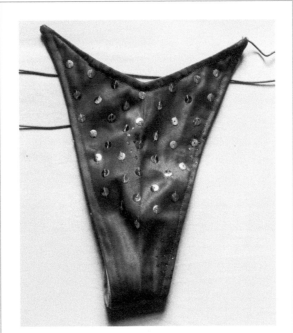

Figure 3.56 The final undergarment is the G-string shown here purple (glitter accented) satin with sequin embellishment.
(Photo by Coleen Scott. Personal collection of Neil "Nez" Kendall and a gift from La Savona)

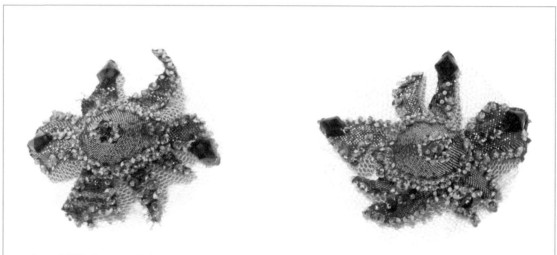

Figure 3.57 La Savona made these early **illusion pasties**. These pasties are especially conical.
Neil Kendall interviewed La Savona and when she talked about her pasties, she said she would make
them pointier to give the illusion that her breasts were larger. The 1950s ideal silhouette was a curvy
hourglass figure, à la Marilyn Monroe. Materials: tulle, fabric, beads, and sequins.
(Photo by Ben Trivett, 2016)

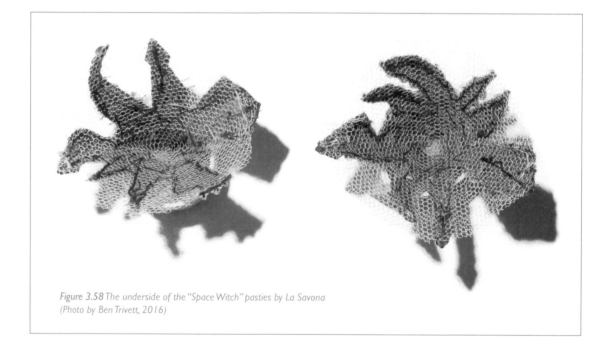

Figure 3.58 The underside of the "Space Witch" pasties by La Savona
(Photo by Ben Trivett, 2016)

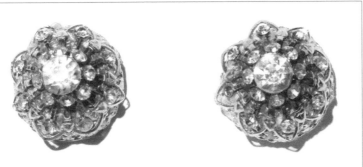

Figure 3.59 A pair of 1940s pasties from performer Lynne O'Neill. These very small pasties are metal with rhinestones and are only about 1 ½ inches in diameter. They are lined in moleskin.
(Photo by Ben Trivett, 2016)

LYNNE O'NEILL   THE ORIGINAL GARTER GIRL

Figure 3.60 Lynne O'Neill wearing the pasties above with a matching rhinestone underwire bra, 1940s. *(Photo by Maurice Seymour. From the personal collection of Neil "Nez" Kendall)*

In the 1940s and 1950s, with the number of burlesque performers working, one could not just be a pretty face. A **hook** was needed as competition rose and pay rates went down due to supply and demand. Some of these hooks were **animal acts**, and **half and half acts**. The animal acts were any burlesque performance done with live animals on stage assisting the performer. Half and half acts portrayed a performer as a beautiful woman being forced to strip by some "other" such as a Gorilla, wolf, a "Chief", or the Devil. Some burlesque performers marketed themselves as the insert-famous-woman's-name-here of Burlesque. For example, Dixie Evans was "The Marilyn Monroe of Burlesque."

Figure 3.61 Dixie Evans, "The Marilyn Monroe of Burlesque" on stage, 1950s.
(Image from the collection of The Burlesque Hall of Fame Museum. Likeness used with permission of Luke Littell and The Dixie Evans Estate)

DIXIE EVANS

Figure 3.62 Dixie Evans in a colorized photo meant to emulate the style of Gene Korman's portraits of Marilyn Monroe.
(Image from the collection of The Burlesque Hall of Fame Museum. Likeness used with permission of Luke Littell and The Dixie Evans Estate)

ANIMAL ACTS

Figure 3.63 shows just a few well-known and creative animal
acts, including Shiva, Lili St. Cyr, and Rosita Royce with her doves.

Figure 3.63 *Clockwise from top left: A performer with a horse in her act; Diane Ross and Squeaky the monkey; Rita Atlanta and Fraulein Stinky; Shiva and one of her snakes; Lili St. Cyr and her tropical parrot; Rosita Royce and her doves.*
(Gene Laverne, Gene Laverne, Garbo Chicago, Maurice of Chicago)

HALF AND HALF ACTS

Maxine Holman featured twice on this page was known for her half and half acts including her dance with a "Chief" that was accepted and even celebrated at the time, but would be completely inappropriate today. All of the half and half costumes required creative engineering and design to make the acts work convincingly.

Figure 3.64 Clockwise from top left: Faith Arlen in a Leda and the Swan half and half act; unknown performer with a devil; Miss Kelly Barton with a soldier; famed half and half performer Maxine Holman with a wolf and a stereotyped "Native American Chief." (1. n/a, 2. Conner Geddes, Cleveland. 3. James Kriegsmann, 4 and 5 n/a)

NATIVE AMERICAN ACTS

The trend to appropriate Native American ceremonial costume continued in the 1940s and 1950s. These acts were used as a hook as well, with their impressive headdresses and promises of a "wild" "tribal" dance. Even big stars created Native American acts, including Lili St. Cyr. Some performers claimed their actual Native American heritage, like Princess La Homa, but the costume stylings of most of the dancers on this page are inauthentic stereotypes. It is important to share these images and emphasize that this is a part of burlesque costume history that should not be repeated.

DoMAY
The Cherokee Half Breed

"PRINCESS LA HOMA"

Figure 3.65
There were countless Native appropriation acts in 1940s and 1950s burlesque, and this continued in later decades. There was a rare occasion where a native woman was performing this type of act; for example, Princess La Homa (top right) was 1/16 Chickasaw and her family lived on a reservation and practiced the culture. The other three performers here: Do May (top left), Princess White Wing (bottom left) and, particularly, Lily Christine (bottom right) who has bronzed her skin in this Maurice Seymour photo, did not claim to have any native heritage. The photos are included as a reminder of the offensive costuming that was accepted at that time, and what should NOT be repeated. Clockwise from top: Maurice Seymour, Ray Barry, Maurice Seymour, James Kriegsmann- all images from Janelle Smith)

By the 1950s burlesque films screened in movie theaters for less than the cost of a live show. You could see your favorite performer in action even if she hadn't come through your town. Blaze Starr was a 1950s burlesque queen and was immortalized in Irving Klaw's 1956 burlesque film *Buxom Beautease*. Blaze was a curvaceous redhead and high-energy dancer. Her tagline was "The Hottest Blaze in Burlesque." Her signature act involved an exploding couch that smoked and blew flame-shaped streamers as she feigned being hot and bothered. Blaze was featured in countless pinup and cheesecake magazines, and wrote a memoir of her life, including her love affair with the Governor of Louisiana, Earl Kemp Long, about which the movie *Blaze* was made in 1989 starring Paul Newman.

BLAZE STARR

Figure 3.66 Blaze Starr appropriates an African drum and wears a leopard print bikini in this image by James Kriegsmann, 1950s

Figure 3.67 A 1950s gown hand-beaded and worn by Blaze Starr. From the personal collection of Leslie Zemeckis.
(Photo by Leslie Zemeckis)

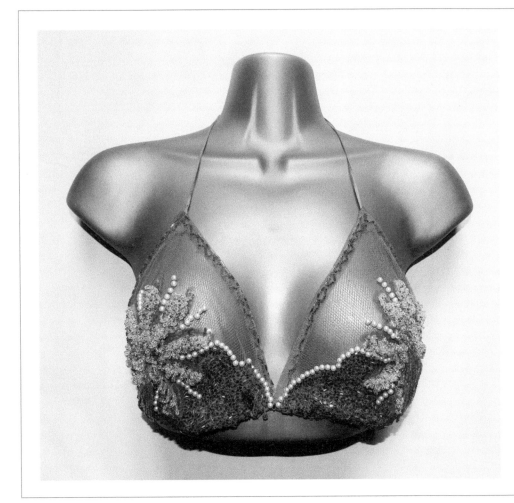

Figure 3.68
A double-layered tulle bra heavily beaded. Worn by Blaze Starr. From the personal collection of Neil "Nez" Kendall. This bra looks very similar to those beaded by a seamstress named Caroline, who was based in Brooklyn, New York. Caroline trained the well-known burlesque costumer Kiva in beading techniques. According to burlesque legend April March "everyone who came through Brooklyn had at least one set from Caroline." In the late 1950s a five-piece set including pasties, bra, garter belt, brief and G-string cost about $65. Dancers would get them in multiple colors to match their gowns.
(Photo by Coleen Scott)

Figure 3.69
A close-up of the beading on the bra. The center of the flower has a looped beaded tassel attached. The density of these beads is signature in sets by Caroline. The edge of the tulle is turned and finished with a zig-zag row of orange **bugle beads**.
(Photo by Coleen Scott)

Figure 3.70 Quick-release brief with dense hand beading and looped fringe. Worn by Blaze Starr. (Photo by Coleen Scott)

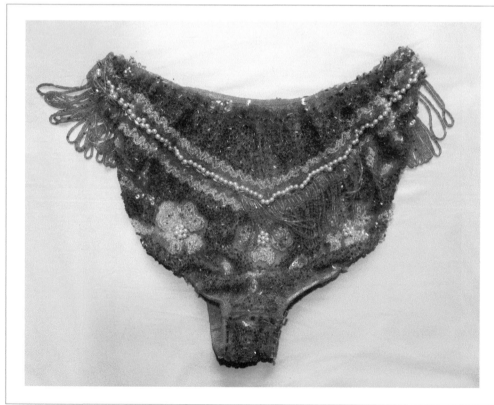

Figure 3.71 The back view of these briefs shows a beaded floral detail that corresponds to the bra. (Photo by Coleen Scott)

Figure 3.72 *Close-up of the center front of these briefs.*
(Photo by Coleen Scott)

Figure 3.73 *Detail of the inside and plastic lining of the panty, as well as the overall garment shape.*
(Photo by Coleen Scott)

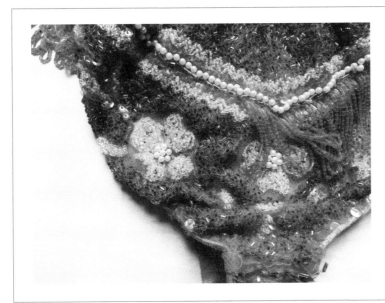

Figure 3.74 *Beading detail on the back of the panty.*
(Photo by Coleen Scott)

Figure 3.75 This spread shows just a few performers and a variety of costumes from the 1940s and 1950s. Clockwise from top left: Joy Barlow and Diana Mumby in Earl Carroll's Vanities; Val de Val lies on a skirt of ruffles; Baby Scruggs with feather fans; Ginger and Javoil; Zorita in a sheer gown; Chez Paree with Alan Carney, Margery Behr and June Cabot, 1942; Tirza in her famous wine bath; Unknown (Author's collection); Coby Yee. (From the collection of Janelle Smith and Neil Kendall)

Figure 3.76 Clockwise from top left: Dee Milo; Lottie the Body; Rose La Rose; Lorelei; Jean Idell; "The Sizzling Comet"; La Wanda; Rita Atlanta; Naja Karamuru. (From the collections of Janelle Smith and Neil "Nez" Kendall)

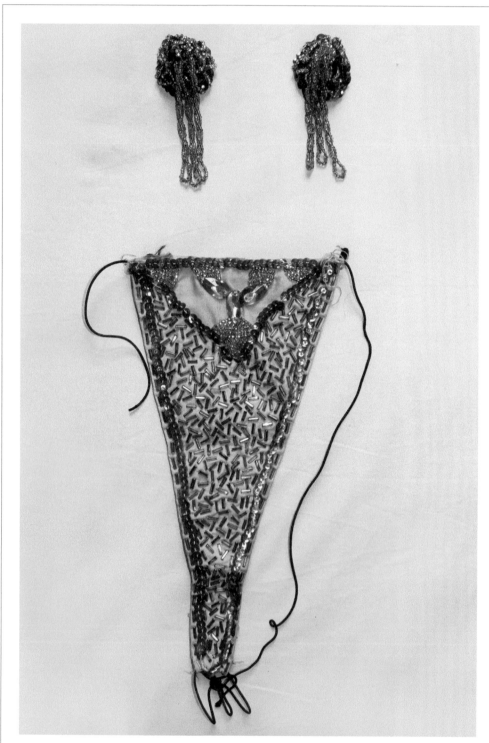

Figure 3.77 *1950s pasties and G-string from performer April March. These pasties are made from buckram, tulle, sequins and seed beads with looped seed bead **tassels**. The g-string is signed inside on the plastic lining and reads "Best Wishes, April March – worn on stage 1953." The set is part of one from Caroline in Brooklyn, New York, and pieces are comparable to the accessories that would have accompanied Blaze Starr's costume in Figures 3.67-3.74.*
(Photo by Coleen Scott. Costume from the personal collection of Neil "Nez" Kendall)

Burlesque performers of the 1940s and 1950s were straying from the expected and the norm like their sisters before them. They were progressive and admirable to many unsatisfied housewives who longed to escape a humdrum life. Burlesquers exhibited glamorous lifestyles, and rubbed elbows with other famous performers. High-end burlesque to this point had become about the presentation of an illusion, an unachievable beauty or glamorous star on the stage posing and demurely removing her gown and undergarments for a split-second final reveal creating anticipation that aroused the audience. In the 1950s, a burlesque performer dancing in sheer, beaded **net bras** and panel skirts to tease and titillate until a final reveal of a G-string and pasties at the last moment was a common sight. More skin was showing and seeing more was becoming necessary to keep an audience. Nightclubs started to require socializing with the clientele as part of the job for non-featured performers. Seasoned burlesquers uninterested in doing full or even partially nude shows began to retire. The encouragement of everyday women to own their sexuality in the feminist movement of the late 1950s and early 1960s, as well as the advent of the pornographic film industry, changed the face of burlesque, and, ultimately, led to its transition from teasing to leaving nothing to the imagination.

Notes

1 The term ecdysiast was coined by journalist and author H.L. Mencken from the Greek word *ecdysis*, meaning "stripping."
2 Irving Klaw is credited for many photos of Bettie Page and other performers from this time, but his sister Paula Klaw was most often the photographer, with Irving running the commercial side of the business.

Figure 3.78 A shimmy belt and **flasher** *handmade and worn by Lynne O'Neill, 1950s. The flasher was worn around the waist to cover the lower private parts and would show a "flash" of that otherwise uncovered area when a dancer did a* **bump**. *The long cord on the center of the shimmy belt acts like a thong would and hooks from the front to the center back of the belt, keeping it in place while dancing. From the personal collection of Neil "Nez" Kendall.*
(Photo by Coleen Scott)

Figure 4.1 A film still of burlesque dancer and Russ Meyer **exploitation film** star Tura Satana in the movie Faster Pussycat, Kill! Kill!, 1965. Tura was a successful Japanese–American burlesque performer known for her athletic dance style influenced by her martial arts training. She gained a cult following after playing a murderous femme fatale in the film. Used with permission from Tura Satana Productions. (Tura Satana Productions)

CHAPTER 4

THE DEATH OF BURLESQUE
1960S – 1970S

INTRODUCTION

In the 1960s the next wave of feminism was on its way, and burlesquers embraced their ability to be sexual creatures both onstage and off. Ann Corio taught women "how to strip for your husband" with a chart topping record in 1963, and Fredericks of Hollywood sold novelty matching pastie and G-string sets for the modern woman. Amateur **go-go** contests changed the burlesque landscape. Big name headliners were still using agents and negotiating contracts with remaining burlesque theaters, but young women who came to the club to get a little wild were cost effective. This transition from nightclub dinner dates to solo dancing club nights tipped the pay scales and changed the business. Laws about toplessness or nudity in theaters still required performers to be in a static pose as seen in the Broadway production of *Hair*,[1] but the introduction of fashion trends, and even **full-nude nightclubs**, led burlesque's performance equation to result in less clothing at the end of an act to keep up with the times.

Burlesque performer and actress Tura Satana's persona went through an obvious shift from her first days overemphasizing her exotic Japanese features to her career as a hired "man-eater" post the Russ Meyer film *Faster Pussycat, Kill! Kill!* In burlesque, Tura became known for her flexibility and her **tassel twirling** skills. Pasties with tassels were not new in the 1960s as we know, but twirling them became a trend in this decade. Many feature dancers of the 1940s and 1950s desired a presentation of elegance and beauty. Twirling pasties was considered vulgar, and in speaking to the living legends from that time, this author found that some still hold that opinion. Tassels made from **chainette fringe** as opposed to beaded trims were the choice of twirlers for ease of replacement and less risk of dangerous breakage on stage. Additional hardware like **grommet**s or fishing **spinners** helped the tassels to spin more easily. An example of Tura's pasties is on the next page.

Figure 4.2 Tura Satana with the tagline "Miss Japan Beautiful" in a promotional portrait by Gene Laverne. The entire composition presents a general **orientalism** as opposed to an authentic display of Tura's Japanese background. The costume itself looks to be beautifully constructed and embellished despite the lack of authenticity. (Photo by Gene Laverne. Courtesy of the Burlesque Hall of Fame Museum with permission from Tura Satana Productions)

Figure 4.3 A set of Tura Satana's pasties made by Kiva. Late 1950s/early 1960s. The pasties have a fabric rim that might have been easier for adhesion to the breast, and in the center of the pastie there is a metal grommet, through which the silver ball-chain is run. It is then glued into the peak of the pastie. The large tassel on the end of the chain looks to be a bound piece of chainette fringe trim. From the personal collection of Miss Indigo Blue.
(Miss Indigo Blue)

Figure 4.4 *Burlesque dancing was such a part of American society that even lingerie catalogs like Frederick's of Hollywood marketed novelty gifts like this pastie and g-string set. It is important to notice that Frederick's designers were thinking about twirling tassels when they created these pasties—the tassels are attached to a spinner for ease of movement, especially for an at-home burlesque novice.*
(Photo by Ben Trivett, 2016)

Most models shied away from the suit until California cutie Joyce Willis posed in one—but only for her photographer father.

Figure 4.5 Joyce Willis modestly models the Rudi Gernreich monokini in the July 9, 1964 issue of Jet Magazine. (Photo by Chuck Willis)

THE NUDE DISCOTHÈQUE

san francisco's wild swim clubs—the current craze is an eye-filling, acrobatic, erotic indoor sport

GRANTED THAT A LANDLOCKED LASS undulating in a topless (and often bottomless) swim suit is a far cry from rock-'n'-roll idol Chubby Checker mesmerizing adolescents with 1959's niftiest new dance, the twist; nevertheless, San Francisco's swim clubs owe their existence to twist pioneer Chubby's initial efforts. Not since the Twenties has any dance had the impact of the twist and its progeny (bug, frug, hully gully, pony, monkey, swim, watusi, et al.). The twist spent several post-Checker years as a teenage tribal rite before café society discovered Gotham's Peppermint Lounge, a somewhat raffish twist temple that overnight became ultra-in. The jet set took the twist to Europe, which soon came up with a "twist" of its own—the *discothèque*. An amalgam of deejay (*disquaire*) and dance floor, the *discothèque* was born in Paris where devotees of *le tweest* made boites such as Chez Regine, New Jimmy's and the original Whisky à GoGo *de rigueur* for tourists. The GoGo's Hollywood namesake added glass-showcased, short-skirted watootsies, and a flock of facsimiles quickly appeared. Society has its own favorite watering holes—Le Club, L'Interdit, Il Mio and Shepheard's in New York, The Id in Chicago. But it remained for San Francisco's roisterous Barbary Coast to provide the final fillip. Fashion designer Rudi Gernreich's sensational topless bathing suit supplied the costume gimmick that turned a multitude of Barbary Coast swim clubs into bare-bosom bistros. (The proliferating swim clubs proved the major attraction—outside of Goldwater & Co.—at last year's Republican Convention.) The twist and its exotic offshoots, prime targets for gloom-and-doom prophets, have been characterized as "neo-primitive dances of fear which foster segregation of the sexes," as "sick sex turned into a spectator sport" and as "symbols of a mad and often frightening era." Conversely, one sociologist has defended the practitioners of the pony and such as "a new generation, anxious to achieve its own independence and expression, adopting new sounds and gyrations as its red badge of courage."

Above: Conspicuously cantilevered Carol Doda, shown very much in the swim of things, is a pioneer held by West Coasters in equal esteem with Pike, Frémont, the Forty-Niners and Lily Langtry. Miss Doda (39-26-36) was the very first of the swim girls to don designer Rudi Gernreich's topless bathing suit. No dumb Doda, Carol knew a good thing when she didn't see it, has been a major attraction at the Strip's Condor Club ever since. Her breast strokes have done more to popularize the latest swim suits than Eleanor Holm and Esther Williams combined.

The trend for topless women did not stop with the novelty pasties of Frederick's. In 1964 fashion designer Rudi Gernreich introduced the **monokini**—a topless bathing suit for women. The American public responded with disgust, but it was these exact feelings of shame about the body that Gernreich was opposing. The suit posed the idea that women and men should be equal in their rights to be bare from the waist up. Little did Gernreich know, but he would change burlesque costume history forever. At The Condor Club in San Francisco, cocktail waitress Carol Doda was asked by her manager to wear the monokini for her act, making her the first modern topless dancer in the United States. This started a monokini trend in all of the local San Francisco clubs. When Doda was arrested for indecency after a Playboy feature on her dancing in 1965, protesters called for her release, and she became a national symbol for sexual freedom.

Figure 4.6 Playboy Magazine, April, 1965, pages 74–75, features Carol Doda and another San Francisco **swim club dancer** "Tasha the Glo Girl"[2] in topless swimsuits. Doda was arrested for indecency on April 22, 1965, after the publication of this feature.
(Playboy Magazine, 1964, Author's collection)

Below: The near ultimate in air-conditioned swim suits glitters ephemerally on Tosha, the Glo Girl, the Strip's only Oriental swimmer. She undulates every hour on the hour at Big Al's, a pseudo speak-easy where Big Al himself—resplendent in a Gargantuan-lapelled, double-breasted white suit—greets the callipygia connoisseurs corralled by Tosha's stern wheeling. Tosha, in her renowned topless-bottomless suit, has been a big draw on the Barbary Coast for almost a year, proved to Republican Conventioneers the eye-filling virtues of terpsichorean extremism.

Figure 4.7 A yellow gingham Rudi Gernreich monokini. Wool knit, 1964.
(Copyright The Museum at FIT)

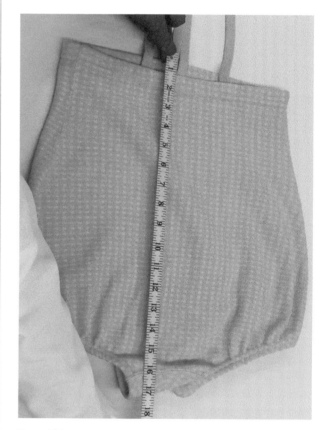

Figure 4.8 A museum assistant measures the bathing suit trunks. The
16-inch back length denotes a very high-waisted garment.
(Photo by Coleen Scott. Suit from the collection of the Museum at FIT)

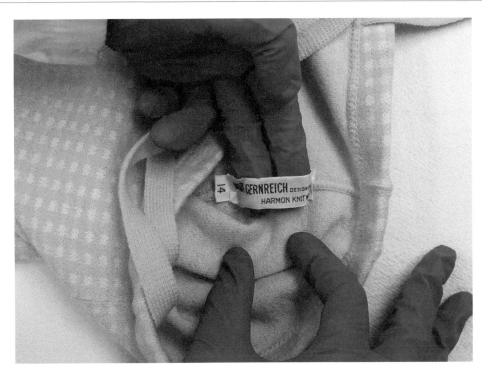

Figure 4.9 The Rudi Gernreich label for Harmon Knit Wear, and size 14 tag.
(Photo by Coleen Scott. Suit from the collection of the Museum at FIT)

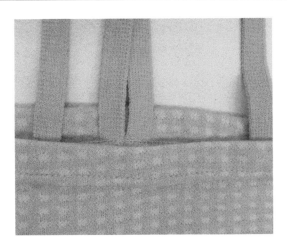

Figure 4.10 Close-up of the straps and double-stitched waistband. This stitching was developed specifically for knits.
(Photo by Coleen Scott. Suit from the collection of the Museum at FIT)

Figure 4.11 This image shows the (possibly cotton) lining in the bathing suit crotch, the seam finishing, and the wrong side of the knit fabric.
(Photo by Coleen Scott. Suit from the collection of the Museum at FIT)

THE LADYBIRDS
THE WORLDS FIRST AND ONLY ALL-GIRL TOPLESS BAND

*Figure 4.12 Promotional photo for The Ladybirds known as "The World's First and Only All-Girl Topless Band," 1960s.
(Author's personal collection)*

The topless bathing suit's use in clubs changed the burlesque scene by creating an environment where audiences wanted to see more of dancers. Laws varied from state to state and even city to city with regard to nudity in clubs, but by 1965, some cities, like San Francisco, had legalized topless dancing. Another shift came with the arrival of new dance crazes like "the twist," encouraging young people to dance solo. Nightclubs with seated couples in the audience and live bands transformed in the 1960s into clubs and discotheques where people went to dance, not to watch live entertainment. The Whisky A Go-Go in Hollywood is the birthplace of the go-go dancer. Joanna Labeann designed the fringe outfits with white boots worn by the dancers at the club. Dance clubs adopted the go-go dancer idea to add atmosphere. Unlike the virginal 1950s young lady, the free-spirited 1960s woman was willing to participate in popular amateur go-go and burlesque contests. This was a much more economical source of entertainment for a venue than a big name burlesque star.

Figure 4.13 Three girls are seen dancing in a raised cage and fringe costumes showing bare midriffs at the nightclub Whisky A Go-Go, in Hollywood, California, on January 25, 1965. (Associated Press Photo)

Figure 4.14 *A fringe go-go costume worn by Blaze Starr, late 1960s or early 70s. Chainette fringe is sewn onto a store-bought bra.* **Hot pants** *are homemade in black satin. Author's collection.*
(Photo by Ben Trivett, 2018)

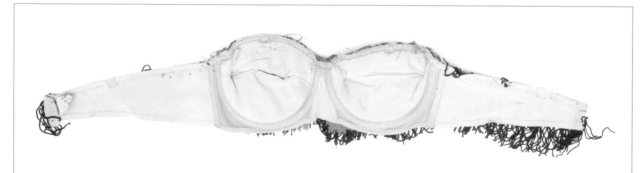

Figure 4.15 *The backside of the bra. This is a store-bought piece that has been covered in trim.*
(Photo by Ben Trivett, 2018)

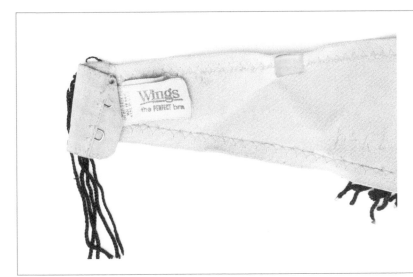

Figure 4.16 The label on the bra shows that it is a flesh tone everyday-bra-turned costume-piece.
(Photo by Ben Trivett, 2018)

Figure 4.17 A back view of the hot pants made of non-stretch satin.
(Photo by Ben Trivett, 2018)

Figure 4.18 A close-up of the left side hook and loop closures on the hot pants.
(Photo by Ben Trivett, 2018)

Figure 4.19 Sheila Ray wears a burlesque costume by designer Gussie Gross. Late 1950s, early 1960s.
(Photo by Gene Laverne)

Despite the clubs with go-go dancers and discotheques full of young people, burlesque survived because the older generation was still paying for the entertainment they enjoyed in their youth. Still, established burlesque performers from the 1950s who continued to work in the 1960s and beyond had to be willing to transition to the new style of clubs, and the new rules of stripping. Even with all the change, remaining burlesque headliners still needed fabulous costumes, and Los Angeles designer Gussie Gross realized their visions. Gussie designed costumes for a number of burlesque queens including snake dancer Shiva and Lili St. Cyr. She was known for her quality work, and for making beautiful costumes inside and out. She understood that the linings of burlesque costumes would be seen as performers shed them, and she prided herself on her finishes.[3]

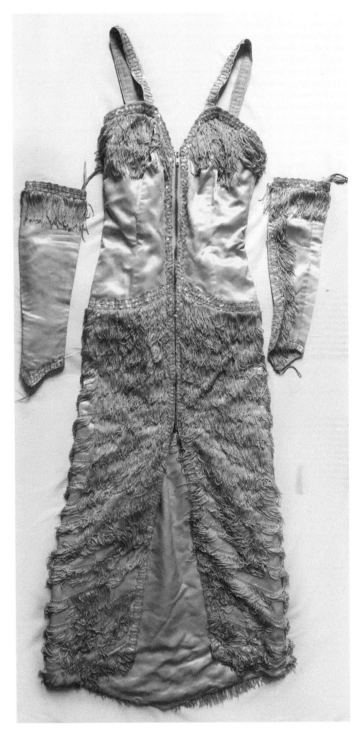

Figure 4.20 A chartreuse satin gown and gauntlet gloves designed by Gussie Gross for Sheila Ray, 1960s. The fit and style of the gown are reminiscent of Gypsy Rose Lee's famous beaded fringe dress from the 1958 film Screaming Mimi.
(Photo by Coleen Scott. Costume from the personal collection of Neil "Nez" Kendall and The Striptease Museum, Chester, England)

Figure 4.21 *The inside of Sheila Ray's gown by Gussie Gross. The lining shows some wear and tear from age, but the use of self fabric through the entire bottom half of the dress to finish all sides, the binding at the neckline, matching thread, and the careful stitching of the bone casing show's Gussie's beautiful finishing techniques. The seams that are visible are stitched to prevent fraying and clipped to lie flat.*
(Photo by Coleen Scott. Costume from the personal collection of Neil "Nez" Kendall and The Striptease Museum, Chester, England)

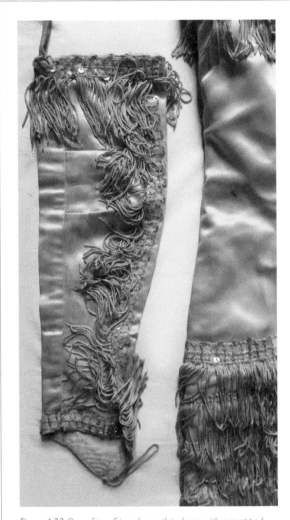

Figure 4.22 One of two fringed gauntlet gloves with a snapped placket at the wrist.
(Photo by Coleen Scott. Dress from the personal collection of Neil "Nez" Kendall)

Figure 4.23 A close-up of the top front of the dress showing the perfect zipper application, with chartreuse plastic sequin trim and three rows of fringe on each bust.
(Photo by Coleen Scott. Costume from the personal collection of Neil "Nez" Kendall and The Striptease Museum, Chester, England)

Figure 4.24 A close-up of the lower half of the dress demonstrating the impeccably sewn fringe and trim. The angles and spacing of the trim show a mastery of dressmaking.
(Photo by Coleen Scott. Costume from the personal collection of Neil "Nez" Kendall and The Striptease Museum, Chester, England)

Burlesque performers in the 1960s had to get creative in a different way than the 1940s and 1950s dancers who used a hook to set them apart from the sea of ecdysiasts. These dancers had to do something new or different that burlesque and maybe even modern audiences haven't seen or tried in their own homes. One creation born out of this was the **fire tassel**. Satan's Angel has stated that she was the first to perform with fire tassels, and she patented her star-shaped designs. A sample of her star fire tassels is shown in Figure 4.26.[4]

SATAN'S ANGEL   The Devils own Mistress

Figure 4.25 Satan's Angel promotional photo. Gene Laverne, 1960s (Gene Laverne. Used with permission from Satan's Angel)

Figure 4.26 Front and back view of star fire tassel pasties by Satan's Angel. The lining is made of flame retardant material coated in layers of Sobo glue. The chain and filament on this set is just for show. Angel emphasizes that metal chain and spinners cannot be brass because of its ability to conduct heat. The "filament" at the end of the chain would normally be a fuel-soaked piece of material, but for aesthetic purposes of the photo shoot, a piece of stuffed gold lamé has been placed there. Fire tassels are to be used by specially trained fire performers only, and are not to be constructed or worn by the uncertified. (Photo by Ben Trivett, 2016. Pasties made by Satan's Angel, 2016, from the author's collection)

CAMILLE 2000: AN INTERVIEW

Camille 2000, known as "The Girl for Yesterday, Today and Tomorrow," was a burlesque performer in the late 1960s through the 1980s. She shared her experience and her burlesque costume stories with the author, and the following is a partial transcript of the interview.[5]

A: What years did you perform full time?

C: I was in the business for 20 years. From 1968 to 1988.

A: Wow, OK. That's a great span because a lot of people talk about burlesque kind of falling off the planet during that time period, but it didn't!

C: Yeah, I was on the tail end of burlesque. My first ten years in the business, I did classic dance and wore classic gowns and costumes and fans, but then my last ten years I started doing **Aggressive Art** and Marquis de Sade, and numbers like that.

Figure 4.27 *Camille 2000 wears "fake nipple" pasties in a promotional photo by Maurice Seymour. Late 1960s. (Photo by Maurice Seymour with permission from Ronald Seymour)*

A: OK, so, you started doing more classic acts and then you moved into the Aggressive Art. What were the factors that made you choose that style of performance?

C: We were losing our audiences to something called live nude dancing. So, that's why I started doing numbers like that—performance art, Marquis de Sade, Black Widow, Nunchucks, and things like that, and boy, it's kind of like **neo-burlesque** today!

A: Exactly! It is on the forefront of what edgier neo-burlesque is, that's what I think is so significant about your career. So, with that change in style, how were you getting hired? When you started, were you getting hired one way, was it through an agent, and did that change through your career?

C: I always had an agent—Jess Mack. He was my agent when I was in New York and he eventually moved to Las Vegas and he was still my agent. Back in the day you had to have an agent, and they booked you. And, if you wanted to be a feature headliner, you had to have the best flippin' wardrobe made usually by a professional like Simon Soar, or Hedy Jo Star, or Caroline—someone that had a famous burlesque name. Because the star of the show had to have wardrobe like "Oh, that's Simon Soar's" or "Oh, that's Hedy Jo Starr," or "that's Bobby Gerstein." You had to have wardrobe if you wanted to be a headliner. You had to invest in it, and I believe that today, the wardrobe is very important.

A: Yes it is, especially, to actually get paid. You know a lot of the gigs now are very low pay.

C: Yes it's different now than from our day. I see that. People do it now more like a hobby, or something, whereas we got into it to make a living from it.

A: Exactly. So, when you were investing in your costumes, when you were working with a costume designer, was anybody helping cover the cost of that upfront, and then you were, paying it off? Or did you have to invest?

C: I had to (pay). The costumer, because they were so expensive, they would let you pay so much a week as they were fitting it. They would come and do fittings and fit it to you. Say if it was $500; that's kind of like a gown that's not like really elaborate, that was just you know, your basic gown that would have some stones and everything on it, but it would be by a famous designer. He would let you pay so much a week, or a month, and when it was finished, you would have it paid off and he would give it to you. But, he came and did fittings, and he sketched it. Simon Soar did—he sketched it, and made it to fit you, and it was beautiful. So, he let me pay so much, until, you

know, I got it paid off. Of course, you would try to pay it off fast because that's your wardrobe—it takes money to make money, you know?

A: You've got to have the clothes to take off, to do the job.

C: Mmmhmmm!

A: Now did you tour as well, or did you stay more stationary?

C: No, I travelled on the road. That's how you get your name, you travel.

A: Right.

C: I worked the burlesque theaters, and, it took me about a year to become a feature. I moved to New York, and had photos done by Maurice Seymour; you had to have a famous name there for the photos. Then I started having wardrobe made by Simon Soar, and Carlos made some of my wardrobe, but Simon Soar was really famous, and Hedy Jo Starr was really famous.

A: And Carlos? Does he have a last name?

C: No, I just remember Carlos.

A: That's what people say about Caroline too.

C: Yeah, I just remember Caroline was just Caroline. I had a lot of her beaded under pieces.

A: Exactly, I talked to April March and she said, "Everybody had at least one set from Caroline."

C: Oh yeah, those seed beads. You *had* to have that, and they could go with any gown, the under pieces you know?

A: Right, you could mix it up. So did you have costumes mostly from Simon? Did you have Hedy do something specific?

C: I have a gown by Hedy Jo Star. Simon Soar did most of my wardrobe. A lot of it got stolen, but I still have that blue velvet gown. I didn't have that at the club the night that I got robbed.[6]

A: Oh my God!

C: It was at home, because I wasn't using it! That blue velvet gown—the one with the ass out? That's a Simon Soar gown.

A: Yes that's an amazing piece.

C: I still have that and I still have a Hedy Jo Star gown.

A: Thank goodness!

C: Yeah, I know! When I pass on, I'm going to donate them to The Burlesque Hall of Fame. I might do it before I kick off, I don't know.

A: So, working with Hedy, do you want talk a little bit about how that was?

C: Hedy Jo Star?

A: Yeah.

Figure 4.28 Camille 2000 wears her Simon Soar backless gown. Late 1960s.
(Photo by Maurice Seymour.
Used with permission from Camille, 2000)

C: She came to Baltimore and made my gown. Her and, there was another woman that made gowns, Tony Midnight. I never had one by Tony Midnight but their work was very similar with the sequins (and embellishments), because Hedy had a sequin machine.

A: I do know that they do get grouped together a bit style wise and they were close friends.

C: Yes, they come from the same era, their work looked alike. I think they probably had the same sequin machine or something.

A: Heavy embellishment is a signature for both of them.

C: Yeah, it was just really popular back then, you know?

A: Yes, well, it always looks so amazing under the lights, too.

C: Mmmhmm. Bobby Gerstein was another famous designer. He made costumes for me. He was out of Las Vegas. He made a lot of Tiffany Carter's and Kitten Natividad's. I saw Kitten's gowns and I said, "oh man, I

want a costume by him," so he made an orange costume for me. I don't have that one though, it got stolen.

A: That's so sad! Did you ever sell any of your costumes to other performers?

C: No.

A: How much got stolen?

C: Thousands and thousands of dollars—everything. Everything except what I had at home that I wasn't wearing. That was the blue velvet gown and the Hedy Jo Starr gown.

A: Oh, God.

C: I know, it crippled me. It really put me in a depression. I wanted to retire because that was the wardrobe. I wasn't travelling back then because this was towards the end of my career, you know?

A: So that happened later …

C: So, then I was doing those Aggressive Art numbers, and I didn't really need the gown. I had to do something else, you know?

A: Yes—so did you start doing that, like, late 70s or even later than that?

C: The late 70s. The first one was The Black Widow—late 70s—when that music was popular with Alice Cooper and Lester Price.

A: Yes and then the Marquis de Sade act too. So, when you were doing those pieces, is any bit of that wardrobe from another person, or were you able to put it together (yourself)?

C: No, I never bought used wardrobe. I always had my wardrobe made for me. My body harness I had made by a guy that made leather—that was a real body harness—and the mask, that was real.

A: Those little, really round cups that squeeze your boobs—that harness?

C: Yes, that was a real body harness. That was the one I wore, in the day. That got stolen also, in Miami.

A: That's terrible. I'm glad that you still have some of these amazing things.

C: I am too. I've got a really sexy rhinestone piece that's just all rhinestones.

A: Ooooh—and who did that one?

C: Oh, gosh, it's been so long! It wasn't someone who was really famous—you know? I'll think of her name later—it was like one name, but she wasn't really known, she just did that kind of work.

A: That's the kind of thing I like to know too. I want to know about the bigger names in burlesque costume, but, there are these other lesser-known people who made a

Figure 4.29 Camille wears her Marquis de Sade costume, 1970s/
early 1980s.
(Mendoza of Miami)

Figure 4.30 Camille 2000 in her "Jesus Christ Superstar
Costume," 1970s.
(Used with permission from Camille, 2000)

lot of costumes for burlesque performers. Do you have
a favorite costume ever?

C: Yes. My favorite one got stolen. It was a Jesus Christ
Superstar costume. It was all beads … and the same
woman that did the rhinestone work—Gabriella knows
her name, but I can't think of the right name … I
designed it, and she made it.

A: Did you say Gabriella Maze knows?

C: Yes. She was in the Carolinas. When I think of her name
I'll message you. (Suddenly remembers) SASSY! I think
her name was Sassy. I might be wrong, but I think that
was her name. She just made things, she wasn't really
expensive. The more famous with wardrobe, the more
expensive. If you could catch somebody that didn't have
a name so big you could get some similar stuff, but it
wouldn't be made by them, you know?

A: Right, you're paying partially for the name and then for
the labor.

C: Yes—"this is a Simon Soar gown."

A: Right. So you mentioned a couple of photographers.
Maurice Seymour,[7] was that one you mentioned?

C: Yes, he did my first photos.

A: He was in New York?

C: Yes—New York. And then 20 years later I had Mendoza
of Miami because I was in Miami at the time—I got him
to do mine.

A: Maybe talk to me a little more about when you started
doing the Aggressive Art.

C: I designed my costumes myself, and got a drag queen
friend of mine to make them for me. Because I didn't
have to spend all that money on gowns like I used to
when I was first starting and wanted to make a name
for myself. By then, I already had a name, you know?

A: Yes! And so you were headlining and doing these types
of pieces.

C: Yes. I designed the Black Widow, and Wendy the Snake Lady made it for me. It was just black chiffon, and the black fishnet bodysuit, and then we put red lamé in the middle with rhinestones on it. And then we had a black headdress with chiffon hanging from it—I had it cut jagged. I still have the Black Widow costume.

A: So even though you were still using an agent as your career progressed, what kind of places were you performing in?

C: Burlesque theaters. I worked mostly burlesque theaters.

A: They still were calling themselves burlesque theaters even into the 70s and 80s?

C: Yes there were a few—the Gaiety in Washington DC, the Gaiety in Miami Beach, The Town in Detroit. Yes, it was a smaller burlesque circuit, but there was still a burlesque circuit. The LeRoy Griffith, The Mayfair in New York. They were burlesque theaters, and they used to have live bands when I first started, but that changed, you know.

A: You were using tracks toward the end?

C: Yeah, we had live bands in the beginning though. And then they started the tracks.

A: Were the theaters showing films or was there pole dancing in between …

C: No. No pole dancing. They showed movies in burlesque theaters in between.

A: I'm trying to get a feel for what was going on then, because it's not well documented.

C: Yes, they were showing movies in the theater. I worked some clubs, but I worked mostly theaters, because I didn't like to socialize. The only clubs I would work were clubs where you didn't have to socialize with the audience.

A: Ah—

C: I didn't like mixing, and I didn't like hustling drinks.

A: Right. You wanted to just do your headline gig and be done.

C: Yeah, I liked the theaters much better.

A: It's good to know that there was still a circuit. People talk about it like it was gone, but there was a little bit still going on.

C: Yes! There was a circuit when I first started—Toledo, New York, Cleveland, Canada …

A: I'm learning that Ohio really kept it going the longest. What were the theater names in Ohio, do you remember?

C: The Todd Art was one, I think it was, Rose La Rose's theater was one, and I worked The Roxy in Cleveland. The Roxy Theater.

A: OK great, thank you for that. Will you talk about how you ended up involved with The Burlesque Hall of Fame Museum?

C: Well, they wanted me to come out for years and perform,[8] and I wouldn't perform. For a long time I would come out, but I just didn't want to perform, I wanted to be remembered how I was …

A: I get that.

C: Then after Eddie [her brother] died I did a tribute to him to R. Kelley's "I believe I can fly"—a fan dance, and that was my debut. So now I perform almost every year, although this year I MC'd.

A: I remember, I watched you! My husband was taking pictures—he got an amazing shot of you riding away on a motorcycle and flipping everybody off!

C: Cool, put it on Facebook!

A: I'm going to send it to you.

C: Yeah! For real for real!

A: OK! Well, I think that's enough for tonight. You gave me so much info Camille, thank you very much!

C: Oh, it was my pleasure, thanks for calling, and you have a great evening!

A: Thanks, you too!

C: Bye Bye Baby!

Camille truly was a trailblazer, headlining with her Aggressive Art. She will be remembered how she was, but she will also be remembered how she is—a strong, wild, burlesque queen who was part of the tail end of the burlesque movement in the twentieth century.

Figure 4.31 Camille 2000 at the 2016 Burlesque Hall of Fame Weekender. (Photo by Ben Trivett, 2016)

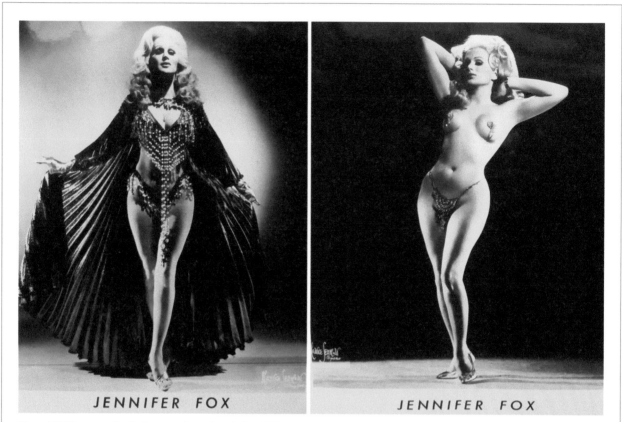

Figure 4.32 **Transgender** *burlesque performer Jennifer Fox, 1960s.*
(Photo by Maurice Seymour. From the personal collection of Neil "Nez" Kendall)

Burlesque has always been a platform for societally identified **deviant**[9] women, and therefore, was more accepting of other similarly identified "deviants." This is not to say that most of the gay or transgender community wanted to be identified publicly *at all* at this time.[10] It *is* to say that burlesque was a career option for closeted or out transgender artists in the 1960s. The most well known of these performers was Hedy Jo Star. Hedy began her career in carnivals in the 1930s as a burlesque dancer and sideshow act. She underwent the first successful sex change operation in the United States in 1962. She continued to perform burlesque, and built a notable career in burlesque costume design. Her garments were heavily embellished and beautifully made. She was a close friend with another well-known queer burlesque costume designer, Tony Midnight, and their work is aesthetically similar.

Figure 4.33
Promotional
pamphlet for
Hedy Jo Star with
headlines about her
book I Changed
My Sex written in
1963.
(Private collection)

Figure 4.34 *Hedy Jo*
Star wears a sequin
halter mermaid shaped
gown and gauntlet
gloves. Late 1950s/early
1960s. This dress was
either made by Hedy or
costumer Tony Midnight.
(Photo by Maurice
Seymour. Used with
permission from Ronald
Seymour. From the
personal collection of
Janelle Smith)

The costume featured in Figures 4.35 to 4.41 is a Hedy Jo Star original from the 1960s. It is from the personal collection of Janelle Smith. All photos are by Fatema Gharzai from the personal collection of Janelle Smith.

Figure 4.35 A Hedy Jo Star gown from the 1960s in nude woven fabric with heavy sequin trim, set rhinestones, feather tassels, and beading.
(Photo by Fatema Gharzai from the personal collection of Janelle Smith)

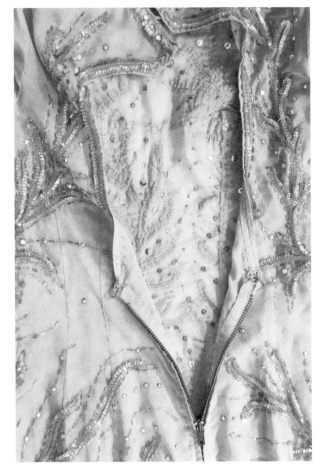

Figure 4.36 *A view of the low zipper and open back of the gown.*
(Photo by Fatema Gharzai from the personal collection of Janelle Smith)

Figure 4.37
Close-up of the
hook and loop on
the back neck of
the gown.
(Photo by Fatema
Gharzai from the
personal collection
of Janelle Smith)

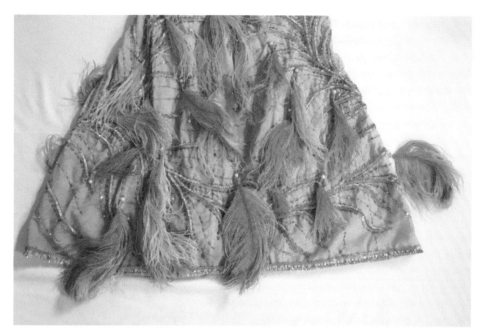

Figure 4.38 The bottom of the gown has a mermaid-shaped skirt with multiple ostrich feather tassels. The sequin-trimmed hem is an excellent example of the extra detail that Hedy Jo Star was known for in her costume designs. (Photo by Fatema Gharzai from the personal collection of Janelle Smith)

Figure 4.39 Close-up of the feather accents on the gown. The ostrich feathers are bundled into a tassel, and are attached to a beaded loop with a pearl bead at the point where it attaches to the gown.

Figure 4.40 A close-up of the embellishment all over the gown. Hedy Jo Star has created her own original textile for this garment. (Photo by Fatema Gharzai from the personal collection of Janelle Smith)

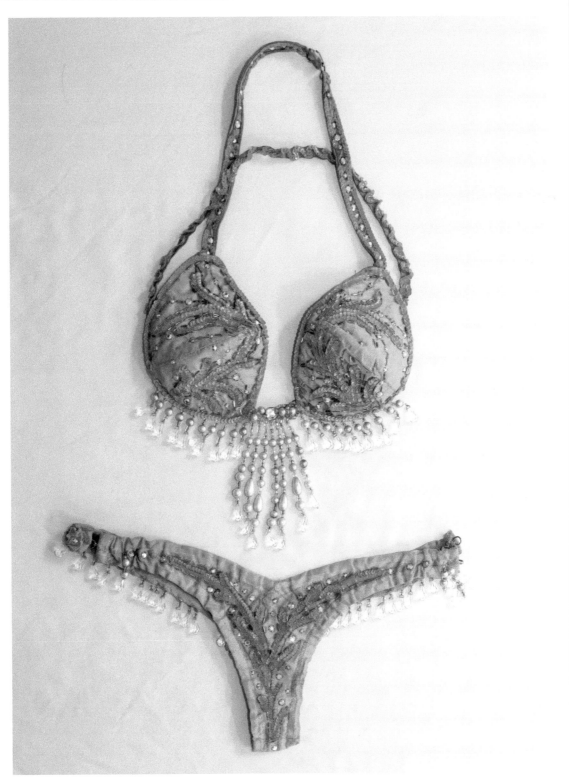

Figure 4.41 *The matching bra and quick-remove thong by Hedy Jo Star. The thong has hook and loops on the sides. A G-string would have been worn underneath.*
(Photo by Fatema Gharzai from the personal collection of Janelle Smith)

BIC CARROLL'S BURLESQUE BULLET POINTS

Bic Carroll is a burlesque legend with worldwide performance experience. He turned 81 in 2018. Working in show business since 1953, he has learned a thing or two about how to impress an audience, how to get paid, and how to get a lot of bang for your buck when it comes to costume design. The following bullet points highlight Bic's career, his costume design experience and style, and his advice to modern burlesquers.[11]

•   Bic was a performer first. He became a costumer out of necessity, and never really enjoyed it. His first costume designs were for the shows at the Follies Theater in Chicago beginning in 1955. The theater was looking for two new numbers a week with different themes and costumes. He choreographed the numbers and made the costumes!

•   Bic initially learned to sew from burlesque performers backstage. He learned how to make G-strings and bras first. His solution to changing the costume designs so frequently on a small budget of $25 per week for everyone (!) was to reuse garments by dyeing them and adding different embellishments. He would make headdresses out of decorated cardboard, sometimes using shampoo bottles to hold fake flowers and feathers. For inspiration, he used to collect images of circus acts and showgirls. He always loved the look of showgirls in costume.

Figure 4.42 *Bic Carroll promotional photo, 1960s. (Used with permission of Bic Carroll)*

- When he was 21, Bic moved to Paris and worked in a nude show at the Chez Noir. He is considered to be one of the first male burlesque stripteasers.
- By 1958, Bic was working in New York City at the Latin Quarter, which had its own costume shop. Bic apprenticed in this shop and learned French couture techniques including muslin draping, finishings, and embellishments, like crochet beading, from the classically trained seamstresses.
- Lou Walters who ran the Latin Quarter suggested Bic do an act. Lou was looking for a man to be on stage so that women would be more enticed to come to the show.
- Lou said he brought Bic to the Latin Quarter because he knew Bic would dance in a G-string.
- Previous to his time in the Latin Quarter, Bic learned how to do a snake act from Zorita. She gave him his first boa constrictor; little did he know it was because that one was getting too big for her to handle. When he had hecklers he would go out into the audience and hand them the snake and go back on stage. Then he would retrieve it when he was done dancing!
- For a big opening number performance, Lou Walters told Bic to cast four showgirls to dance behind him. Bic choreographed 20-minute show numbers with the girls that went on to become a show of its own with an even larger cast. It travelled all over the world, including three years in Japan. His production did two shows a night—early and late, and they would perform a completely different show each time, which would keep the audiences there and buying drinks.

Figure 4.43 Bic performing at The Latin Quarter, late 1950s, early 60s.
(Used with permission from Bic Carroll)

Figure 4.44 A promotional photo of "Bic Carroll's WOW Show" in the 1970s. Bic designed and made all the costumes. (Used with permission from Bic Carroll)

- Bic learned from and occasionally worked for legendary costumer Tony Midnight, known for her ornately embellished costumes.
- Bic got his first **Cornely sequin machine** around 1958, which is the same type used by Tony Midnight and Hedy Jo Star. He still owns two of them. With this machine, you buy **slung sequins** (sequins on a string) and you operate the machine from under the fabric while you place the sequins onto fabric in custom patterns and shapes.
- Bic was known for his heavily sequined costumes. He says the great thing about sequins instead of beading is that you can roll up the costumes and they don't get caught or damaged. The sequins keep their shape and shine. He explained that he didn't use many rhinestones back in the day because they were expensive and heavy.
- Throughout his career, Bic was performing nearly every night. He primarily designed and made costumes for himself and the casts of his own shows. He didn't have time to make costumes for other productions. So for his own show, Bic took all the tricks he had learned from his career and from the costumers and applied every one of them to the costume designs.

- In the 1970s he was asked to design costumes for the Flamingo Hotel's newest show: "Razzle Dazzle On Ice." His production beat Bob Mackee that year for the Best Costume Design in Las Vegas.
- "Razzle Dazzle on Ice" was full of Bic's signature, absolutely breathtaking ensembles. According to Bic, the newspaper headline for the review was "The Only Show in Vegas You Come Out Whistling the Costumes."
- In the 1980s, after Razzle Dazzle's success, Bic ran the **Ice Capades** costume shop.
- After he stopped performing regularly, Bic took on the role of producer for his shows. He also became a specialist in circus animal costumes for Ringling Brothers and Siegfried and Roy that carried on his signature, sequined style.
- Bic says: "With burlesque you should realize you are satirizing the illusion of glamour. New burlesque makes burlesque about stripping, but it's not. Some of the more successful modern acts know they are satirizing themselves. They have a tongue in cheek attitude. There is a playfulness between the performer and the audience."
- Bic says: "If burlesque performers want this art to survive, they should get out and expand their audience. Go back to glamour and remember the goal of sexual arousal of the audience. Make them want to make love to you."

MALE EXOTIC DANCERS

Bic Carroll was an early male ***exotic dancer*** who began his career in the 1950s as a man performing in a primarily female revue. Having a male exotic in a show that presented a variety of acts with performers of mixed gender was becoming a regular sight. The show "Pouf" from New York City in 1976 was

a take on Paris nightlife featuring a male dancer as the central character. Male exotics did not reach a height of popularity until the late 1970s and 1980s with organizations like The ***Chippendales***. In the United States these were the first shows of male dancers that catered to a female audience.

Figure 4.45 The cover of After Dark Magazine, *October 1976, features a male exotic dancer from a show called "Pouf" at La Vie en Rose in New York City.*
(Photo by Roy Blakey. From the author's personal collection)

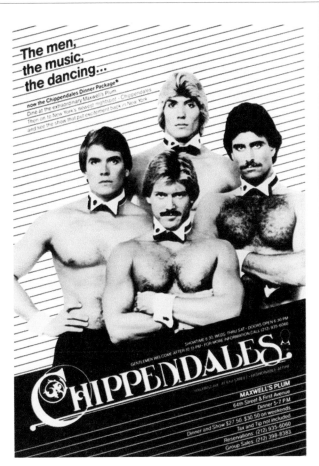

Figure 4.46 An early Chippendale's ad, 1979. The Chippendales were organized in New York City in 1979 and were the first organized group of male exotic dancers in the United States.

F BEAUTY is skin-deep, then the Miss Nude Universe Contest, held each year outside San Bernardino, California, puts more sheer pulchritude on parade than any other pageant in the world. Unlike the Miss America competition —which confuses amateur theatrics and adolescent etiquette with the genuine article—the Miss Nude Universe

THE MISS NUDE UNIVERSE CONTEST

this annual search for beauty in the buff is a refreshing answer to those parades of the vestal virgins

Figure 4.47 The lead image on the Miss Nude Universe Pageant in Playboy, February 1968. The image shows the stage set up for the "Mayan" theme, and the contestants lined up poolside at The Oakdale Guest Ranch. The magazine declares this competition "a refreshing answer" to beauty contests like the Miss America pageant. (Playboy Magazine, February 1968)

As burlesque striptease became less fashionable for couples to watch during a night out, and live nude dancing became the more popular evening entertainment for male audiences, the pornographic film industry was growing. The objective of the audience became much less about being teased, and much more about being aroused, usually by watching full nudity or sexual acts on stage or screen. Another cultural attitude at the time was "natural is beautiful," and the "illusion of glamour" that burlesque provided was not desirable. The Miss Nude Universe pageant started in California in 1965 as an anti-Miss America competition,

declaring that the contestants were a false presentation of beauty. To be fair, the audience, attendants and judges were all required to be nude to attend and participate. Even though being crowned Miss Nude Universe seems like it would not involve wardrobe, each year had a theme. In 1968, *Playboy* magazine featured the current Miss Nude Universe, Kellie Everts, a topless go-go dancer, and contestant images from the appropriated "Mayan" theme. With a prize of a screen test and "motion-picture contract," the contestants competed in hopes of furthering their acting careers.

Judges and audience alike review the 17 candidates for the title of Miss Nude Universe as the girls promenade around poolside at the Oakdale Guest Ranch; an appreciative gathering of more than 1000 spectators has also doffed its duds in deference to contest rules. After much deliberation on the judges' part, the well-rounded field is narrowed to five finalists. While the judges make their final choices, the shapely quintet receives the crowd's plaudits. Seen from behind, the girls are (below, from left to right) Kellie Everts, Bobbie Rogers, Bunny Meeks, Daniél Munsun and Linda Marie Francis

At last, the choices for the queen and her court are announced. Daniél Munsun, a 22-year-old photographer's model (above, left and center), is awarded fourth-runner-up honors and is congratulated by her escort. After Bunny Meeks, 23, a dancer, is named second runner-up, the two girls (above right) view the coronation of the new Miss Nude Universe, 22-year-old Kellie Everts. Moments later, Miss Everts—whose regal dimensions are 39-25-35—poses exuberantly for photographers. First prize was a screen test and motion-picture contract; Kellie, a topless go-go girl, is intent upon an acting career

Figure 4.48 A spread from Playboy's February 1968 feature on the Miss Nude Universe pageant shows the contestants and the loose "Mayan" theme for the year. The winner, Kelly Everts, is shown on the bottom right. The fact that this mainstream national men's magazine found the Miss Nude Universe pageant noteworthy (as opposed to outrage worthy), speaks to the culture's changing attitudes about nudity and constructed beauty.
(Playboy Magazine, February 1968, pages 122, 123. Author's collection)

With the extreme cultural attitude shifts in the US around sexuality and nudity, how did burlesque survive, and what did it look like? There's no arguing the fact that the reveals of burlesque by the 1970s were at least topless, if not fully nude, but there were still burlesque acts happening with featured dancers. It *can* be argued that by the 1970s the tease was gone from striptease because in the end all was revealed, but the extravagant costumes and glamour were not completely gone, they were just different, and adapted for the time.

A perfect example of a performer that embodied the sex appeal and glamour of burlesque in the 1970s was Mexican-American actress, dancer and porn star Kitten Natividad. Kitten held the title of Miss Nude Universe for two consecutive years, in 1970 and 1971. She became a feature in Russ Meyer's films and his romantic partner for well over a decade. Kitten augmented her body with breast implants, which was becoming a more common occurrence for performers in the 1970s. Her film appearances and pornographic photo shoots increased her fame and her pay as an exotic dancer. Kitten had a large champagne glass act à la the legendary Lili St. Cyr, and she modeled her burlesque costume designs after fashion inspirations and Bob Mackee designs for Cher.

Figure 4.49 *A promotional poster for Russ Meyer's film* Beneath the Valley of the Ultra Vixens, *1979, featuring Kitten Natividad.*
(© RM Films International/ Courtesy: Everett Collection)

Figure 4.50 *Kitten Natividad in a costume made by Bobby Gerstein inspired by a Bob Mackee design for Cher, 1970s.*
(From the personal collection of Janelle Smith, used with permission from Kitten Natividad)

Figure 4.51 *Kitten Natividad in another of Gerstein's creations, 1970s.*
(Courtesy of Kitten Natividad)

Figure 4.52 *Kitten Natividad with Comedian Milton Berle, in a mink and rhinestone coat by Bobby Gerstein, 1970s. Kitten says the gown and coat cost $5000 at the time. The coat is featured on the following pages.*
(Courtesy of Kitten Natividad)

Figure 4.53 Mink and rhinestone coat by Bobby Gerstein, made for Kitten Natividad.
(Photo by Coleen Scott. Coat is from the personal collection of Stephanie Blake)

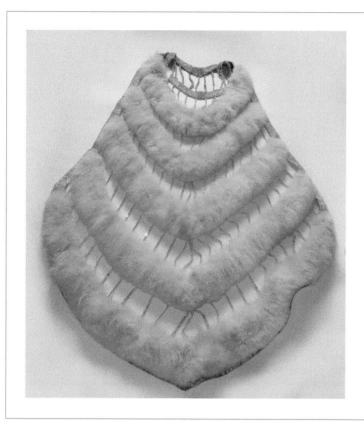

Figure 4.54 *A view of the coat shape, from the right side and back.*
(Photo by Coleen Scott. Coat is from the personal collection of Stephanie Blake)

Figure 4.55 *Close-up of the neckline construction and armholes of the fur and rhinestone coat.*
(Photo by Coleen Scott. Coat is from the personal collection of Stephanie Blake)

Figure 4.56
A full-length view of the coat from the inside. (Photo by Coleen Scott. Coat is from the personal collection of Stephanie Blake)

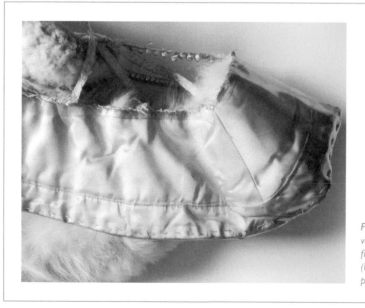

Figure 4.57 Close-up view of the vinyl-lined hem of the coat to protect it from dirt.
(Photo by Coleen Scott. Coat is from the personal collection of Stephanie Blake)

Figure 4.58 Close-up of the construction of the coat. The strips of grosgrain look to be machine sewn into the bagged out lining and the lining edges whipstitched to the fur. The rhinestone trim looks like it was handsewn to the grosgrain ribbons. (Photo by Coleen Scott. Coat is from the personal collection of Stephanie Blake)

Figure 4.59 Close-up of the rhinestone trim. The trim is made of the white settings with stones and a cord running through both sides of the bottom of the settings. The trim is then handsewn to grosgrain ribbon. The coat has had many repairs and the strip on the top of the image has been backed with twill tape for extra strength. This rhinestone trim is useful because it does not have pronged settings, which might have caught on itself or the fur more easily. It makes the rhinestones easier to replace as well. (Photo by Coleen Scott. Coat is from the personal collection of Stephanie Blake)

Tiffany Carter was Miss Nude Universe 1975, and was known for her ornate burlesque costumes. She owns a coat in black like the one in Figures 4.52 to 4.59, and she worked with Bobby Gerstein to execute her costume visions.

Figure 4.60 Tiffany Carter in ostrich feather **chaps** with keyhole cutouts. Late 1960s/early 1970s.
(From the personal collection of Janelle Smith with the permission of Tiffany Carter)

Figure 4.61 Tiffany Carter in a sequined mermaid gown with an
ostrich feather skirt. Late 1960s/early 1970s.
*(From the personal collection of Janelle Smith with the permission of
Tiffany Carter)*

Figure 4.62 Tiffany Carter in a big cat-inspired costume with large
feather headdress, 1970s.
*(From the personal collection of Janelle Smith with the permission
of Tiffany Carter)*

As stated by burlesque legend Camille 2000 on page 147, there were burlesque theaters in the 1970s, but they were few and far between. There is a stark difference in the costume styles from stars of the early 1960s to those in the late 1970s. Figures 4.63 and 4.64 give an example.

Figure 4.63 Clockwise from top left: Miss Toni Elling; Etta Cummings; Feline; Alexandra the Great 48; Unknown; Shawna "The Black Venus"; Satan's Angel "The Devil's Own Mistress."
(From the collection of Janelle Smith and Neil "Nez" Kendall)

Figure 4.64 Clockwise from top left: Marinka; Gypsy Louise; Holiday O'Hara; Berbette; Big Fanny Annie; Dusty Summers. (From the collection of Janelle Smith)

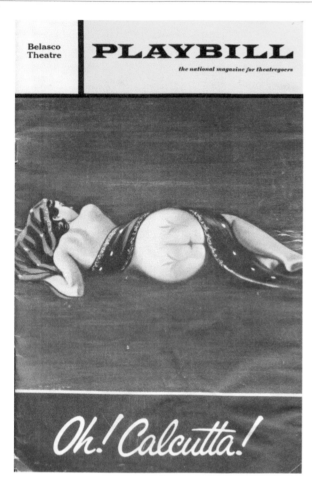

Figure 4.65 The Playbill for Broadway's Oh! Calcutta!, 1976. The controversial play opened off-Broadway in 1969 and contained full nudity. It was successfully revived on Broadway in 1976. (Author's collection)

Burlesque went from glamorous and elegant mainstream entertainment in the early 1960s to a campier, raunchier version of the performance style that catered to the expectations of a male-dominated audience with occasional nods to its golden age. The sexual revolution in America affected cultural views on nudity and sex, and the tease was no longer desired. Burlesque performers had to compete with Broadway plays, pornographic films, and clubs that promised full nudity in order to keep up with the times. Audience wanting to see live entertainment without interest in **pornography** or full-nude venues might be more likely to see a drag show that promised glamour, **camp**, and comedy, go to the legitimate theater for the "tasteful nudity" of *Oh! Calcutta!*, or *Hair*, or watch a new film like *The Rocky Horror Picture Show* or the burlesque-centric *Peeper*. Live burlesque may have faded out in these decades (the term **exotic dancer** was used to describe most strippers by the 1970s), but the remnants remained. Even without the word burlesque in their job title, headliners were using the same basic structure of a burlesque routine in performance. Acts became significantly shorter, usually three songs as opposed to 20 minutes, and **canned music** was used instead of live. Still, the threads of the golden age of burlesque stayed connected through the next two decades, and a new group of young women began to weave their own designs with each link to the past they uncovered.

Figure 4.66 Rocky Horror Picture Show, Nell Campbell, Patrick Quinn, Tim Curry, Richard O'Brien, 1975.
(™ and © 20th Century Fox Film Corp. All rights reserved. Courtesy: Everett Collection)

Figure 4.67 Liz Renay as a stripper in Peeper, 1975. The film is supposed
to take place in the 1940s, but the burlesque costume design and hairstyle
are obviously interpreted through a 1970s lens.
(™ and © 20th Century Fox Film Corp./courtesy Everett Collection)

Notes

1 The nude scene in *Hair* was originally done with actors undressing under a parachute that had slits cut in it and when they were naked, they would slip through a slot and stand still, in keeping with the theatrical nudity regulations.

2 Tasha is inappropriately (though accepted at the time) described as "Oriental" and it is noted that she is the only Asian dancer at the club.

3 First-hand testimony about Gussie's construction methods can be found in Liz Goldwyn's book *Pretty Things*.

4 Satan's Angel created these fire tassels for *The Pastie Project*, (2017) a book about the history of the burlesque pastie.

5 Interview date: October 20, 2016. The full interview was featured on BurlesqueBeat.com in May 2017 as part of the "Legendary Costumes" column (by author under the pen name Rosey La Rouge).

6 Camille's dressing room in Miami was robbed in the 1970s and all of her costumes were stolen.

7 Maurice Seymour was actually a duo of brothers. One was in Los Angeles and one in New York. The name Maurice Seymour was a combination of both of their first names.

8 The Burlesque Hall of Fame Museum in Las Vegas has an annual weekend fundraising and burlesque event in June that honors living legends of burlesque and showcases some of the best performers currently in the business.

9 In the 1960s, stripping was considered a deviant profession (not much has changed today), and homosexuality was considered a deviant behavior, and in some journals a mental illness by psychologists and sociologists.

10 There is difficulty in applying the modern openness, terminology, and statistical information about gay, trans, queer, and any other non-heterosexuality to the past, when those who might have been part of the community remained closeted, and in some cases, did not even have an accepted term for their sexuality in their lifetimes.

11 The facts about Mr. Carroll and costume tips presented here were discussed during a phone interview with the author in April 2018. This bullet point list was published in its full form on burlesquebeat.com, September 7, 2018 as part of the Legendary Costumes column.

Figure 5.1 Burlesque legend and iconic costume designer Catherine D'Lish performs her famous spider web act. Catherine began her career in strip clubs, became famous for her burlesque acts as a two-time Miss Exotic World winner (1992 and 1994), and is more recently known for her costume designs worn by Dita Von Teese, and her clothing company company Boudoir by D'Lish. (Photo by Kaylin Idora)

CHAPTER 5

THE STRIP CLUB MEETS NEO-BURLESQUE
1980S – 2002

By the late 1980s, the ***burlesque theater*** had given way to the ***strip club***, many of which had a different set of aesthetics than golden age glamour. There was a changing of the guard of sorts with a mass retirement of dancers who had no interest in full nudity in their performance, and a barrage of new dancers who never knew a time when stripping wasn't about taking it all off. Costume documentation on this time period is limited, as it was the age before the internet, and the archival interest in strippers seems unsurprisingly inadequate with the exception of the McCaghy collection at The Ohio State University and personal collections. Luckily, many of the people who were stripping and involved in the vintage revival scenes are alive to show and tell their experiences from a costume perspective. In addition to costume documents, this chapter and the next will focus on case studies in the form of oral histories from significant designers and performers who continue to have their fingers on the pulse of the neo-burlesque movement and it's aesthetic.

Neo-burlesque pioneer Jo Weldon, headmistress of the New York School of burlesque, author of *The Burlesque Handbook* and *Fierce! The History of Leopard Print*, spoke with this author about her experience as a stripper and sex worker in the 1980s and 90s.[1]

Figure 5.2 Jo Weldon as Tanya Hide in 1992, wearing a fishnet and lace bodysuit.
(Photo by J. Stephen Hicks)

Jo was a house dancer at the Cheetah Club in Atlanta between 1980 and 1995 when she moved to New York to dance. According to her, narrative or character-driven acts were a common occurrence in her 1980s club. Jo also stated that the average clientele of some clubs tended to be one to two generations older than the dancers, which allowed for features like Madison Stone, Venus Delight, and Yvette Paris to create classic burlesque style acts involving fans, gowns and vintage glamour that reminded their patrons of the past. One of Jo's acts presented her as a nurse who gave out phony prescriptions to audience members. She danced with fire and did a ***fan dance*** as part of her repertoire. When she arrived in New York in the mid-1990s, she saw that similar style acts were presented by featured entertainers at club nights, and she was immediately interested in bringing her stripping repertoire into this scene. The classic elements of burlesque performance where dancers have chosen music, costumes, and a routine that involves systematic clothing removal is exactly what signifies that burlesque did not die, it evolved with the times. Cultural anthropologist Judith Lynne Hanna spent years of her career helping to argue in legal cases that these theatrical and performative elements are exactly what make stripping an art form that should be protected by the first amendment.

Figure 5.3 The interior of a 1984 program for Don Arden's Jubilee! at the MGM Grand Hotel. This was one of Las Vegas' longest running classic showgirl productions.
(From the author's personal collection)

As in decades before, the look of the "desirable woman" changed, and strippers needed to fit that mold. By the 1990s, in commercial strip clubs the billion-dollar pornography industry had transformed beauty standards and aesthetics that were reflected on some strip club stages in the form of breast implants, and later, hairless bodies. This physical transformation was not only reflected in clubs and in men's magazines, but on the mainstream stages of Las Vegas. In costuming, **strip club style** varied from showgirl style in Vegas mostly because of the expensive embellishment applied, including Swarovski crystals and ostrich feather boas. In showgirl costuming there is more theatrical use of nude fabrics and nude tights to create the illusion of nudity versus the actual nudity on a strip club stage, and the pieces are not designed for onstage removal like that of a stripper. However, the actual size and shapes of base garments are similar, including a bra and a g-string or **thong**. These two very different performance and costume styles can be traced back to roots in burlesque.

Figure 5.4 Vegas Showgirl Leah Marie poses on this Las Vegas postcard from the early 1990s. Her physique is representative of the showgirls at this time, and differs from that of the dancers in the Don Arden's Jubilee! 1984 program above.
(Author's collection)

Figure 5.5 Stephanie Blake in the 1992 LA Drama Critics Circle Award winning production
Melody Jones. *Stephanie wears the 1970s fur coat that she purchased from her friend
Kitten Natividad, and her rhinestone Hedy Jo Star bra, underwear and jewelry.*
(Photo by Ron Link from the personal collection of Stephanie Blake)

Burlesque dancer, strip club owner and actress Stephanie
Blake worked in clubs in Kansas City, Arkansas, Las Vegas and
Hollywood in the 1970s and 1980s. She toured with Sid Caesar
in "A Touch of Burlesque" in 1981. She has had a successful
career acting on stage and in film, including a role as a sexy
singing nurse in 1986's *Ferris Bueller's Day Off.* Blake shared her
experience both dancing in clubs in the 1970s and running
the club The Star Strip in West Hollywood in the 1980s.[2] She
explained that when she first started dancing, her acts, including
a champagne glass act, were 20 minutes long. She says: "You
had to wear extra layers of costume so that you had enough to
take off!" It wasn't until she moved to Las Vegas to work at the
Royal Casino in the late 1970s that she started doing an eight-
minute **show**.[3] Blake explained that in Vegas, the rhinestone
bra and bottom was a very popular costume look, and she was
fortunate enough to purchase a stunning set from Hedy Jo Star.

Figure 5.6 *Stephanie performs her step down number at Miss Exotic World in Helendale, California, 1999.*
(Courtesy of the Burlesque Hall of Fame Museum)

After living in Vegas for a couple of years, Blake moved to Los Angeles to pursue her acting career. She heard about Miss Exotic World competition from the first winner,[4] Toni Alessandrini, while living in Hollywood, and decided to enter. She won the title in 1997 and 1998, even after they had introduced a rule that the same person couldn't win the title twice when Catherine D'Lish took the title in 1992 and 1994. The Miss Exotic World pageant and the Helendale museum of the same name celebrated the history of burlesque, and its founder Jennie Lee, along with her loyal friend Dixie Evans, kept the flame of the American art form alive for the next generation to discover. Exotic World has been a beacon for the neo-burlesque movement. It is now known as The Burlesque Hall of Fame Museum and is located in downtown Las Vegas.

Figure 5.7 *Dixie Evans stands in front of the entry gate to the Exotic World Museum, 2004. (Photo by Don Spiro)*

Figure 5.8 Aurora Borealis crystal bra made by Hedy Jo Star. From the collection of Stephanie Blake. (Photo by Coleen Scott)

Figure 5.9 Close-up view of one bra cup. (Photo by Coleen Scott)

Figure 5.10
Rhinestone shimmy belt with rhinestone g-string attached. From the personal collection of Stephanie Blake. Blake noted that the two pieces were separates originally, but were joined together for the play Melody Jones in 1992.
(Photo by Coleen Scott)

Figure 5.11 Burlesque legend Judith Stein poses in a metal rhinestone bra, g-string and accessories similar to the one above. Early1980s. Judith is a Canadian burlesque performer who toured extensively in the United States.
(Courtesy of Judith Stein)

Figure 5.12
The matching rhinestone
necklace for the set. The
clasp for this piece is a
costume hook and loop.
(Photo by Coleen Scott)

Figure 5.13 *An arm band accessory. This is worn around the bicep*
and there is a set of two.
(Photo by Coleen Scott)

Figure 5.14 *Matching earrings for the costume. The tape on the*
backing is to help the piece stay in place when dancing on stage.
(Photo by Coleen Scott)

The Miss Exotic World pageant brought together strippers from the early days of burlesque and modern women working in clubs. The competition included themed acts and interesting costumes. Toni Alessandrini won the first contest in 1991 with a devil themed act. Stephanie Blake competed in gowns that actually belonged to her mother, who was a Kansas-based burlesque performer in the 1960s named BB Love. Blake added extra embellishment to the dresses, including rhinestones, feathers and sequins. Photos of her title-winning costumes are showcased on the following pages.

Figure 5.15 *Front view of a Toni Allessandrini gown, 1990s.*
(Photo by Coleen Scott. Dress from the personal collection of Stephanie Blake)

Figure 5.16 Red velvet 1960s gown worn by Stephanie Blake for her 1997 Miss Exotic World win. The rhinestones and feathers were added by Blake. The photo shows that the **mermaid skirt** splits directly up the middle in the front and back. There is a Velcro closure that replaced older snaps. (Photo by Coleen Scott. Dress from the personal collection of Stephanie Blake)

Figure 5.17 Close-up of the rhinestone trim additions made by Blake. This gown belonged to her mother, 1960s Kansas burlesque performer BB Love. (Photo by Coleen Scott)

Figure 5.18 A black
sequin dress and
single gauntlet worn
by Stephanie Blake for
her second Miss Exotic
World Title in 1998. This
gown belonged to her
mother, 1960s Kansas
burlesque performer
BB Love. Blake added
the sequins all over the
knit dress. The beaded
waistband accent is
original.
(Photo by Coleen Scott.
Dress from the personal
collection of Stephanie
Blake)

Figure 5.19 Close-up
of the original beaded
waistband.
(Photo by Coleen Scott.
Dress from the personal
collection of Stephanie
Blake)

The costumes of the 1980s and 1990s exotic dance world and Las Vegas showgirls retained stylistic elements of burlesque, but there were other scenes in the country that inspired performance and costume experimentation leading to burlesque's revival. Susanne Bartsch[5] is a queen of the New York party scene. Bartsch and her diverse group of friends created ornate and ever-changing wardrobe that led the charge in keeping beautiful nightlife alive from her first party in 1986.

"It was about seeing and being seen," says Bartsch. Bartsch and her friends have long constituted a fashion underground of creative individuals who take dressing up to the level of **performance art**. From the FIT exhibit:

"Style is about expressing yourself," says Bartsch. "You can be whatever you want to be: a silver-screen star, a Marie Antoinette baroque creature, a Victorian punk. I love that about fashion and makeup." A muse for fashion designers and makeup artists, Bartsch has also been a catalyst for the cross-fertilization of ideas between creative people in a range of fields.

Figure 5.20 *Susanne Bartsch and her crew, 1991. Susanne is wearing a Mr. Pearl ensemble.* (Photo by Michael James O'Brien/The Licensing Project)

AN INTERVIEW WITH LAURA BYRNES
OF PINUP GIRL CLOTHING

The **swing dance** craze centered in California in the 1990s led to a new generation's love of vintage glamour. Laura Byrnes was working and costuming the strip club scene when she was invited to perform her 1960s burlesque style routine for a party full of **swingers**.[6] Her **stripper-wear** designs and love of **retro** style combined to form Pinup Girl Clothing. Laura's crossover experience performing and costuming on the strip club scene and her business growth during the burlesque and **vintage revival** make her an expert in what people in these scenes wanted to wear. The author interviewed Laura about this experience and her company.[7]

CS: When and why did you create Pinup Girl Clothing?

LB: I started Pinup Girl Clothing in 1997. I was a photographer for a few years before that, and my goal was to be a fashion photographer. But I ended up doing mostly portrait editorial and working with a ton of creative types. You know, there were a lot of musicians, some actors, and some models. So I ended up, just, getting to the point where I was working mostly with creatives, and I was on track to become a magazine editorial photographer. But at that time in the mid-90s, there were a lot of independent magazines that were all

Figure 5.21 Heather models a signature cherry dress from Pinup Girl Clothing. (Photo by Laura Byrnes)

starting to go out of business very quickly. It was a kind of rough thing where you knew you could get work, but you just had to hope that you got paid before the magazine went out of business, and that was very stressful. Right around the same time, I got married. I was pregnant in 1996, and at my baby shower my husband's aunt had made baby clothes for my daughter. And I thought they were so beautiful, I was so impressed that I was like, "I want to learn how to sew so I can make clothes for my daughter." So I started sewing just by accident. Ultimately, I really liked it. I really enjoyed pattern making and I'm kind of an OCD person so there was something I really got out of making clothes. So first I was making clothes for my daughter, and then some for myself, and you know, a little for my friends.

Since I was working as a photographer and, you know, shooting this editorial stuff and hoping I would get paid, I was supplementing my income by stripping at Sam's Hoff Brau three days a week. It was kind of amazing. I worked the day shift so that I would drop my daughter off at babysitting, and go strip to make some money and then go pick her up.

CS: Where was the club?

LB: Sam's Hoffbrau is in Los Angeles. Still one of my favorite clubs, and it became my favorite club to sell stripper clothing to.

I worked as an exotic dancer between 1992 and I'd say mid-1995. Then I tried to go legit. I mean, I was. I moved out to California in 1992 to pursue photography. So I was pursuing that at the same time I was dancing, and I was actually doing a little bit of acting. Which was coming just by accident, since I had no problem being nude. I went to casting agencies. They said "Are you ok with nudity?" I was like "Oh yeah, sure." So suddenly I'm doing body doubling. I'm a **body double**.

CS: Oh yeah?

LB: In a movie for three minutes. You know, I just, I ended up getting work because I said I would be nude. I was like "This is great!" Ha-ha. I had been a stripper for years, and I actually enjoyed it way more than a day job. Which is why I didn't really want to go back to work doing a day job. But in '95 I went to work at a photo lab, which is what I had been doing in New York before I moved. So basically, I started Pinup Girl because I had gone back to stripping just two days a week to support myself, and while I waited for these magazines to pay me, I was making clothing.

One day (in the strip club) a woman, there's always clothing ladies, that's what we call them. There was never any other name for them. And they would come in, and they would have stripper outfits that they would make for people to buy. And a woman comes in, and again I'm very OCD, especially if it's something that goes into an area I know. I got into it with her because she was selling a dress, it was sheer from the bust down. It was a little A-line that just covered your booty. It was sheer, so I said "that's great, but where's the matching underwear?" Like what is anyone going to wear [with it]? And she wanted $40 for it. I looked at the stitching, and I'm like, "the stitching isn't really good; if this opens up the whole seam is going to come undone. And why don't you have matching underwear? You know, no one's going to find anything to match this." She gave me the wave—"You don't know what you're talking about. You don't understand what goes into sewing." And I'm like, "I'm pretty sure I do. I could make something like this but better, and add some underwear and actually sell it for less than what you are selling it for." Then this woman, who was not very bright (we were in the dressing room, and there were like a dozen other dancers in there, because again it was day shift so it wasn't very busy), she said straight up to me, "Well I don't see you doing that. I just see you stripping."

CS: Oh, no.

LB: Which is the worst thing you can say.

CS: No more business for her!

LB: Literally! I mean within a year. She hated me, and the other strippers thought it was so funny because she had started out selling this stuff at $40 a piece and people were buying, but a year later she couldn't sell her stuff for $15. People hated her because she was selling to the girls, but she had no respect (for them).

CS: Clearly.

LB: You know what I mean? She was not a dancer, she never was. And you know, I'm just an asshole. Everyone knows it. [That day] I said to her straight up, "I will go home, I will stay up all night, I will come back here with outfits, and I will sell them for less than what you are selling." And the girls were like "Oh hell, yeah!" They gave me their little booty shorts to copy, and their bikini tops. I literally stayed up all night and I came back with six outfits. They sold out. Six weeks later, I stopped dancing, and I started going around to all the clubs selling the dancewear. That was 1997. I did that for two years. I had a whole set-up. I had a two-week schedule where each week one I would hit 12 clubs and the following week I would hit another 12 clubs, and then do it again.

CS: Wow

LB: So I was hitting 24 strip clubs in in LA and Orange Country.

CS: Were you producing it all yourself then?

LB: I was in the very beginning. Yes, I was cutting, sewing, designing. Literally everything. **Sourcing** the fabric. I was a one women show, and I had a six-month-old; no, at that point she was about a year. She came with me everywhere. I mean, she literally grew up in swap meets and you know in the fabric district. She works at my company now.

CS: Amazing!

LB: I'd say about six months in I said, "I have to put an ad out for a seamstress. I need somebody to help me sew this stuff." Because, of course, that takes the most time.

CS: Yes.

LB: I was also starting to do custom orders. I still have my little loose-leaf folder. I had one folder that had photos of all my designs, and I had another folder that had fabric swatches. So when I went around to these clubs, I had my little rack with clothes. Then I had this catalogue that had order forms. And since I was on a two-week schedule, the girls could pick literally anything. You know, I want this dress in this fabric and I'll give you 50%

deposit and you'll bring it to me in two weeks. So I was doing that as well. That was great, because the girls were always trying to make sure that they didn't have the same outfits as another girl in the club and so they started ordering custom stuff. Then I got a seamstress to make it, and that was Maria. She eventually became my first production manager. First, she just sewed for me, then she said, "Look, I'm gonna cut, I can cut the stuff too." So basically, I started taking orders, and she would cut the orders, and then she hired other [employees].

CS: Wow.

LB: Yeah. We got a place in 2001, and we started the website. I was with her, before we even started the website. Then I finally moved [production] out of my house, and into an office in 2001. She came in and we had six sewing machines. She was pattern making, everyone else was sewing and it was like this little factory in the back of my showroom on San Pedro Street. So we started out essentially doing exotic dancewear. It morphed from that. We were still doing exotic dancewear in 2001. I went from that into swimwear. Because after you've done all that exotic dancewear—they always say swimwear is the hardest thing to design and fit, but that was the first thing I was doing.

CS: It makes sense.

Figure 5.22
Mosh models a vintage-style swimsuit from Pinup Girl Clothing. (Photo by Laura Byrnes for Pinup Girl Clothing)

LB: That was the amazing thing about me coming up. People are amazed that I can do what I do with no fashion training. I didn't go to fashion school, I just took a couple sewing lessons. I went to the library. I got a book on pattern making. But, I think, making clothing for exotic dancers where it's fitted, it has to stretch, it has to look really good. It has to look great when you're hanging upside down from a pole. [It's good training.]

CS: Yes.

LB: So I was doing stuff that was actually quite difficult at the time. Now it's like- "you want me to make a gown that looks like *blank*" it's so easy. I guess that's why I started Pinup Girl, because I wasn't getting paid as a photographer. At that point, stripping was paying and making clothing for exotic dancers was paying, and it continued. We didn't even venture into swimwear until 2002. Then in 2003 we started the dress line.

CS: So, the first things you were making—the strip club wear—what were you doing? What kinds of shapes were your garments? I'm guessing you were doing some bikini tops, did you have any pieces that you invented, or types of garments that were in the most demand at that time?

LB: Yes, I used to have a cat suit that is still my all-time favorite thing, and it was full-coverage. That was always the funny thing. Sometimes that stuff was most popular. I think part of that was that these girls could go out dancing in it. It was just called the "zip front cat suit." It has a zipper in the front, that started right below your bellybutton then came all the way up, and it had a collar and three-quarter sleeves. This was 1997, so it had slightly flared legs.

CS: Nice.

LB: I would do it in black velvet, and then there's also that stripper fabric … that thick nylon tricot but they put that coating on, with clear sequins, or not so clear sequins. The black Lycra with clear sequin in that costume—I started just making it in sizes to always have it for people. I still have mine at home. My zip-front cat suit was my jam. It was weird. Obviously I [also] had bikinis and I had booty shorts, which you sell hand over fist.

CS: Of course.

LB: I even made pants, but the things that sold the best were the things people could, also go out clubbing in.

CS: Right.

LB: I think that the dual use stuff did the best. I'm sure that's how we transitioned. (laughter) You know, it's funny. I still have dancers, a lot of dancers that shop at Pinup Girl, that were some of my earliest customers. Now they're just like "How did this become *this*? You had this

little dinky stripper website that we used to buy from, and it's big now." And I'm like "Yeah, it's great!"

CS: It is!

LB: My favorite thing is to talk about how it started because it's awesome. I would say, everything I've learned about sales, I've learned from exotic dancers. They're the toughest customers, and the best because you can learn everything you need to know.

CS: Yes, I love that this is the history. I think it makes Pinup Girl such a special company. You talked about other women selling to the clubs, and not having respect for the dancers, but you started there. So you started it in a place of respect and wanting people to have quality garments in that industry.

LB: Yes.

CS: That's just so good.

LB: I'll say, just to credit, there was one other person around who was like that, selling clothes at the time, and she's still in business as well. She's kind branched off to do her own thing as well—J. Valentine.

CS: Oh. That is ringing a bell in the back of my head.

LB: I would look her up. She specializes mostly in club wear now, but she was about the same age as me. I would meet other clothing ladies sometimes, and finally the clubs would figure out to keep us separated.

CS: Hmm.

LB: Because not everyone would have me. I remember going, and she was there, and I said: "Oh, I'll leave." And she said: "Oh no don't worry about it, we can sell together." She was looking at my stuff and said: "Oh wow, your stuff's actually good." We became friends, but we never really worked together. Then the funny thing was [at one time] I was selling her clothing on my website.

CS: Oh cool.

LB: We stayed friends for a while. She was the only other person that started out as a dancer and had complete and utter respect for her customers, and it showed. That's why she's successful now. Like I said, I think everyone should train by having exotic dancers as customers. I don't know if you've done just burlesque or just exotic dance, but exotic dance is like the nitty-gritty version of burlesque. It's rough, you don't get an ounce of respect as an exotic dancer. If you did burlesque, people were like "Oh *Burlesque!*" It's kind like for some reason it's more respectable. I don't see it that way. To me exotic dance is essentially the same. They just can't afford the costumes, or they don't have the time for that. They're just trying to make their $200 dollars and go home.

CS: YES. Exactly, they don't have the time to be sparkly for free. Basically that's what a lot of people are doing in burlesque. Pay rates are changing in some scenes, but it's nothing like strip club money for most. Some girls do both and supplement their burlesque dancing with strip club stripping.

LB: Burlesque is a labor of love.

CS: It is.

LB: It's a labor of love, unless you can get on the tour. [Dita Von Teese's tour]

CS: Yes.

LB: You're never gonna get paid. I used to do it, back in the day. When I was stripping, I would do burlesque, but it was 1992, 93. No one cared, you know. It was so bizarre.

CS: Can you talk about anything you did that was influenced by burlesque when you were working in the club? Or act that you saw that was burlesque-like?

LB: Well, the funny thing is when I was just working in the club, that didn't influence me to do burlesque at all. I already knew about burlesque. I loved Kitten Natividad. I've been obsessed with her from like the moment—I don't even remember how old I was when I saw a movie with her in it. She's my favorite Russ Meyer[8] girl. I got to meet her and be friends with her. The day I met her I was like "Could you be my mom?" and she said "Absolutely." And there you have it.

CS: Awesome.

LB: I loved Tempest Storm—I was all into that stuff. I do a burlesque act that is based on the Bettie Page and Tempest Storm *Teaseorama* reel where she's getting dressed. So I knew about all that stuff. Then I go and become a stripper, and I thought "Oh, this is great, but it sucks cause there's no opportunity to do that old style." I didn't see it as something different ideologically, it was just back in the day as strippers you got to wear sequins. The audiences, whooped and hollered at you, instead of starring at you with a blank dead look in their eyes. That was actually the weirdest thing about stripping in the 90s—how repressed everyone was.

CS: Hmm.

LB: Like: "I'm going to watch you strip, but I can't make it look like I'm enjoying watching you strip—because that would be weird." But no, what's weird is I'm up here shaking my butt, and your just looking at me like you're watching television. So it was more that I started doing burlesque at that time wherever I could get it. There was a club called The Mint, it was 1993 or so. Somehow, I got to know the manager. I said, "You

know what would be cool? If I just came in and did burlesque in between like when you had bands." And he said OK. I said, "Just pay me like $60." I remember going, showing up, and thinking, "I'm going to go do burlesque at The Mint!" This is the crazy part of the story, and again, it was 1993—during the "90210" years.[9] I'm getting ready to go back stage, and there's a girl hanging out near me when I'm trying to find the entrance, and it's Jenny Garth![10] I said: "I'm going to be doing a strip tease and I …" and she says "Oh, let me help you." She brings me backstage and helps me get dressed. She gets me on stage, and gets things moving, and people started throwing 20s at me.

CS: Oh my god.

LB: I made like $300, because no one had done it [burlesque]. I still have photos I've got to dig out. My ex-husband shot slides of this. I'm in burlesque mode. I've got my pasties, and I used to do a whole black and gold thing. There was a place up in San Francisco near me that you may have heard about—Piedmont.

CS: Yes, I know Piedmont!

LB: Oh god, I used to go up there and get my outfits made. They would embellish these padded bras and make stuff that looked like 60s burlesque wear. So that became my schtick. Like even when I went clubbing, I would go to clubs wearing this stuff. And I would look like a 60s burlesque girl. So it was more like I was stripping [in clubs], but it wasn't living up to my aesthetic expectations. It wasn't what I wanted. I started doing burlesque so I could pretend I was Tempest Storm.

CS: I was curious about that—I mean, you were at that one club, and I know that in some clubs there were featured dancers that were bringing burlesque-style acts to other clubs. Did you ever see anybody else doing a burlesque-style act at a strip club?

LB: Well. Not at Sam's Hoffbrau. It wasn't that kind of place. It was working class, but that's what I loved about it. It was a very tight community. The customers, the dancers, and I've got to say the owners of Sam's were some of the best owners of any strip club. They really were. I don't know if they are still the owners, but they were Allen and his dad.

My very first stripping in a club experience was when my friend was working briefly at Market Street Cinema. That place was trash. It was basically a lap dance club. I mean trash. No stalls in the bathrooms, so girls wouldn't do heroin in them. The thing is the girls were great, but the club was gross. It was just nasty. But they would have featured dancers. At that time, it was like you went and got surgery to have boobs that were way too big. The features were people like Kayla Cleavage and Honey Moons, and I can't remember everyone's names. Me and the friend that I went up with to dance, we were there for three weeks, and we worked there. We just loved seeing the featured performers. We actually have a scrapbook. We would take stuff—like if their boas dropped a feather, we'd pick up that feather, and we would take a picture. We would always do the $5 polaroids after the show.

CS: YES!

LB: So we have this whole scrapbook of us with these girls. So, again, I think it was more that I wanted stripping to be better than it was.

CS: Yeah.

LB: Normally, the strippers and the featured performers, they resented each other, for whatever reason, but we were like "No, this is fun!" And this was the only thing we really got to see, so it was no one really doing burlesque [in strip clubs]. In the very late 90s and early 2000s you started hearing about Dita and Catherine D'Lish, and then you were like "Oh thank god."

It was around 2002; there was a Burlesque Hall of Fame benefit in one of the theaters downtown. They asked me "do you want to vend?" I mean, literally, I had one of those tables you buy at Target, and I was set up in the lobby selling magnets, or whatever crap I had. It was funny. I remember my husband manned the table so I could run in and see them perform. I thought "Oh my god. Someone's doing it. Thank fucking god."

CS: So did that transition feel gradual? Or did it feel like you thought, "Yeah it's here now! It's arrived!"?

LB: Well, it felt like, in Los Angeles, I think Dita was probably influenced by the same things that I was. Like looking at Tempest, and Bettie, and all those guys. But also, in LA we had the movie *Swingers*.[11] There were exotic dancers but then there was also the swing dance scene that was happening and The Derby and all these other places.

CS: Right.

LB: That was actually the precursor to the rockabilly scene and that became the pin-up scene here in LA. So I was part of that. In fact, I started doing bachelor parties because I found a really great agency, it was run by a bunch of swingers—they all met at **swinger clubs** and were like "Why don't we just do this for money?"

Most of the bachelor party agencies tended to be fronts for prostitution, and the owners were on drugs. It was just a nightmare. But these guys were just—they

were swingers. They were very sex positive, and so it was all these swinging couples, that the dudes would drive and the girls would do the dancing for bachelor parties. The guys, the husbands, were obviously getting off seeing their girlfriends dancing for all these guys. They, this agency, turned the bachelor parties into real parties. I remember going to one in Silverlake, and, you know, I had my old Piedmont, burlesque-y thing. That's the thing—if I did a bachelor party I had a whole burlesque outfit that I did.

When we got there, they were all rockabilly boys. And we thought—"Oh shit!" When we came out the place went "Who are you?"

It was so funny because, they couldn't objectify us. They were just like "who are you?" and I had not heard of The Derby[12], this was so early—I think it was 1993/94. There was this dude who asked "The Derby, do you go to The Derby?" and I said "I don't." He [insists] "You have to go to The Derby. I'm giving you my phone number, you don't have to call me, but I'm going to be there Wednesday. Come to The Derby." And I go, and he says "Oh my god. You made it!" And we swing danced all night. We would meet Wednesdays just to dance.

CS: That's awesome.

LB: It was the craziest thing. At least, for me, it felt like a bunch of disparate things coming together. So all of a sudden there were people in LA who were like "You know what's great? Mid-century everything. Mid-century burlesque. Rockabilly. You know swing dancing, the fashion, all of it. So it all came together. That's why I started making dresses—because I started going to The Derby. I had these stripper clothes, but I wanted to make some stuff for going out. At that point the swing dancing thing turned into rockabilly and Viva Las Vegas and all that. So that's how it happened. There have always been elements of all of that in Pinup Girl because that's what I was into at the start of it; I always have been, really. I mean, I called the company Pinup Girl. It just aligned with all my interests.

CS: From getting a storefront in 2001 until now – how has Pinup Girl evolved? Once you started doing full garments and dresses in 2002, the pin-up and rockabilly scene existed—talk about how business was.

LB: We got very popular first obviously among exotic dancers buying my stuff. Then, a lot of the bikini girls, and also porn stars were buying. People like my friend who was a pin-up photographer back in the day. He was always DP-ing and PA-ing on porn movies and then just

Figure 5.23 La Cholita
models a classic satin
wrap-dress from Pinup
Girl Clothing.
(Photo by Laura Byrnes)

ended up shooting his own … He literally said "My
dream is to shoot porn" and then he went and did it.
But his style, It was very rockabilly. So, first it was exotic
dancers, then we added bikini girls and porn stars, and
they all knew who we were. Heff's[13] girlfriends were
wearing my stuff. Then from there it became the
rockabilly scene who discovered us. So we moved into
that, and again that all aligned with my interests. Like, a
dress with cherries on it? Not a problem. Boom. Then it
was funny, because I started getting bored. We were the
biggest thing in the rockabilly scene, the biggest website,
and you know everyone bought their stuff from us. Our
dresses were doing well. But I'm always sick of

something if there's too much it, for too long. I wanted
to move on to the next thing.

CS: You're an artist. I totally relate to that.

LB: I think everything has to evolve. Burlesque and
everything should evolve. People are like "I've seen that
a million times" and they get bored and move on. So
yeah, I'd say that around 2008–2009 I [decided] "OK,
we have to get a little bit less rockabilly." That's why I
started moving into more vintage-type prints and things
like that. That did really well. Then [we did] more cuts
that were less rockabilly and more classic and even less
pin-up if you will. Just sexy glamourous. I remember
there's a collection I did in 2011 that had influences of

Bladerunner, Alexander McQueen, and—pretend Dita Von Teese was a lawyer—what would she wear. I made a jacket like the *Metropolis* jacket and thought "she'd wear that, OK." If she was going to fight in a [court] case, she'd walk in with that jacket. It was taking that glam feel, and that became pin-up style. Which was great, but by 2014–2015 I started to feel pigeon-holed by that. Like "Oh, look, another novelty print, another vintage floral." Then, of course, the last couple of years, every company in the world has decided that that model is the way to go: "Let's do a million novelty prints!" I'll go to the trade shows, like there's London Edge, which I used to love. I don't need another floral, I don't need another print with ice creams on it, or cactus, or whatever we're sticking on a fricking print. So I've actually been, the last year or so, trying to do a little less novelty and to be more classically glamorous and referential. Whatever, we'll always have a leopard print,

we'll always have a cherry. But I'm trying to move things a little more forward, because I feel like we're all growing up. Which I don't think is a bad thing. I'll say it, I'm 49, I'll be 50 in December. That's fantastic, and I remember the last time I met with Dita [Von Teese], we talked about how we're aging and that's a good thing. What needs to happen now is, she said something, and don't quote me on Dita, but she said something along the lines of "now it's time to make aging glamorous"; to show the glamour in being hot older women. We have to step into that now. I feel that's the new way to be a role model. For people like Dita, for people like me, because we've not really shown that before. Normally, people age and they go [away] and they groom some younger person. Younger people are great, but I don't see Dita stepping out of the spotlight anytime soon, and I don't plan on it either.

Figure 5.24
Laura Byrnes.
(Laura Byrnes)

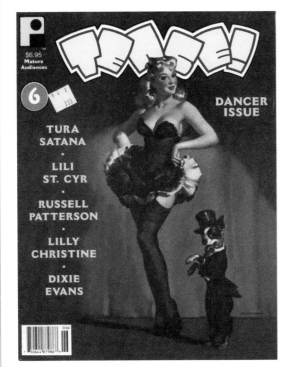

Figure 5.25 1996 issue of Tease magazine featuring
burlesque dancers.
(Tease Magazine)

In the early 90s burlesque was just a twinkle in the eyes of
its pioneers. In 1996 the pin-up and vintage culture was large
enough to generate its own magazines. The burlesque revival
was just beginning as evidenced by this issue of *Tease*. The
"dancer issue" features a southern burlesque show, a feature on
Lili St. Cyr, and an interview with Tura Satana. Publications like
Tease, the Miss Exotic World Competition and events like Tease-
O-Rama[14] were resources and gatherings where like-minded
and trans-coastal trailblazers could learn and network.

Figure 5.26
A spread about
the French
Quarter Follies
burlesque show
in Atlanta,
with images of
performers in
costume. The 1996
article touts
"Who knows?
In a little while
every major city
may be offering
burlesque."
(Tease Magazine)

THE SHIM SHAM-ETTES
AND THE SHIM SHAM REVUE

Figure 5.27 The Shim Sham-ettes circa 1999. From left to right: Stacy Sheer, Bethany Lemanski, Kryss Statho, Allyson Garro, Veronica Oliver, Johanna Rivers, Marcy Hesseling, Samantha Hubbs, Nina Bozac. Costumes by Oliver Manhattan. (Photo by Jian Bastille)

One of the early classic burlesque revival shows, The Shim Sham Revue ran from 1999 through 2001 at The Shim Sham Club in New Orleans. From creator Lorelei Fuller:[15]

> I was approached by Morgan Higby to create a burlesque troupe, at the old Maxwell House, which became The Shim Sham Club after he and partners took it over. I created the Shim Sham-ettes, and as a no-brainer Morgan wanted Ronnie Magri to put a cream of the crop jazz band together—The Shim Sham Revue. … Later on my troupe had 24 dancers, including many individual acts, and multiple group numbers. Costume wise- every number's costumes were paired with the year or era of the song. All music was live.

Fuller says the costumes were made by Sarah Levine and Oliver Manhattan, both designers who still reside in New Orleans.

> An obsession with Rodin, Isadora Duncan- Busby Berkley … merged with Morgan Higby's vision and his trust fund. Throw in Ronnie Magri's genius, putting music to dance, movement. Hello Shim Sham-ettes! International recognition was easy. Bringing Neo-Burlesque back was a given. I loved the beauty of everyone's hard work doing that.

Figure 5.28 The Shim Sham Revue's album cover. Recorded in 2001. (Ronnie Magri)

DUTCH WEISMANN'S FOLLIES

Dutch Weismann's Follies was a New York City speakeasy burlesque show that began in the early 1990s. Burlesque superstar and Miss Exotic World 2008 Angie Pontani was part of this enterprise, and later went on to form her group The World Famous Pontani Sisters. From Dutch Weismann's co-creator Billie Madley:[16]

I was the first (and only for a while) with Dutch Weismann. Tony Marando arrived [in New York] in 1992 from LA and wanted to do a backers audition for a script about a burlesque club. Very similar to the movie *Lady of Burlesque*, a murder mystery from 1943 (with Barbra Stanwyck). He had heard there was a girl doing burlesque who was also an actress and contacted me. I think it was his 3rd week in New York. We became friends, I did numbers for some for backers and parties for investors in his loft. Then we staged the play; we cast through people we knew. We started to do just numbers in the loft to pay the rent and named it after one of the characters in the script (Dutch Weismann) who was the owner of the club in the play.

I cast through girls (dancers) I had known in strip clubs who had interesting personas. I was a fashion stylist and actress, so I had been casting for magazines and theatre. So we did all the early stuff together, finding girls that could embody characters, then costuming them. There was an awesome choreographer, an older women that was a dancer and actress but also worked at strip clubs in the early 60s. She was amazing. A couple of years before, I met a girl who did performance art and stripped, her name was Otter. We stayed up all night when I first met her, scheming. I had had the idea that burlesque and women doing their own material as artists would have an audience with a broad appeal. To take control of sexy. We were totally on the same page. So around the same time we wanted to mount more shows Otter called me and said "I'm doing it! You're the first call I'm making" ... she started a club called Fallen Angel (with a German woman named Eta who had a space and was a dominatrix), later it changed to Blue Angel. I was too busy at the time, but I took Tony and we met more great girls like Ami Goodheart. So Bernadette Brooks was the choreographer, and Tony Marando and I were really the beginning of that. Tony and Bernadette molded a lot of the real first **firebrands** of neo-burlesque.

Figure 5.29
Billie Madley by Stephanie Foxx, 1990s. (Photo by Stephanie Foxx. Courtesy of Billie Madley)

The New York Times

The City

cv   Section **13**

NEIGHBORHOOD REPORT- CHELSEA

Chelsea Moulin Rouge? Lavishly-clad Showgirls in a Legitimate Speakeasy

Tony Marando has brought real showgirls back to New York in Dutch Weismann's "Winter Follies" at his Speakeasy on 18th St.

The Victorian furniture, velvet drapes, marble busts and spectacular mahogany bar make you believe you're in a very real speakeasy. Cigarette smoke and expectation fill the air as latecomers scurry for seats in the gorgeous showroom at midnight on a cold Friday in Chelsea.

It's time for "Dutch Weismann's Winter Follies" which has been playing since early November at this exclusive Speakeasy. And although the show bears Mr. Weismann's name, the production, (and environment) have been created by Tony Marando, an innovative theatre /cabaret entrepreneur who takes us back in time. The fiction is carried out to make us believe this show is made up of highlights and history from Dutch Weismann's past successes, tracing his history of Minstrel from the 1850's, through Vaudeville and Burlesque, to the nightclub Revues of the 1950's.

Luc Sante, whose 1991 book, "Low Life" (Farrar, Straus & Giroux) is partly a history of live entertainment in New York, said, "The time is ripe to revive the down and dirty aspects of old-time (Burlesque and Vaudeville) theatre; there is a sentimentality about it now that is relevant."

The time must be right, because Dutch Weismann's Speakeasy on 18th St. in Chelsea is quite successful. Mr. Marando, who came back to New York in 1992 from Los Angeles, was a live theatre / nightclub producer for The Walt Disney Corporation. The first Weismann shows were produced at a secret location on West 23rd St. in a second-floor loft. The only way in was a secret word-of-mouth password or concierge referrals from The Waldorf, The Paramount, Ritz-Carlton, or for the very soignee, The Sherry-Netherlands. That Speakeasy was credited for starting the retro-trend in New York's late-night scene.

The Weismann character is a creation from Marando's 'live' film noir murder mystery, "Die Stripper Die!" for which he did recieve a rave notice- from the NYPD who raided the "last, real, illegetimate speakeasy" in Manhattan. It seems they had a problem with his charging for liquor- without a license. A quick call went out to Weismann who was in Langkawi on business, and financing was found for this-his newest and legal Speakeasy in the Chelsea district. Perfect.

After-theatre, hungry-for-entertainment New Yorkers, and a surprising demographic of extremely international travelers have made reservations months into the New Year to come to Weismann's. With such strong word of mouth and the classy concierge referrals- did we mention the celebrities who swarm the club?- Mr. Marando is making his point. "It's time quality and class were put back in Manhattan nightlife." We couldn't agree more.
EDWARD LEWINE

Figure 5.30 A clipping from The New York Times *column "The City," early 1990s.*
(Courtesy of Tony Morando)

Figure 5.31 Three images of Dutch Weismann performances including Laurel Sanders in a Brecht number with live neon, Chicago Sheila Champagne, and Angie Pontani with host Max Berman.
(Courtesy of Tony Morando)

Figure 5.32 Angie Pontani started The World Famous Pontani Sisters (Helen, Tara and Angie)
in "'97 or '98" after her time with The Dutch Weismann Follies.
(Photo by Orlando Marra)

THE VELVET HAMMER BURLESQUE

In the late 1990s, The Velvet Hammer Burlesque introduced neo-burlesque stars Kitten DeVille, Miss Astrid, Bobbi Pinz, The Poubelle Twins, and founder Michelle Carr's burlesque persona, Valentina Violette, among others. The Velvet Hammer was most certainly the home of the Los Angeles neo-burlesque movement, and featured guest performers from the New York City scene like Julie Atlaz Muz, World Famous * BOB *, and Dirty Martini.

From Carr:

Born and raised in Los Angeles, I felt repeatedly insulted by the prevailing surgically altered cookie cutter design of unrealistic, idealized femininity. I can find beauty in just about everyone, the more eccentric and unusual the better. I believe there is room for all, not just the standardized beauty society holds high. The women portrayed in [vintage men's] magazines, on the other hand looked like they were in charge—in an era when women were anything but in charge—and I wanted to be just like them, those sanguine sisters of Salome. For better or worse, they made their own way in the world as travelling performers. Tough misfits and **firebrands**, these were true individualists. And I felt an immediate affinity as it jived with the punk rock ideology I embraced.

As a woman, I would naturally dream of myself up on stage. "What song would I choose, what would I wear, would I end up breaking my neck on that pole?" … and my fantasy version would invariably turn into an over-the-top Busby Berkley flight of fancy.

… The Velvet Hammer Burlesque would evolve into what has become a feminist revolution of sorts, sweeping the nation and even crossing international borders.[17]

Figure 5.33 Michelle Carr is the founder of The Velvet Hammer Burlesque and co-founder of the long-running wrestling and burlesque show La Lucha VaVoom in Los Angeles, California. Her burlesque persona is Valentina Violette, captured here in the early 2000s by Jody Ake. (Jody Ake)

Figure 5.34 Miss Astrid by Jody Ake. Early 2000s.
(Photo by Jody Ake)

Figure 5.35 Bobbi Pinz by Jodi Ake. Early 2000s.
(Photo by Jody Ake)

Figure 5.36 Kitten DeVille, Miss Exotic World 2002, by Jody Ake.
Early 2000s.
(Photo by Jody Ake)

Figure 5.37 orld Famous *BOB* by Jody Ake. Early 2000s.
(Photo by Jody Ake)

Figure 5.38 Burlesque revival pioneer and Miss Exotic World 2008 Angie Pontani, in a Garo Sparo ensemble.
(Photo by Patrick D. Wade)

AN INTERVIEW WITH
DESIGNER GARO SPARO

Garo Sparo is a fashion designer, artist and burlesque costume genius. He sat down with the author to discuss his career and his burlesque costume designs.[18]

CS: *Thank you* for agreeing to talk to me about this.

G: Of course! It's a really good thing—you're [making this book] when, well, drag and burlesque are really becoming things that, kids even, are very exposed to these days. The generation coming up, it's crazy—they're going to be like "I want the sexiest corset ever…!" My friend's daughter she's only 12 and she already wants to be a burlesque dancer! I love the concept of the book.

CS: Thank you for sharing the enthusiasm! So—let's start with how to properly pronounce your name.

G: I grew up on Long Island for part of my life and lived in North Carolina for part of my life, so it's just Gare-o. Gare-o Spare-o. A little bit of New York a little South …

CS: Where are you based, Garo?

G: I was based in the East Village for 15 years on 10th Street between B and C which used to be no man's land and now is like ridiculously expensive. And I have now moved to 37th Street between 7th and 8th.

CS: And how long have you been up there?

G: I have been here since September of 2015.

CS: OK, and I know you worked in factories early in your career, so you've been building clothing for how long?

G: Oh, I started my business when I was 19 years old, and I've been in business for 23 years. Basically, it formally went into real business around 1995. I was a total raver and I sold hats. I started in millinery, so I sold hats at clubs. It's been in my family—my family has been in the garment industry in Sicily. I'm a descendent of Sicilian background and my family has been lace makers, and doing all sorts of things in the garment industry.

Figure 5.39
Garo Sparo in his studio dressing room.
(Photo by Coleen Scott)

When they moved to America to flee the war they worked in factories, and my grandmother was a hat model, and she learned how to make hats. She's the one who taught me how to make hats, my mom taught me how to do flat patterns, and my nonni, my grandmother on my mom's side, she taught me how to use an industrial machine, and she had all the accoutrements. That's how I got interested in piping and bindings and things like that, she had a piping foot that I was obsessed with. So, I was the only kid who was allowed in the sewing room, and I probably sewed my first thing when I was like, four? Because my dad wouldn't let me have dolls, so I was like "the hell with you! I'm going to sew hair on all of my stuffed animals!" My first experience was sewing hair on all my stuffed animals so that I could make clothes for them so that they would all be female. (laughs)

CS: Yes! That's amazing!

G: And being obsessed with Barbie dolls, that's how I got into corsetry. It was the manipulated silhouette. Which, I don't think her silhouette is perfect, I mean it's not my ideal silhouette, I like a fuller silhouette than that, but that severity is what really got me into manipulating the body and the silhouette through corsetry.

CS: Wonderful. So, you had all this family experience in garment making, did you also go to school and train in more specific skills, like corset making? Or was that from family background too?

G: Corset making was something that just came naturally. I just did everything super body-conscious and then began to manipulate and create my own original modern corsetry because period corsetry crushes the ribs from the front and the back, and I have a specialized style, it's the most comfortable corset anyone could ever wear because it's cinching in the soft tissue of the body. It fools the eye into thinking you're at 19 inches but you're really at like 21.

I did formally go to school. Originally, I was like, oh no, you can't be a designer, that that would be too gay, you're gay. I was coming to terms with the fact that I was gay. But, I love the weather, and I'm obsessed with things I can't control. So I went briefly to school for the preparatory courses, one semester, at University of North Carolina, for meteorology, and then I was like, math? No. I'm all about geometry and visual math, but not that kind of math, so I went home for a semester, and I came to terms with the fact that I was coming out of the closet. At home, my mom was getting ready to

send a bunch of stuff to Goodwill, and I picked up the whole box and went down into the sewing room and I just started to morph things. I made my first hat, back when everyone was wearing those huge Cat In The Hat hats at rave parties. I made my first jug head raver hat, and I tried to make everything reversible, which is something I still try to do. I try to make everything transformable.

So I started with hats, and then I started making clothes for my friends, and then I went back to school after taking the semester off, and switched to UNC Greensborough, which has a clothing and textiles program. That's where all the textiles and Levi's is, and a lot of our American basic clothing companies are based out of North Carolina

CS: Yes, because that's where the (cotton) crops are.

G: Exactly. So, I went to UNC G and started doing textiles there, but I already was way ahead of a lot of the students, so my teachers kind of let me have my own itinerary because I had some sewing and sketching background and everything else. So, I kind of got to do my own thing which was awesome—it was kind of cool being a big fish in a little pond. I don't know what life would have been like if I had come straight back to New York. It was cool, and I learned a lot about textiles because that was a very manufacturing based school. I continued there, started taking trips back and forth to New York, randomly ran into this **drag queen** who was arranging this Absolute™ sponsored event called Absolute Subluxation™.

I started to dress people for **raves** and we would do things like weird fashion shows and clubs would pay me to dress performers in North Carolina, and I would document everything. So I had all the documentation with me in New York, I got this meeting with Absolute™, and they sponsored me. As of my last semester, I was due for my internship, and looking back I wish I had done my internship because I would have made a lot less mistakes in business! But I ended up getting the fashion show [through Absolute™] in New York in '95, and I was like well—"screw this! I'm done! I should just move to New York, I don't need to be in school anymore!"

So I never graduated. And it doesn't bother me that I never graduated because no one has ever asked me whether I graduated or not. The proof's in the pudding!

So that's how it all started.

CS: Was it through the raver crowd and the club scene that you encountered burlesque performers and costumed them as well?

G: Yes, it was because basically, that was the beginning of neo-burlesque. Jo Boobs [Weldon], she was one of the first, it's hard to say really who was the first, but you know, neo-burlesque was beginning, even in the rave scene. It was a performance. Everyone was trying to outdo each other. And in the process of trying to outdo each other, the performer's outfit had to transform, slowly, slowly until the girl was in nothing but a bikini and pasties. They (the raves) were all underground, so she would be in pasties and an underwire or a bikini, or whatever.

It began to teach me the mechanics of burlesque, and how to fool people into thinking that something is one solid garment and then it breaks into a million pieces. That was the beginning—it's where the quirky side of what I do kind of injects itself. You know there's a classic and a quirky side, so the rave scene kind of like, ate my brain a little bit.

CS: Ha-ha, in a good way. So, that was the mid-nineties; would you say you've been a burlesque costumer since '95? Because that was the beginning (of the revival).

G: Yes!

CS: At this point you have owned your business that long as well. Were you ever represented by an agent or were you ever in (or are you in now) a union?

G: I have been word of mouth almost my whole life. I've had numerous investors over the years that have come in, and tried to change me, and in one way or another I broke away. I'm in a[n investment] relationship right now that's a good one. I've had PR before, [but] I feel like PR is just an outdated concept, you know what I mean? People should have agents these days or marketing companies. So it's mostly word of mouth. 90 percent.

CS: Right. Social media has kind of changed everything, so do you find that that has made a difference for you with self-promotion?

G: Absolutely. I get an inquiry multiple times a day, nonstop. I get inquiries from all over the world thanks to social media. I have people flying in from Spain to get things made, and all sorts of things.

CS: That's wonderful. As far as your style goes, we know you've done burlesque. Generally, what types and styles of fashion are you most known for?

G: Mostly, I'm known for corsetry, corseted anything, and millinery to underpinnings—a top-to-bottom look with many

layers involved. The [ensembles] are made to be orchestrated beautifully and fool the eye into thinking its one piece. You don't know what's going to come off first or second or third. And if it's going to come off, it's not going to be some little nothing, it's going to have a—each part has got to have a "boom" "boom" "boom" because otherwise, why bother?

CS: I love that you do take on the whole ensemble. It's wonderful being able to see that someone has envisioned the whole thing, and the way your pieces deconstruct, it's amazing to watch that.

You have your studio, and you've had the company for over two decades, so now, who is doing the construction of these pieces? What is your role in the construction of everything?

G: We most often tackle pieces that require technical expertise and mechanics or engineering, so what I do is, I start out by sitting with a client, figuring out what they need, these days over social media a client will tell me what they want, and I give them a budget, they say "Yay" or "Nay," and then we start from there. Once we've initiated the process we start with a technical sketch, and that's when I really come in the strongest because it's the sketch that drives the patterning that drives the construction that drives the act. It's always centered around the performer. I have a staff that expands and contracts. I have a base staff of five but we expand to 20 if we have to on different jobs when I have piece workers and such.

I jump in and, I usually do the cut. I usually am a cutter. I'll **drape** it, I'll pattern it, I'll cut it, or I'll have Sarah, who's my right hand girl, do it. After every performer comes through now we have a whole system. We have a meeting about it afterwards. We talk about the top of the budget, what's possible, what's not possible, and then we go in and we just drape the thing and different things are handed off to different departments of the studio. One girl, she's my corset girl, and then I have my crystal queen—she does all the embellishment—and I have the person who does anything that's a tailored look. We specialize in things, and then I am of course the jack-of-all-trades, so any time we're overflowing or there's a technical issue that can't be figured out, I'll just jump in and do it myself.

CS: With that being said, what's an average number of different projects you're working on at once in the studio?

G: I would say between 15 and 20?

Figure 5.40 Dallas burlesque performer Minxie Mimieux "The Texan Tigress of Tease" in a Garo Sparo ensemble. (Photo by Michael Sauer)

CS: You need that support. You can't be the one person running around and doing all that.

G: No. I have an excellent, excellent team. Instead of having a larger constant staff, I've pared it down because you need that really good team behind you. You can't do everything yourself because then your quality of work, and the level people want, will just decrease. It's important to delegate and not to micro-manage.

CS: Yes, and to hire people for their specialty and appreciate that skill.

G: Exactly and their craftsmanship in a dying industry of "hand-made" and "made in New York."

CS: Definitely! It is dying and you're keeping it alive, thank you very much!

G: Amen sister! I will till the day I die!

CS: Good! What might a full ensemble cost? I know it ranges, based on materials and things, but do you do it based on an hourly rate, or supplies and hours, or some other way?

G: Yes, well, this is the thing. I break it down, I have my like $2500 special.

CS: OK!

G: Which is underpinnings and a corseted or boned gown that goes over it, some embellishment, but not an insane amount of embellishment. But it includes a corset base, pasties, a g-string, garter belts if they want, I even do hosiery as well if they want that, and then there's the overdress. Recently, I did something for Minxie Mimieux from Dallas that would be considered like a $3000 special …

But our burlesque rates start, for just a basic boned dress like something Amanda LePore[19] would wear—we do make a dress that's like $800 with just pasties and a g-string. Where it's just stretchy. It's all stretch fabrics. I don't want to scare people off completely. Because a lot of people get intimidated when they come here. But once they have giant ideas they do need to know that it's not cheap.

CS: They have to understand. Yes, I come from that background too. People really need to understand what goes into it, and what the cost, the *real* cost is when you're getting something that is the best it can be, you know? It is intimidating, but it depends what your goal is for your act, and what you are able to do.

G: Totally. And my caveat is that I guarantee it for life. (Basically three years.)

CS: (laughs)

Figure 5.41 *"The American transgender model Amanda Lepore special guest at the Fausto Puglisis party at late night in Milan during the fashion week." Milan (Italy) February 23, 2017. Amanda wears Garo Sparo.*
(Mondadori Portfolio/Archivio Marco Piraccini/Marco Piraccini/Everett Collection)

G: Because people get tired of it or they shelve it. But I will fix it anytime anything has any problem. Just bring it back in and I'll tweak whatever.

CS: I mean that's everything! You think you're going to get your badly made 15 dollar corset from China and someone's going to do something with that when it breaks?

G: (laughs) Those tubular garments they call corsets?

CS: Yes, exactly.

And back to Amanda LePore, you wouldn't consider her a burlesque dancer, but she performs on stage. She was my very first client in New York, and I made her a leopard burlesque look that's kind of iconic for her. Her pieces are all made to come off in different layers and she ends up naked by the end of the night, but she's usually just paid to be there or perform her album at events. I wouldn't necessarily consider her a part of the burlesque scene.

CS: No, but influential in the whole club and underground scene for sure.

G: Yeah, completely. And she's my first client and we're still working together. She still gets stuff like once or twice a week to this day!

CS: Wow, that's a lot of work! So she's a huge client—what about other famous burlesque performers you work with or burlesque costumes that are some of your favorite?

G: I would say … there's so MANY! It's so HARD!

CS: That's why I'm talking to you!

G: I knooooowww! Recently, one of my favorite feats of engineering was of course Gin Minsky's Ice Cream Cone (Figure 6.41 to 6.54 see page 000). I'll never forget us in final tests, and we were like "OK, we've got to snap it all back together now and try it again!" And the number of times we had to snap it together to get it to unfurl properly and then the other parts and everything else … that was a great feat of engineering. I love Gin Minsky, she is in my top five—I don't like to put people in my you know, top ten, top five, but definitely Gin Minsky, everything I've ever made her has always been a feat of engineering and I love that she loves it as much as I do.

CS: Yes!

G: You know, Bambi (the Mermaid),[20] I've done hundreds of mermaid tails and weird—she's like such a neo-burlesque-y kind of girl because—one of the craziest looks I've ever done for her, I think she only did it once, it's a "germ" look. We were studying bacterium and all this stuff!

CS: (laughs)

G: Really, to figure out how to get really "germy" but pretty. I did her shrimp look, so many mermaid tails, even the swimmable ones, what else? I did so many things for Bambi it's hard to say. I just did her wedding dress for when her and Chuck got married …

CS: Yes, I was there and I saw that in person—amazing!

G: Angie Pontani is another client—she's just such a sweet person, and I love doing anything for her because she's the classic side of burlesque.

CS: Yes, she is.

G: We've done lots of mechanically driven things for her where things have to come off a certain way but it looks like it's a full gown, but then it's five pieces and that sort of thing.

CS: Yes, and she always looks impeccable in those **classic acts** (see: classic burlesque), and in early neo-burlesque she was trend setting how refined those things needed to look. She was a model for that because of your work too. I mean, she's also impeccable with her choreography; she's an exceptional person to put classic looks on for that reason.

G: Absolutely. You know somebody else who I've been working with for almost three years, is Mosh from California. Yeah, and we're about to do a whole bunch of crazily engineered looks, but one of the hardest ones I've ever done for her is the Gypsy Rose-inspired, hand-beaded fringe dress—it's silver and [it weighs like 65 to 70 pounds.] Anyhow, we're about to embark on a whole batch of craziness, so, stay tuned!

G: I'm about to do an awesome act with Hovey (Burgess), you know Hovey?

CS: Yes!

G: Yes, Hovey the "polar bear" and (Lil Miss) Lixx being his tamer. His **dominatrix** tamer! So I'm doing this amazingly engineered, and Hovey is sparing no expense, he is just like "just tell me how much it costs, I want it to be perfect—I want it to be the best costume I've ever seen, touched, been a part of, anything!" and he's the sweetest guy and so fun. [In the act] He's basically, she's his trainer and he's a mean polar bear who's acting up, and ripping her costume off bit by bit. So, it's gonna be *really* good.

Figure 5.42 Bambi the Mermaid in a Garo Sparo mermaid gown with wired tail fins and her husband Chuck in his own custom-molded creations on their wedding day at The Mermaid Parade, 2017.
(Photo by Norman Blake)

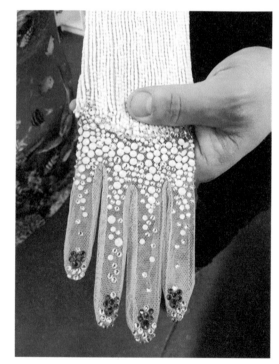

Figure 5.43 Garo holds a beaded and rhinestoned custom glove for Mosh.
(Photo by Coleen Scott)

Figure 5.44 Lil Miss Lixx as the trainer and Hovey Burgess as the polar bear in costumes by Garo Sparo.
(Photo by David L. Byrd)

CS: That is SO good!

G: And Lixx is one of my favorite people on the planet too. She's Bambi The Mermaid's daughter and that pretty much says it all.

CS: Exactly.

G: I've done unbelievable things for Lixx as well, that's why it's so hard to pick one!

CS: Oh, I know. I mean, those are people who I love very much too in my own life, so it's nice to hear, and Hovey, did he just turn 80? He's a legendary circus performer.

G: Yes, and he got finished with his (literal) hundredth semester teaching at NYU, and he just retired, and he is like—now I'm going to be a polar bear!

CS: (laughs)

G: And already they're booking the act, so it's going to be great.

CS: Yes we'll see it as Best Duet at Burlesque Hall of Fame in a year or so, it'll be great!

G: Amen!

CS: I'm excited for that! So, you've had all these amazing clients—what do you think makes a great burlesque costume?

G: What makes a great burlesque costume is to really come up with an original idea even if it's taken from a classic perspective, or it's taken from completely outer space. It's really important for the performer to come on stage, to be as covered up as possible in just the right ways, and peel away the pieces in new ways. It's a

Figure 5.45 A wall of gloves available for rent and purchase at Garo Sparo's studio. (Photo by Coleen Scott)

constant battle to try to find new ways of taking things off.

CS: Yes—

G: And to fool the eye into thinking that your dress is all one solid gown head to toe, when it's all broken up into little bits and pieces and you hide it all via embellishment, all sorts of hidden closures and flaps and zippers and magnets and pulley systems.

CS: It's being able to create new elements of surprise. That to me is what makes burlesque costumes different from other types of costumes–do you have any other thoughts on what makes them different?

G: What makes them different is also just thinking outside the box. Like thinking "I want to be a …" I'm just looking at my wall in my fitting room, and it's covered in pictures of all my burlesque girls. It's all about coming up with something special and being true to what your aesthetic is and sticking with it, you know what I mean?

CS: Yes. Do you have any other favorite costume building tricks or tips or hacks?

G: Well, yeah! Some of them are top secret, but I will give you one that's kind of gotten out there a lot—and it's nothing new, but it happened a lot back in the Golden Age of burlesque. It's the old string trick, where you pull a string and the whole thing falls off. Basically it's just made by interlocking loops with one string running through it, or something stiff and you just yank it out and the loops all come apart and then that's how the gown falls off of you.

CS: And it's a quick reveal, just like *flash*, and it falls off you!

G: Exactly. And magnets of course. Magnets have become so amazing. Because I work with magicians and stuff, they are the ones that turned me on to them. They make them so strong now that they will snap your fingernail off if you are not careful when you're working with them.

CS: Yes, and then if you have one backwards and they flip back on to your finger— aaaah!

G: Yeah that's like blood blister city.

CS: But they are great. So, last question for today—What does burlesque mean to you?

G: I love the relationship between the costume and the performer, and how the garment worn becomes a part of the performer's persona and their act. It seems so simple, but it's very true. I'm always honored when I do a burlesque performer's look to be a part of that moment for them, making sure that it's a well made, jaw-dropping thing with unexpected releases. A costume can change the impression an act makes, of course. I just love to collaborate with a performer as an artist to make the costume an integral part of what they are trying to make the audience see. Sometimes people who don't have that whole concept, they just confuse people.

CS: Yes, thank you for that. It is my humble opinion that you have been an integral part of making burlesque costume and the burlesque scene respected for the art form that it is, and I thank you very much for this and for your time!

G: Thank you! Thanks! That means a lot to me.

Figure 5.46 This is a small collection of neo-burlesque stars representing a variety of styles primarily within the New York burlesque scene (performers from other states indicated). 1. Miss Indigo Blue, costume design by Danial Webster (Seattle, WA), 2. Brown Girls Burlesque, costume design by Dame Cuchifrita, 3. Julie Atlas Muz, 4. Margaret Cho (Los Angeles, CA), 5. Jo "Boobs" Weldon 6. Tigger!, costume design by David Quinn, 7. Fancy Feast, costume design by Wae Messed, 8. Pillow in her own creation (Anchorage, AK). (1. Paul O'Connell, 2. Adrian Buckmaster, 3. Jody Ake, 4. Albert Sanchez, 5 and 6 Ben Trivett, 7. James Andrew Ridley 8. Ben Trivett)

Figure 5.47 Clockwise by number: 1. Little Brooklyn, 2. Divina GranSparkle, 3. Kitten La Rue, 4. House of Noire, 5. Mr. Gorgeous, 6. Bonnie Dunn, 7. Jezebelle Express, 8. World Famous * BOB *, 9. Johnny Porkpie, 10. The Schlep Sisters.
(1 and 2 David L. Byrd, 3. Ben Trivett, 4. David L. Byrd, 5. Ben Trivett, 6. John Patrick Naughton, 7. Ben Trivett, 8. Don Spiro, 9 Leland Bobbe, 10. Ben Trivett)

Q & A WITH BURLESQUE LEGEND CATHERINE D'LISH

The following interview is with Miss Exotic World 1992 and 1994, burlesque costume maven, and costumier for Dita Von Teese, Catherine D'Lish.[21] Catherine is unquestionably one of the most influential costumers in classic neo-burlesque, as her designs for her own acts and for Dita have established a luxe aesthetic exemplified by an obscene amount of rhinestones on all pieces of a costume. Catherine's design influence reaches even further with her line of Boudoir by D'Lish gowns, robes and loungewear that have become coveted garments not only for burlesquers, but for brides, drag queens, and women simply wanting to add glamour to their wardrobe.

CS: How long have you been a performer? Where? Why did you start?

CD: I started performing as a teenager when I saw an ad for "$NUDE$" dancers, and went downtown to a strip club, thinking it would be a funny thing to do one night.

I was right, it was funny. It was so funny that I started working there, and from that night forward, my life took a different turn!

CS: How long have you been making burlesque costumes? Where did you acquire your skill set?

CD: I started making costumes to wear at the strip club, we had to do three-song sets a few times a night, and I wanted fun things to wear. When I first started, I simply pulled elements from my late-night dance-club wardrobe … I already had elaborate plumage, stockings, gloves, **stilettos**, the works. I just took out the elements that made those outfits street-legal, and presto! Instant stripper.

Not long after I started dancing at the club, I bought a sewing machine and some scissors, and started making things to wear on stage. I never really had a "skill set," one cuts up fabric and sews it back together, right? I just made stuff, then I made some more stuff, and eventually was making stuff for the other dancers to purchase too.

CS: Which came first—costume or performance?

CD: Just like the chicken and the egg, costume and performance are intertwined, neither comes first, or last.

CS: What inspires your designs?

CD: More often than not, a costume will begin as a twinkle in its mother's eye. And when I say "twinkle," I mean that I see a Swarovski stone/color I like. Then I buy more of that stone than I can afford, and then I make something with them!

Figure 5.48
Catherine D'Lish.
(Photo by Kaylin Idora, courtesy of Cathrine D'Lish)

Figure 5.49 A chocolate hued Deluxe Cassandra Gown from D'Lish robes.
(Courtesy of Catherine D'Lish)

CS: Please discuss your D'Lish robes—how has your business changed with growth, and how is your original vision for the company different (or better) than you dreamed? What has been the most difficult aspect?

CD: It's been nice to see the feathered gowns that we sell at our online store become popular. I love that we have such a broad customer base, and the enthusiasm of our customers makes them really fun to work with. It warms my heart to see our gowns be a part of someone's special day, whether it's a maternity shoot, wedding day, birthday, anniversary, boudoir shoot, performance, or just something fun to make them feel glamorous on a lazy afternoon! I'm very lucky to have found an incredible team to work with, so all around the business has been a pleasure. We all work (very!) hard, but seeing our customers enjoying their gowns makes it all worthwhile.

CS: Discuss a favorite costume (or costumes!) for Dita and a favorite personal costume. How do you go about putting a full ensemble together for yourself or someone else?

CD: Each of the costumes I've made for Dita has been its own little world of experiences, and each of these ensembles has a special place in my heart. Dita and I are best friends, so it's not really like a "job," it's more like something fun for us to do together. It's lovely to see how gorgeous she is on stage, and I've yet to tire of experiencing a major Swarovski-gasm when the crystal costumes are hit by the stage lights. It's been nice to share that feeling with people all over the world.

My "favorite" costumes are ALWAYS the ones that I haven't made yet. Every project comes with its own specific challenges, and therefore, its own rewards.

CS: What is your favorite costume tip, trick, or reveal?

CD: Just like I mentioned above, the "favorite trick" is something I haven't tried yet. The ones that I think will work, and am about to put into production. There are some new items in the works at the moment, and those are also current favorites!

CS: How has the burlesque scene and costuming changed through your career?

CD: It's been fun to see the burlesque scene embrace costuming as part of the burlesque-experience, and I enjoy seeing what people are doing! I think that the enthusiasm for costuming in the burlesque world is something really special and unique to this particular global community.

Figure 5.50 Catherine in a stunning burlesque ensemble of her own design.
(Photo by Kaylin Idora with permission from Catherine D'Lish)

Figure 5.51 Dita Von Teese in a Swarovski crystal encrusted costume by Catherine D'Lish.
(Photo by Franz Szony, used with permission from Dita Von Teese.)

Dita Von Teese is the most recognizable figure in burlesque today. She started her career in the 1990s in strip clubs where she worked with Catherine D'Lish who became her close friend and costume designer. In 2002 she graced the cover of *Playboy Magazine* and solidified her place in mainstream popular culture. Dita has become known for her style, and her costumes are made of the best materials accented with the most lavish embellishment. Dita has worn garments from the iconic Mr. Pearl and numerous fashion designers including Zac Posen, but it is Catherine D'Lish's costume designs for Dita that have established the model for what classic burlesque is in the neo movement.

Figure 5.52 *Dita in a costume by Dark Garden Corsetry and custom Christian Louboutin boots.* (Albert Sanchez)

Figure 5.53 Dita wears custom Louboutin boots.
(Photo by Albert Sanchez)

Figure 5.54 Dita Von Teese wears a custom yellow gown by Mr. Pearl.
(Photo by Albert Sanchez)

Figure 5.55 A back view of the Mr. Pearl gown.
(Photo by Albert Sanchez)

Notes

1 Interview date: April 8, 2018.
2 Interview date: August 23, 2018.
3 "Show" is another term used for a single burlesque act. Burlesque performers would do four or more shows a day or in a full shift of work.
4 The first Miss Exotic World competition was held at the Exotic World Museum in Helendale, California, in April 1991. It was organized by Dixie Evans as part of a publicity draw for the League of Exotic Dancers 34th Annual Reunion. The League of Exotic Dancers, and the museum, was founded by burlesque legend Jennie Lee, who passed away before the 1991 reunion. Her close friend Dixie took over the museum with a mission to bring it more recognition in Jenni's honor.
5 The Museum at FIT held and exhibit of Bartsch's nightlife ensembles in 2015.
6 The term "Swingers" in Los Angeles in the 1990s referred to people who were part of the swing dance nightlife scene. There is a 1996 cult classic film by the same name starring Vince Vaughn and John Favreau that encapsulates this trend.
7 Interview date: August 8, 2018.
8 Russ Meyer was a well-known exploitation film director in the 1960s and 1970s.
9 *Beverly Hills 90201* was an extremely popular television show produced by Aaron Spelling about high school students in Beverly Hills that starred Jennie Garth, Shannon Doherty, Jason Priestly, and Luke Perry.
10 Jennie Garth played a lead character named Kelly on the very popular 1990s television show *Beverly Hills, 90210*.
11 *Swingers* was a 1996 film about out-of-work actors in Hollywood who are part of the swing dance and vintage revival scene.
12 The Derby was a swingers club on Los Feliz Boulevard in Los Angeles, open from 1992–2009. The club was a center of the 1990s swing dance resurgence. It was called The Derby because it was previously one of The Brown Derby restaurant franchises.
13 Hugh Heffner of the Playboy franchise.
14 More info on the history of the Tease-O-Rama event which began in New Orleans in 2001: www.teaseorama. com/2012/about_the_event/the_people_behind_tor/
15 These excerpts are from an ongoing online conversation between the author and Lorelei Fuller that occurred from August 10, 2018 through September 25, 2018.
16 These excerpts are from an ongoing online conversation between the author and Billie Madley that occurred from August 26, 2018 through September 10, 2018.

17 From the introduction of *The Velvet Hammer Burlesque*, by Michelle Carr, p. 3, Die Gestalten Verlag BmbH & Co. KG, Berlin, 2008. Used with permission from Carr and the publisher.
18 Interview date: January 2018.
19 Amanda LePore is a transgender icon and model. She is a fixture of the New York City club scene and is known for her outrageous fashion and her club music hits.
20 Bambi the Mermaid is a New York neo-burlesque superstar and the founder of Coney Island's Burlesque at the Beach, as well as the Miss Coney Island Pageant. She is always a parade leader at Coney Island USA's Mermaid Parade each June.
21 Interview date: April 2018.

Figure 5.56 *Dirty Martini performs her title winning act at the Miss Exotic World Competition in Helendale, California, 2004. Exotic World Was founded by performer Jennie Lee and after her passing in 1990, was spearheaded by Dixie Evans. The museum has now become known as The Burlesque Hall of Fame in Las Vegas, and the title of Queen of Burlesque is the most coveted in the modern global burlesque movement. The annual Burlesque Hall of Fame Weekender is a source of burlesque networking, education and a celebration of all things Burlesque past and present. (Credit: Don Spiro)*

Figure 6.1 Dirty Martini in her Mae West tribute costume by David Quinn.
(Photo by Ben Trivett)

CHAPTER 6

MODERN BURLESQUE COSTUME DESIGN

INTRODUCTION

In this chapter, the designers and performers with their fingers on the pulse of the current burlesque scene speak for themselves. Case studies of several modern burlesque costume designers are focused on, as are up-close examples of modern costumes. Performance photo series give the reader an idea of what the costumes look like as each reveal happens in an act. Notable burlesque performers are bringing deep skill sets from sister arts like circus, global dance, and aerial. Other art forms like cosplay and modern **drag** have adopted burlesque costume conventions into ensembles and acts. Burlesque is encouraging the art of drag costuming and characterization within its presentation as well. Costume is an integral part of successful burlesque performance and is very often at the discretion of the individual performer. The ability to put together a dynamic look is key, but the price point compared to the pay per performance is very often in disagreement.

With the exponential growth of the global burlesque community, the reality of what it takes to do burlesque for a living and what performers deserve for pay is up for discussion and changing. There is a vast discrepancy in construction and assemblage of modern burlesque costume pieces, which is dependent on both the financial status and the style of the performer. Regardless of these subjects, performers are almost always solely responsible for their costume design and construction costs with few exceptions. Today, hobbyists could easily spend $1000 or more on a full ensemble even if it will take months or even years to make a return on their investment financially at an average of $50–$100 guaranteed per performance. Some performers work with entertainment companies who hire them for large parties and events at good pay rates, but these gigs are dependent on extravagant or original acts and previously developed costumes. Private events and larger-scale showcases pay much better wages than small weekly or monthly productions in bars or small theaters, as do burlesque groups who have residencies in venues that create co-beneficial relationships for profitability. Venues that are centered around burlesque performance are few and far between, but the ones that exist provide the promise of a regular **gig** with dependable income. Whereas burlesque could be a union-supported career for a high percentage of performers in the past, it is currently a hobby for most, with a slim margin of performers making a livable wage, and the top few making a highly profitable living.

Many burlesquers supplement income with Patreon[1] accounts and day jobs, but even the top performers have supplemental income sources with commercial contracts or fashion lines. Mosh is a model for clothing companies like Pinup Girl in addition to her performance and pin-up modelling work. Catherine D'Lish has her line of stunning robes and ***dressing gowns*** that have become a must-have item for those doing classic acts. Dita Von Teese has been a muse for designers like Zac Posen, and the face of Cointreau, Frederick's of Hollywood, Wheels and Dollbaby, and Vivienne Westwood. Besides authoring two best-selling books, she has her own lingerie, perfume, and makeup lines as well as a sponsorship with Swarovski. High-profile performers like Von Teese spend thousands on their costumes and work with professional costume and fashion designers to create them (see Figures 5.51 to 5.55).

There are favorite burlesque costume designers in cities throughout the US, some of whom are showcased in this chapter to give the reader a variety of designer backgrounds and styles from self-taught costumers like Nasty Canasta (see page 264) to professional fashion designers like Jamie Von Stratton (see page 241). Photo captions provide even more designer names and information. The following is a list of designers and companies named by performers throughout the US[2]:

- Allen Ryde (Maryland)
- Amber Ray Acoutrements (New York, New York)
- Angela Ann Kelly (Los Angeles, California)
- Anne Atomic (Knoxville, Tennessee)
- Aurora Clothiers by Allengale
- Beau Rocks Costumier (London, U.K.)
- Burluxe by Delilah (New York, New York)
- Charis Churchill (Vermont)
- Danial Webster (Seattle, Washington)
- Deborah Foster (Louisville, Kentucky)
- Flo Foxworthy (Australia)
- Gorgeous by Gorgeous (New York, New York)
- Holly Dai (Portland, Oregon)
- Liberty Rose (Philladelphia, Pennsylvania)
- London St. Juniper and Vicious Poodle Pinup
- Manuge Et Toi (Ottawa, Canada)
- Nina Nightshade (Portland, Oregon)
- Orange Appeal by Lauren Cohen (San Francisco Bay Area, California)
- Rena La Marr (Ohio)
- Ruby Vixen – Vixenland and Dandy & Vixen
- Sin and Satin (New York, New York)
- Sweet Carousel Corsetry- (Edmonton, Canada)
- Threads by Mayhem (Texas)
- Varla Va Voom (Orange County, California)

When it comes to putting together a burlesque ensemble, even performers with a design and construction background infrequently build full costume ensembles due to time or money factors. For example, if parts of an ensemble can be purchased and embellished to create exactly what is desired for less cost, performers will combine pre-made pieces and build or commission only the items that don't exist or that they want made exactly to their specifications. Most performers are able to make their own pasties and heavily decorate commercial items. Performers with big budgets might have one designer build the gown and another build the underpinnings depending on their preferences for different makers. They may pay a third to make pasties or do their embellishment. There are designers out there who build a full ensemble for performers from gown to headdress, to pasties, gloves and fans like Garo Sparo in New York City (see Chapter 5, pp. 201–209), but being able to go to one person for every part of a costume is a rare option, especially if budget is a concern. With the popularity of burlesque growing, and the complexity of skill sets performers are bringing to the stage, the quality of the costume must meet the level of performance.

Figure 6.2 *Australian-born, New York City burlesque performer and professional dancer, Lilin in a self-made costume with headdress by Tyler Holland Designs.*
(Photo by James Andrew Ridley)

Figures 6.3 and 6.4 (facing page) Neo Burlesque superstar Dirty Martini performs her Mae West tribute act. Costume by David Quinn. *(Photo by Ben Trivett)*

DIRTY MARTINI

This ensemble for Dirty Martini shown in Figures 6.3 to 6.10, designed and made by New York City-based designer David Quinn, is a wonderful example of modern burlesque costume. Dirty Martini is a neo burlesque legend who started her career in burlesque in 1996 while she was getting her Bachelor's degree in Dance from Hunter College. Her thesis was on burlesque dance, inspired by the photos of Irving and Paula Klaw, and vintage burlesque films like 1955's *Teasorama*. She won the title of Miss Exotic World in 2004, and has become one of the most recognized and beloved performers in burlesque.

Figure 6.5 Dirty Martini's Mae West tribute dress by David Quinn. The two images below the dress show a close-up of the dress embellishment and the construction of the horsehair hem. (Photo by Coleen Scott)

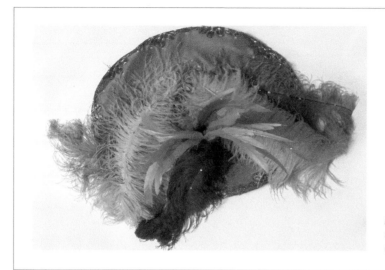

Figure 6.6 *The full-brimmed hat is made of two hats nested together and covered in matching fabric and feathers. (Photo by Coleen Scott)*

Figure 6.7 *The gathered satin lining inside the hat shows the expert finishing in David Quinn's costumes. (Photo by Coleen Scott)*

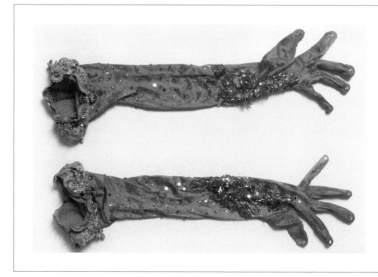

Figure 6.8 *These store-bought gloves were embellished by Dirty Martini. (Photo by Coleen Scott)*

Figure 6.9 Tulle net bra, hand-beaded and made by Dirty Martini.
(Photo by Coleen Scott)

Figure 6.10 Rhinestone pasties made by Dirty Martini.
(Photo by Coleen Scott)

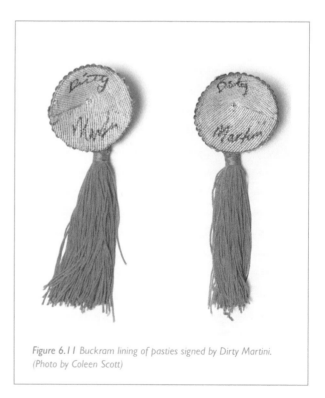

Figure 6.11 Buckram lining of pasties signed by Dirty Martini.
(Photo by Coleen Scott)

Figure 6.12 *Blue silk panel skirt by David Quinn.*
(Photo by Coleen Scott)

Figure 6.13 *Close-up of the embellished waistband.*
(Photo by Coleen Scott)

Figure 6.14 *Close-up of the hem finishing.*
(Photo by Coleen Scott)

Figure 6.15 *Dirty Martini's Brazilian dance shoes, customized for*
the costume.
(Photo by Coleen Scott)

A SIT-DOWN WITH SYDNI DEVEREAUX

Sydni Devereaux is known as "The Golden Glamazon." She is an international burlesque headliner and featured performer, and she is a producer of Wasabassco Burlesque in New York City. Devereaux has worked closely with burlesque costume designer Catherine D'Lish, and she shared some of her career and work experience with the author:[3]

CS: How long have you been a performer? Where? Why did you start?

S: I've been a performer since 2005. I started in Seattle, Washington. Prior to being a burlesque dancer, I was a model and a musician. When I heard there were women dancing in beautiful costumes to the kinds of music I loved, I was intrigued and the rest is history I suppose.

CS: What is the burlesque scene like where you perform?

S: I am currently in NYC. The scene is huge, oversaturated and wonderful. I consider myself very lucky to be a full-time performer and producer here with one of the most well-established burlesque companies in the world, Wasabassco. New York offers an opportunity to every type of performer to get their feet wet and to join the grind. There are shows every day of the week here, and many performers here can make the bulk of their income off of performing. I've performed all over the world but this is by far my favorite place to perform.

CS: What is your experience as a performer of color in the burlesque industry?

S: Burlesque has a lot of growing to do. The racism and colorism in this art form is definitely a problem that needs to be addressed. I've been booked simply because I'm black, but also because I'm light-skinned. I've watched many opportunities pass me, and my brown and black peers by because we haven't been white. Due to this, I work extremely hard to have my business together, to put on a good show, and keep my eyes on my own paper so I don't get too disheartened. I've had a more successful career than that of a lot of other performers regardless of color because I am laser focused on elevating the art form where I am. It's tiring but worth it because I love this job and I'm worth it too.

CS: Who has been the biggest influence on your burlesque performance style and look? How did they influence you?

S: My biggest influence has been my mentor, Catherine D'Lish—and certainly she's impacted my aesthetic in many ways, including showing me how to work with proportions and cuts to accentuate parts of my body in

Figure 6.16 Sydni Devereaux performs at the Burlesque Hall of Fame Weekender in her Catherine D'Lish inspired gown, 2014. (Photo by Don Spiro)

different ways, as well as the osmosis that happens around color theory when you're apprenticing under one of the best costume designers ever to be in this field. I could write odes to Catherine in what she's given to me in terms of movement theory and how to produce charisma and I'm forever grateful that she chose me to be with her for so many years. As far as I'm concerned she's the most compelling entertainer I've ever seen on a burlesque stage.

CS: Who designs and makes your costumes? How do you go about putting a full ensemble together?

S: I design my costumes with the assistance of my costumiers. Over the years I've had the assistance of Catherine D'Lish, Jamie Von Stratton, Medianoche, Mr. Gorgeous, Nasty Canasta, and more. I usually have people make the bases of my costumes and I do the

appliqué, lace, and **rhinestoning** myself. I think first and foremost of color (my light synesthesia makes this imperative once I have my song. The colors of my costume must match my song) and then shapes. From there I think of underwear shapes and how I want it all to come off. I stay pretty streamlined in my costumes as I want to be the focus; not my costume. I usually end up being a little more understated than my contemporaries. I like no more than two colors in my palette, long lines (less fluff is easier to pack in NYC for sure), hourglass silhouettes.

CS: What acts are you known for?

S: I suppose I'm known for my Gold Beads act or Red Bottoms act, which both won me a trophy at the Burlesque Hall of Fame. My Gold Beads weigh about 35 pounds and it's like dancing with physics.

Figure 6.17 Sydni performs her "Gold Beads" act at the Moisture Festival in Seattle, Washington, 2013. (Photo by John Cornicello)

It's a very technical act as the beads need a place to go. My Red Bottoms act is minimal—I take off only a faux fur coat, gloves, and a bra. I don't like taking off tons of costume pieces in acts. Once we get above five pieces I feel like it's just about the costume and not about the movement, so I try to keep my items under four. I have a ton of acts, but the ones I won with were taken in by a worldwide audience at that event so they made a big impression. I perform other acts much more in NYC.

CS: What is/was your favorite costume?

S: Currently my Cowboy costume made by Mr. Gorgeous is, because it's fun and bright and I feel powerful in it. I am also particularly fond of my peach dress that I made with Danial Webster (Seattle designer) for my wedding in 2011, with permission from Catherine D'Lish to copy the design and perform in it afterwards. The color choice was my own but the shape and skirt were based off of Catherine's design. I did all the lace applique and rhinestoning myself including ruffling hundreds of yards of **tulle**. My skirt has 450 yards of tulle and it's heavy but wonderful to play in. Takes about 25 minutes to fluff up before I can wear it. She [D'lish] has used [the style] for a Dita costume if I remember correctly.

CS: When and where did you work with Catherine and for how long?

S: I worked with her while I lived in Seattle—she lives on the islands surrounding. I worked with her there for almost four years, somewhere between three to five days a week. 2010–2014. I still consider her my mentor and friend.

CS: In what capacity did you work with her, and how did that opportunity arise?

S: Just a few of my tasks were dealing with and prepping feathers, cutting fabric, laying out rhinestones, actual rhinestoning of projects under her supervision, hand-stitching, taking inventory of fabrics and feathers, sending out orders, and pretty much anything she needed, especially when she was about to tour. One of my favorite tasks was digitizing all of her VHS tapes. I was happily at her disposal during the time I was with her, and sometimes if we had a time crunch for a deadline I would take pieces of costume home to work on for her. As part of our arrangement she worked with me in movement and personal emotional development. I met her at a Burlycon in 2007 or 2008 during a one-on-one that had become available the same day. I begged my mom to borrow the money to have the hour with her, as we had seen her live in Seattle the year earlier—my

mom just thought she was the greatest entertainer, so she happily paid for the session! Catherine and I got along, she's pretty much the most rad lady I've ever met, and we stayed in light touch until I found out she was moving to the PNW from LA. Once she was up near Seattle it wasn't long before I started small projects and errands for her. Her operation needs many hands, and during my time with her other women would come onto projects for a time, depending on how much help she needed executing all the various projects.

CS: What did you experience or learn by witnessing Catherine's design process?

S: She draws (brilliantly too I might add), she marinates on color options, and I've never met anyone with such an exquisite color palette in her head. She works intensely on her projects and only seems to choose things she's excited about, which is a key to success I think.

CS: What is your opinion of Catherine's significance as a burlesque costume designer?

S: I think she is singlehandedly the most important designer to emerge since the 1990s. Her designs have influenced *everyone*.

CS: What is your favorite costume tip or reveal?

S: Mind the arch in your shoes! It can break or make a killer leg. And find the underwear shapes that are ideal for *your* body. Trends pale in comparison to the perfect shape for your frame.

CS: What is burlesque? What does it mean to you?

S: It is the art of the tease. It is cerebral sex. It's an energy exchange. It is entertainment. It's whatever a performer wants to make of it.

CHEEKY LANE

Cheeky Lane is an endlessly creative New York City burlesque performer. She is also a professional set and prop builder skilled at creating intricate sculptures from cardboard, including costume pieces. Cheeky collaborates with the author on occasion when she designs a costume that she needs technical assistance with. Otherwise, she constructs her costumes herself. Her rose act is a stunning example of a neo-burlesque act employing both glamour and imagination.

Figure 6.18 Cheeky Lane in her rose dress constructed by Coleen Scott. Roses and accessories by Cheeky Lane. (Photo by Ben Trivett)

Figure 6.19 Cheeky Lane performs her rose act.
(Photo by Ben Trivett)

Figure 6.20 The wrap skirt for Cheeky Lane's rose costume.
Costume construction by Coleen Scott.
(Photo by Coleen Scott)

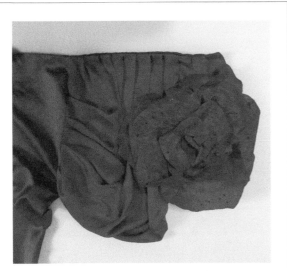

Figure 6.21 Close-up of the skirt front. The skirt was **draped**
on a form to create the shape and pleating. Rose construction
by Cheeky Lane.
(Photo by Coleen Scott)

Figure 6.22 The inside of the rose skirt has a ruffled side crinoline,
which helps the skirt keep an asymmetrical silhouette and an
exaggerated right hip curve.
(Photo by Coleen Scott)

Figure 6.23 This one-shoulder mini-dress goes under the skirt and creates the illusion of a bodice. There are two ribbon ties at the shoulder and two at hip level of the skirt. The bottom straps tie when the skirt is twisted around the body. The ties are attached through a grommet to prevent fraying of the silk dress, and easy tie replacement. The asymmetrical hem is two layers and is meant to resemble the edges of rose petals. *(Photo by Coleen Scott)*

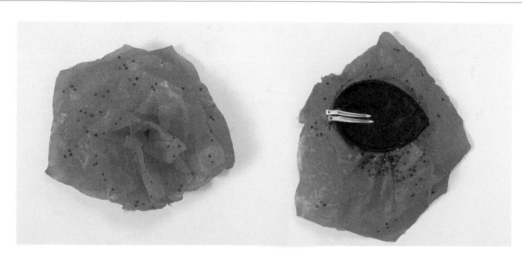

Figure 6.24 The rose hat, top and bottom view. The roses are made of waxed paper, and embellished with rhinestones. *(Photo by Coleen Scott)*

Figure 6.25 *A top and bottom view of the fingerless gloves. Each glove is a different color and has a different arrangement of roses attached. Designed by Cheeky Lane.*
(Photo by Coleen Scott)

Figure 6.26 *The classic style pasties and g-string for this act. Made and embellished by Cheeky Lane.*
(Photo by Coleen Scott)

Figure 6.27 *Jamie Von Stratton in the "Mermaid's Dream" costume that she designed and made. (Photo by Jiamin Zhu/Jajasgarden)*

TALKING ABOUT DESIGN WITH
JAMIE VON STRATTON

Jamie Von Stratton is a fashion and costume designer based in Seattle. Her beautiful construction and imaginative designs are some of the best in burlesque today.[4]

CS: How long have you been a performer? Where? Why did you start?

J: I began my burlesque career in 2004. Kitten La Rue and I did a little show in Seattle, and she asked me to be a part of the troupe she was starting with Fanny N Flames. It's been a whirlwind of glitter, sparkles, pasties, and fabric moments ever since.

CS: How long have you been making burlesque costumes? Where did you acquire your skillset?

J: I've been a ready-to-wear designer since 2002, but moved towards burlesque when I joined the [Atomic] Bombshells.[5]

CS: Which came first—costume or performance?

J: Ooooh good question! As a theater person, the stage came first. I was making my own costumes in junior high and high school for the plays and musicals I was in. In a sense, I suppose I was always making costumes, but burlesque turned them down the glamour stripper path.

CS: What inspires your designs?

J: So many things! I use Pinterest a lot when working with clients. It can be anything from couture images, to pictures of fish, or rocks. Basically, any visual that aids in the design process, and keeps me on the path to the final destination.

CS: What are some of your specialties as a costume designer and maker? How do you go about putting a full ensemble together for yourself or someone else?

J: I think I might be the Fishtail Whisperer. I just *lurve* a **fishtail gown**. I love them, every time, and in every fabric. As for costumes for myself, that's a tricky one. Some things start as a concept I've dreamed about, others as a mass of fabrics and pieces that get made into a whimsical thing. I love looking towards the vintage MGM Grand musicals, and getting inspiration there.

CS: Discuss a favorite costume commission and a favorite personal costume.

J: Favorite Commission is HARD. There have been hundreds! I guess I can say one of my favorite people to work with is Iva Handfull. She and I have been creating her looks for nearly a decade. At this point I know her style so well, but she still surprises me every once and a while.

Figure 6.28 *Seattle burlesque star Iva Handfull in a zebra costume by J. Von Stratton for her 2014 Burlesque Hall of Fame win. (Photo by Olena Sullivan)*

[Regarding] my own favorite piece, I'm really happy with my "A Mermaid's Dream" costume. It took me over a year to make, it didn't have a deadline so I worked on it slowly. It started as a drawing, then I started adding more and more pieces. In fact, there are some parts of it that I had to edit out because they didn't work anymore. Then last spring I was like, I need a coral reef set. Done. Then during the summer I thought, What if I have seahorse confetti cannons? Done. Now I'm like, I need an anchor aerial apparatus? Done? Ha-ha.

CS: What is your favorite costume tip, trick, or reveal?

J: A spray bottle of vodka. Oh it's the jam. Spray in the pits of your costumes to keep them odor-free. Use to disinfect your area, or your hands (in case there is no bathroom to wash your hands before applying eyelashes or whatnot). Clean your mirror, spray the airline tray if you're traveling, clean your house with it, spray it in your mouth if you've stage fright. It's the best!

CS: How has the burlesque scene and costuming changed through your career?

J: I can really only speak to my experience in Seattle. When I first started here, the full on vintage throwback, **high glam**, and **camp** was fresh and new. There was burlesque here, but it was a bit more punk and hardcore, which was cool. As far as I know, Paula the Swedish Housewife, Indigo Blue, and Inga were the only performers I'd seen performing high glam vintage style acts (I could be wrong, but that was just my scope). It seems like the style broadened up and opened its arms as the years passed, and we started seeing more **avant guarde burlesque**, and **boylesque**, and **nerdlesque** (YES!), and now we have this enormous scope of performance styles that sit under the burlesque umbrella.

CS: Do you have any thoughts on cultural appropriation in costume design and how to navigate that line between tribute/celebration and offensive?

J: This is complex. The layers here are controversial. I've always found such beauty and inspiration in garments coming from the rest of the world, both current and historical. I think there is this grey line between bastardizing a culture and genuinely pulling inspiration from a piece, and that line is determined by the viewer, so it's always going to be a bit of a gamble if you're the artist. What's the intention? What is the act's intention? Is it necessary? Will you be proud of this in 20 years, and would you be proud to share it with people from that culture? I suppose those are some questions one can ask themselves.

I've made inspired garments, and some of my favorite pieces and collections from designers are inspired. I would never want to judge or hinder an artist in their creativity, but I caution to tread this path lightly, and be humble and considerate in your decisions.

CS: What is burlesque? What does it mean to you?

J: Burlesque is Helpful. It helps people feel great about their bodies, and their sexuality. It can provide community and social engagements for like-minded individuals, which is excellent for building relationships. Sadly, I've also seen it be harsh and hostile. I've seen the industry lift people and I've seen it throw people to the wolves. I love burlesque like I love my sibling. I love it more than anything, but sometimes it drives me batty and I eye-roll it something fierce.

Figure 6.29 *Jamie Von Stratton.*
(Photo by Jiamin Zhu/Jajasgarden)

Figure 6.30 Gin Minsky performs her quick-change tap act. Costume by Garo Sparo.
(Photo by Ben Trivett)

GIN MINSKY[6]

" I've been dancing and tapping since I was five years old. I started performing in nightlife in 2008 with a non-strip act with the Minsky Sisters, so it's been about ten years. I debuted this act at the NYBF in 2016." About the act inspiratioN:

> "I was watching *RuPaul's Drag Race*[7] and Violet Chotchki had [a] black glitter jumpsuit and then she opened it up and spun out and it was that plaid winged amazing thing, and I thought "I want a quick-change number! I want a quick-change costume!" And so I was brainstorming what I wanted that to look like and a lot of my stuff is 20s, but I pull a lot of my inspiration from old Hollywood in addition to 20s *flappers*, so I liked the idea of transitioning through time, and doing a reveal in burlesque that covered me up more than I already was."
>
> (Gin Minsky)

Gin's thoughts about using turbans in tributing 1920s style:

> "There are a lot of problematic things in the 20s in general. I mean, the dance steps that I perform were appropriated from African Juba dancing…I thought about it since I wear a turban in this act. I do think it's a fine line. It originated in the 20s and people wore turbans in the 1940s still. Yes, Whites in the 20s appropriated it, but it has since been removed generation after generation and now it's a fashion item. I think it's really far removed at this point, unless you are wearing a traditional Middle Eastern turban or [other traditional garments like it]."

Figure 6.31 Gin Minsky in her 1920s to 1930s quick-change costume by Garo Sparo. (Photo by Ben Trivett)

Figure 6.32 A pair of Bella's Tchotchki's "Unicorn" 3D printed pasties. Author's collection. (Photo by Ben Trivett)

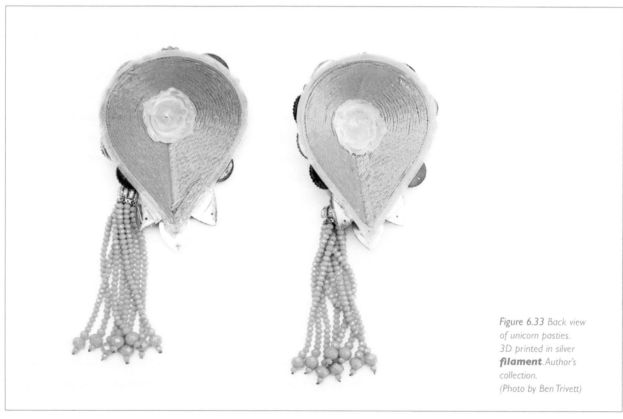

Figure 6.33 Back view of unicorn pasties. 3D printed in silver **filament**. Author's collection. (Photo by Ben Trivett)

AN INTERVIEW WITH BELLA LA BLANC OF BELLA'S TCHOTCHKIS

Technology has taken the fashion world, the entertainment world, and the burlesque world by storm, and there is no shortage of cutting-edge technique in the costumes on the burlesque stage. Upon further investigation, the author caught up with one of the most innovative pastie makers in the country, Bella La Blanc of Bella's Tchotchkis, to learn more about her adventures in making the perfect 3D printed pasties, including engineering her own 3D printers for the job. The following interview excerpt is a personal account of Bella's process and her thoughts about how artists can work together in a competitive field.[8]

CS: Hey Bella! What's your name?

BLB: Well, I'm Bella La Blanc, and I'm the owner of Bella's Tchotchkis!

CS: Where are you?

BLB: I am now based out of Rockville, Maryland.

CS: I know you have a performance background, but when did you start performing burlesque specifically?

BLB: I got into burlesque from the **fetish scene**. It was very big and thriving in Fort Lauderdale, Florida, for a while in the late 1990s early 2000s. I've been a full-time touring performer for a little under a decade. I also had to stop and have real life happen, like I got married, I had children, so there were a lot of very long breaks involved. I can say that I've been going my hardest for the past six years.

CS: So when you started making pasties were you just experimenting, or did you have a guide?

BLB: When I first started getting into the pastie thing everybody did **craft foam**, or craft foam with **buckram**, or just buckram. So with buckram, I thought that was great, but the problem was, after a couple months of wear, no matter what your adhesive was, either you had the gunky stuff inside it or it would just start going flat, it would warp—you had to treat it like it was fine crystal china, or it was garbage.

Figure 6.34 Bella La Blanc by Stereo Vision Photography. (Courtesy of Bella La Blanc)

I was at a fetish event, and saw this gorgeous woman in this amazing costume—a skin tight mermaid pencil dress, and I was like, "your dress is so beautiful what is it made of?" I asked if I could have consent to touch the vinyl skirt, and she said "yes" and something clicked in my head. Then I found out other pastie makers were also using vinyl, and I thought "let me try this."

A performer even said to me "hey, why don't you sell this shit you make?" I always jokingly said "yeah, it'd be really nice if I could glue shit to shit and call it my job." That's actually what I tell people now!

Literally I started Bella's Tchotchkis with a pipe dream and three pots of coffee in my kitchen with a couple friends.

CS: That's how all the best projects start!

BLB: So when I first started selling them I was using a mixture of vinyl and buckram. I'm not knocking them as materials for pasties, because there's another great pastie maker [using those materials] who I love, Gothfox.

CS: Yes she's excellent.

BLB: She is probably one of my biggest supporters. When I told her I wanted to start, Gothfox was very supportive, and even gave me tips and directions on things to do. She actually waterproofed a pair of pasties for me, and showed me how to do that, which was amazing. Those original materials are still good, I'm not ever going to knock the materials used in the past, it's just not what I choose to use anymore.

CS: Some of these materials have been used since the beginning of pasties, and people have been making different combinations of them, but that's why it's good to have multiple types of pastie vendors, because you have options!

BLB: Right! I still make a vinyl pastie on occasion because, honestly, you can't print everything. Or, I'll make a printed base and I'll put some vinyl design on top, and then I'll hit it with a resin so it's still rock solid, but I have to tell them, you still have to treat this like you would a vinyl pastie. Even though the inside is a rock solid cone that you could throw against the wall and it would live to tell the tale, the rest of it might not. That's kind of my thing now, I like to pitch the durability aspect because now I have pasties that have lasted for years.

CS: That's great, because if you're going to get one pair that's going to last you, then you will make your cost back.

BLB: Exactly! Especially if you just buy a neutral like a crystal or crystal AB combo or you go to neutral or nude, you buy something like that, and whenever you think "oh shit

I don't have pasties for this number, oh wait, yes I do, and I bought them five years ago!" That's amazing because it pays for itself after a while.

When you come by my booth you see that my pasties are not only durable, but I make them as inexpensive as humanly possible. Right now you can get a basic pair without tassels for $30, and you can get a basic pair right off the rack with tassels for $50–$60. That's really affordable!

CS: Right! So, how long have you been doing 3D printing?

BLB: Well, we started toying with the idea about five years ago. My husband is a software architect and does computer engineering and stuff like that on the side as a hobby. Yeah, he's a nerd by trade, and a nerd for fun, so, in other words, he's really HOT.

CS: Hahaha.

BLB: With that being said, we started seeing these big Maker Fairs and Tech Fairs, and we'd go to these, and we saw a 3D printer. And he was like, "I really want to get one, I really want to do something with it." And I was like, WTF are we going to do with a 3D printer?

So we bought a Duplicator I-3 and it was a build your own kind of kit (a lot of this was his hard work too!) because if you bought them pre-built it was $5–6000. If you bought your own kit and built it yourself when they first came out, it was only $2000.

We started fucking around with it and making all kinds of cool shit. And we realized that the plastic was hard, that you could print it really thin, you could print it really thick, and then it was literally him and me on the couch one night just talking and I was working on merch, and I looked at him and he looked at me and I held up a pastie and he already knew.

And he said: "we can try…"

So, he literally built all the patterns from scratch. We're talking we probably went through at least two to three rolls of filament

CS: Yes, because you're trying different densities and shapes, right?

BLB: Exactly. A lot of my earlier models were a little thinner, my next models a year or two later were a little on the thicker side, but they were also heavier; it took us years of tweaking. We had to consider what kind of plastic are we going to use? Because there are tons of other kinds of plastics out there now like PLA, PET, a bunch of others, and I have rolls of all of them!

Then we had to figure out high melt temp, low melt temp, warping, cracking, proper temp to print at—things that especially even now, people who are buying 3D printers don't think about. I don't want to admit the amount of money that we spent to figure out exactly the right consistency, the right plastics. I mean, we've gone through a couple of printers too, because, if you're going to buy a printer and work it like a work horse ...

CS: Right.

BLB: I only have two printers right now in my maker space and I've had more than two at a time, and one is currently down for repair, so I only have one active printer at the moment.

CS: How long does it take to print the pasties?

BLB: It takes about two hours to print one pair, but it's not a big deal if you just keep them printing morning, noon and night. You do have to go down and scrape the printer, so I set up a print before going to bed and when I get up in the morning and scrape the printer and get the next print started. The truth is, the machine does all the work.

CS: Oh yeah, after the two years of engineering where you figured out what you wanted to do and how to do it right!

BLB: Yeah, I mean, it was not fun! We figured it out on our own, we didn't reach out for help.

CS: Well, there weren't people out there doing this specific thing for those specific needs.

BLB: Exactly, and to be completely honest with you, I didn't really talk to anyone about it because I didn't want to be copied. I wanted my product to stand out. I wanted it to be different.

It was funny because I started going to festivals and selling my product and I started noticing that some of the people I sold my stuff to started doing it, and I was like, "OK, I guess I have to let this go ..."

CS: Yeah, it's a good point. I mean, in some ways it's inevitable. On the other hand, there is the option to patent things ...

BLB: I was considering doing that, I looked into it, but it was so vague ... you can't patent a basic pastie.

CS: Yes it has to be one type of pastie with one specific design element and/or engineering to patent.

BLB: I mean, there are other people who have made a 3D printed pastie now that have done things different to it and had theirs patented. Good for them!

I was so heartbroken when I saw multiple makers around year three or four of my business, and I didn't know what to do. The one thing I did start doing was on advice from Gothfox, who told me to advertise that I was the original maker of the 3D printed pastie. And I did. It felt nice to say that, and it's true!

Some people like my products, some people like other products more, and that's fine—capitalism I guess?

CS: Well, yes!

BLB: There's plenty of room in the seven kingdoms for all of us to play.

CS: Yes, if your business is doing well and you're still producing a great product, people are still going to be coming to you.

BLB: Exactly, but it did take me a while to get to that level of acceptance.

CS: It's hard to do, it's your *art*!

BLB: It is my *baby*! It still is my baby, let's be honest. Those machines get treated better than some people's pets.

CS: So, do you have a different printer now that you prefer, or are you still using the same brand but an updated model?

BLB: So, now we use printers that my husband has built from scratch because we know what we want and how we like things done.

CS: Wow!

BLB: Even the parts for the printer are 3D printed!

CS: That's amazing!

BLB: It's become a science of exactly what we want and how we want it. So, you can't buy the printer, because he made it!

CS: That's what you want, a product that no one else can get!

BLB: I do suggest for someone who wants to get into 3D printing—don't buy a MakerBot, they are really outdated. If you have one, great, just make sure you have the updated stuff for it. But I've seen a lot of positive things come out of the Prusa brand. That's my suggestion. Don't spend thousands of dollars perfecting it like we did!

CS: Have you taught any workshops on this technology, or on using technology for burlesque?

BLB: The one class I did teach for years, and it's still on my website as something I teach; it's a 101 and a 201 class about pasties on the cheap.

I teach you how to make pasties out of all the products you can use. I do bring my 3D printed bases into class, but I will not teach you how to make them. I will teach you how to make them out of everything else.

My higher level pastie making class is getting into details like what trim you can use, hand sewing, adhesives, what's right, what's wrong, alternatives to **E6000** ...

I recommend **E6000 Fabri-Fuse** because it doesn't soften from warmth over time, and you won't have as much stone shift.

It's sad but true with my product because it's plastic, I'm stuck with the toxic shit indefinitely because I also like to say my products are waterproof.

So, that's the kind of stuff I teach, but I don't teach 3D printing and I probably never will.

CS: Right. The other thing about your pasties specifically that I'd like to know is what you are embellishing them with. Are you printing things? Are you making resin pieces, or are you buying all of your embellishments?

BLB: Some things I have printed and added gloss to, but very little. I do buy a lot of my **resin stones**. And what I do for those and other stones with a foil or acrylic base, because I have to use E6000, is use clear nail polish. I take all the stones and I coat the underside with two coats of clear nail polish and let them sit out for 48 hours before I apply them, so the E6000 doesn't eat away at the foil.

CS: Great tip! I was very curious about your stones because they make the pasties look so different.

BLB: Go to New York. B&Q trim—ransack their bins of stones. I go to the garment district once a month to buy stones and I buy my tassels now too. I'll share where I get my stuff, I don't mind. That is one of the things a lot of makers shared with me—where to buy certain things. I also have a couple wholesale accounts too.

CS: Yeah, of course, for the regular stones.

BLB: But once in a while you walk into a store, and you're like, "Oh my God, that stone is amazing, and all the amazing things I can make with it." I also buy extra so that when I have a custom order, I can send a larger bag of excess stones so they can put that on their costume to match.

CS: That's excellent. Do you think you'll ever stop making pasties?

BLB: Originally, it was a joke that it was going to be my retirement plan when I quit stripping at 40, which by the way is slowly looming closer.

I don't think I'm ever going to 100% quit stripping, and also I'm a sideshow performer. I graduated Coney Island in 2015. I might slow down, but I don't think I'm ever going to quit performing. Let's be honest, I fucking doubt it. Yes, give me all the applause. I want to wear the sparkly shit I make too!

In regards to making pasties – I love making pasties. It's actually something I love to do, and that's why a lot of my customers keep coming back. Even when I'm in a rush preparing for a festival, even in that moment, I love making the patterns [of embellishment]. I try not to make a lot of things alike, and that's really hard to do.

Sometimes patterns will duplicate themselves with different sizes and shapes.

As of now I don't plan on stopping. My goal for this year was to slow down on performing and focus more on my business. I have a couple of big vending events coming up.

The thing I love about this business, especially when you're vending in a public space, is that you get to talk to people.

I'm an ambivert—I'm a hardcore extrovert then I run away and hide in my house. I love getting to play somewhat of a dress up, or just putting on my face and getting to wear my normal clothing which is goth girl regalia, and then being able to talk to performers and see what inspires them, what inspired them to buy the product or a certain piece. Then I know what I need to make more of, what I need to keep in stock, what I probably need to tweak and/or change. I do take input seriously. What I really love is talking to performers and then giving them a piece of me to take home, and knowing that the piece is going to have its own history. To me, that's really special, and it's what makes me want to continue making.[9]

Figure 6.35 *A sampling of some of Bella's Tchotchkis.*
(Photo by Bella La Blanc)

MODERN PASTIES[10]

There are currently hundreds of pastie vendors in the US, and the pasties featured in Figures 6.36 and 6.37 are just a few samples from important makers in burlesque costuming. Gothfox specializes in pasties with additional accessories available like g-strings and body harnesses. She has begun sharing her rhinestoning knowledge by offering video demos online under the hashtag: SchoolofGothfox. Glorious Pasties began as a pastie company and has expanded to offer luxurious fully-embellished bra, corset and skirt or shimmy belt sets. The company also offers chiffon dresses, rhinestoned shoes, and takes custom requests.

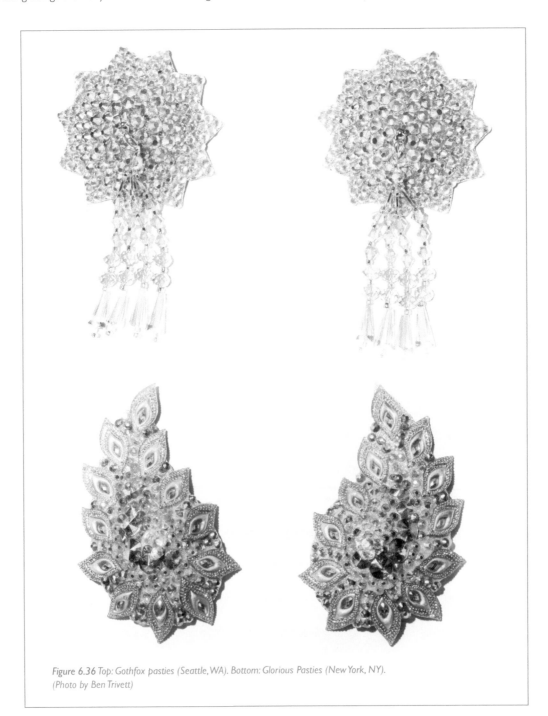

Figure 6.36 Top: Gothfox pasties (Seattle, WA). Bottom: Glorious Pasties (New York, NY).
(Photo by Ben Trivett)

Manuge Et Toi (figure 6.37 top) is actually a Canadian burlesque costume company, but the work of designer and owner Christina Manuge is highly recognized in the United States and in *21st Century Burlesque's* Top 50[11] lists as a favorite costume designer for several years. Manuge Et Toi offers custom orders, and specializes in original pastie designs, multiple g-string styles, gauntlet gloves, and body harnesses. Penny Starr Jr. is the granddaughter of burlesque legend Penny Starr, and an early member of the neo burlesque movement, taking a prize at Miss Exotic World in 2004. She is a professional costumer in Hollywood, and makes pasties and custom commissions under her label Movie Starr by Penny Starr Jr.

Figure 6.37 Top: *Manuge Et Toi (Ottawa, Canada). Bottom: Movie Starr by Penny Starr Jr. (Hollywood, CA). All pasties on these pages were featured in* The Pastie Project, *2017.*
(Photo by Ben Trivett)

Figure 6.38 Darlinda Just Darlinda performs her rainbow act. Costume by Garo Sparo.
(Photo by Ben Trivett)

From Darlinda[12]: "Garo Sparo made the costume in 2007 for my *Year In Rainbow* project.[13] I wanted to make a costume that showed the history of burlesque in a costume. It starts out looking like an 1800s ballet costume, then it's a little more 1950s—Marilyn Monroe showgirl line, and then the shimmy belt, which is a little more 60s, and then the wings—which are timeless."

Figure 6.39 *Darlinda Just Darlinda in a costume by Garo Sparo.*
(Photo by Ben Trivett)

Figure 6.40 Cheeky lane performs her Ganesha tribute act. Costume by Cheeky Lane. Skirt by Coleen Scott.
(Photos by Ben Trivett)

From Cheeky[14]: "I wanted to explore the concept of glove peel with more than one option. I tend to pick archetypes. I researched into what I did, how I costumed, and how I bedazzled and jeweled everything. I worked with a choreographer who does both traditional and Bollywood style dancing. I did do quite extensive study building and doing dance choreography for [the act]. It is to ensure the act celebrates Ganesh."

Figure 6.41 Cheeky Lane in her Ganesha costume.
(Photo by Ben Trivett)

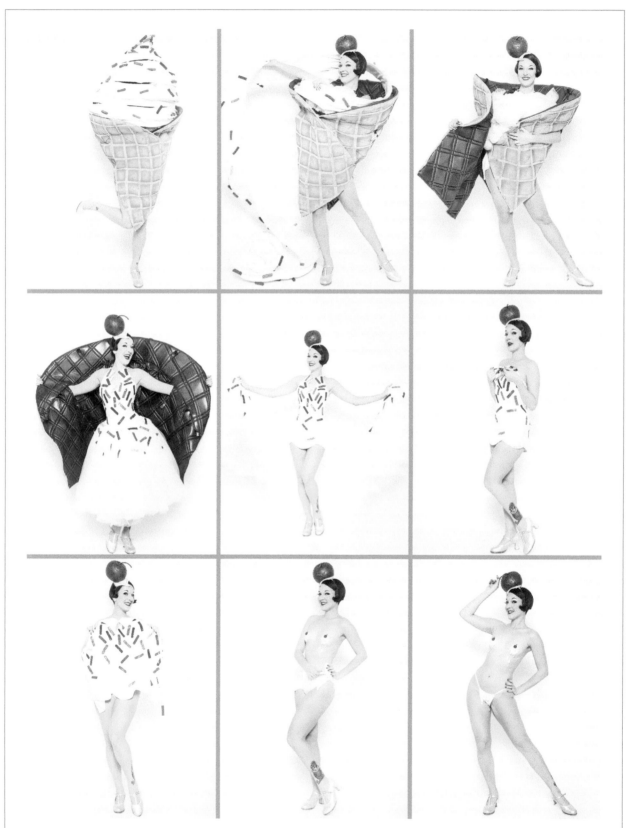

Figure 6.42 Gin Minsky performs her tap dancing ice cream act. Costume by Garo Sparo.
(Photos by Ben Trivett)

About this costume from Gin[15]: "Those that know me know that I have a big ice cream thing … and it's become a joke in the burlesque community so I figured it was time to have an ice cream act, and I figured I would be a giant ice cream cone! … When I went to Garo and I told him I wanted to do this act, I was like "so I want to be an ice cream cone" and he started designing this very fashionable couture outfit with like a little swirl hat, and I was like "no. I want to be a mascot. I want to be a cartoon."

Figure 6.43 Gin Minsky in her ice cream costume by Garo Sparo.
(Photo by Ben Trivett)

Gin Minksy's ice cream cone costume is a feat of engineering by designer Garo Sparo. The intricacies of modern burlesque costumes are copious. It would be complicated enough to build this ice cream cone costume, but it is also a costume that has to break apart in visually creative ways. The costume is a perfect example of the originality in construction and design that makes burlesque costume its own category deserving specialized study.

Figure 6.44 The cone portion of the ice cream costume by Garo Sparo. (Photo by Coleen Scott)

Figure 6.45 The red metallic lining inside the cone when it is "unwrapped." There is **steel hooping** in the top of the cone helping it keep its top edge shape, and the closure is a plastic three-prong clasp. The straps are more like wide shoulder supports you might see on a backpack. (Photo by Coleen Scott)

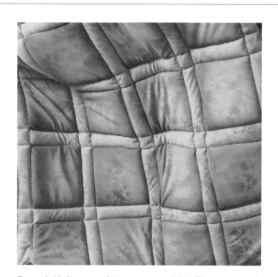

Figure 6.46 Close-up of the outer cone fabric. The matte knit has been quilted and then airbrushed for shading, with stencils used for texture. (Photo by Coleen Scott)

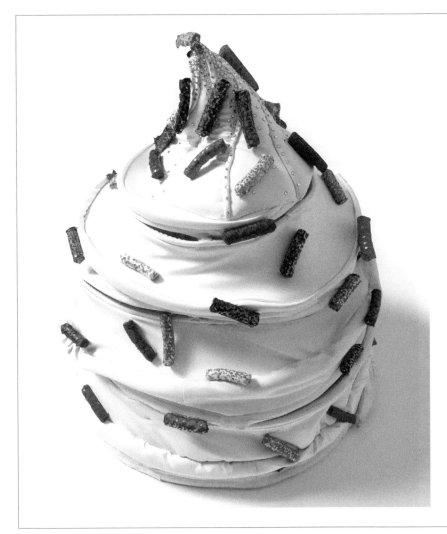

Figure 6.47 The top of the ice cream costume. This piece is also made with hooping that has been spiraled into this shape with the help of the foam liner and neoprene fabric form and individual plastic snaps on tabs that keep the spiral closed until it is unraveled. The top of the piece is constructed similarly to a pointed hat with seven panels. The outer seams of this encase additional boning or wire. (Photo by Coleen Scott)

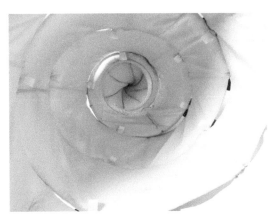

Figure 6.48 A view of the ice cream from the inside. You can see the seaming of the spiral and the **grosgrain** tabs that can be pulled individually to separate the layers of the spiral. (Photo by Coleen Scott)

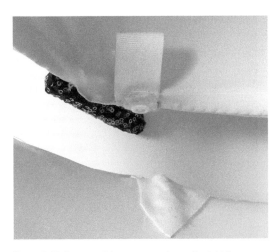

Figure 6.49 Close-up of the top snap, where a "sprinkle" gets placed between the spiral layers to allow a sliver of space for Gin to see out of as she tap dances. (Photo by Coleen Scott)

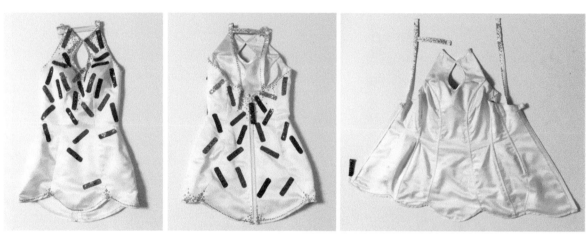

Figure 6.50 The tap dress that is worn under the ice cream cone. A snap at the right shoulder and a zipper all the way down the center back allow the dress to open completely for easy removal. The inside of the dress is completely finished for a beautiful view if seen from the stage.
(Photo by Coleen Scott)

Figure 6.51 This very full mesh skirt with "sprinkles" is worn over the dress above and pulled up around Gin's body inside the top part of the ice cream cone so that it cannot be seen until she reveals it. The skirt snaps apart into two pieces.
(Photo by Coleen Scott)

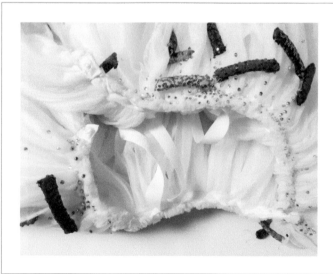

Figure 6.52 Close-up of the waist and grosgrain waistband of the full skirt.
(Photo by Coleen Scott)

Figure 6.54 **Tear-away** ice cream shorts. The shiny spandex shorts have been built with accent layers to replicate dripping ice cream. They pull apart with snaps at both sides.
(Photo by Coleen Scott)

Figure 6.53 The inside of the cherry hat, which can be seen on Gin in the previous pages. There is a fleshtone, sheer elastic strap to keep the hat on through the tap number. The hat does not come off during the act. Garo Sparo's label can be seen inside.
(Photo by Coleen Scott)

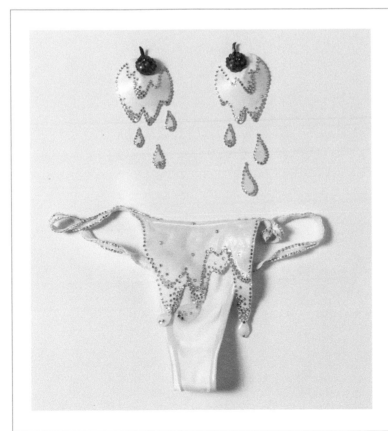

Figure 6.55 The pasties and g-string for the ice cream costume. These pasties are especially creative with the extra "drops" that need to be individually adhered to the body.
(Photo by Coleen Scott)

NASTY CANASTA: AN INTERVIEW

Nasty Canasta is a New York City burlesque performer known for her intelligent acts and pop culture references. "The girl with the 44DD Brain" has been called a mother of nerdlesque, the category of burlesque that celebrates all things nerdy. Examples include: literary, anime or comic book references, films and television, or general popular culture. Nasty makes her own costumes and many for her fellow performers. She has a knack for designs and acts employing simple brilliance. Her car alarm fan dance is a perfect example of captivating an audience with an original soundtrack and two fans. The transcript that follows is a portion of an interview with the author.[16]

Figure 6.56 Nasty Canasta wears a crown of crowns. Her own creation. (Photo by Ben Trivett)

CS: Well, hello Nasty Canasta.

N: Hello.

CS: How long have you been a performer? Where have you performed? And why did you start?

N: I've been a burlesque performer for about 14½ going on 15 years. I've been in the theater since I was a little kid, and mostly New York based. But the last couple of years I got to travel more, with is great.

… So when I started performing. After college I moved to New York to be a serious actor, and I did that for years, and it was miserable. I don't know if I was a good actor or not, I mean I wasn't terrible. I probably wasn't brilliant, but I was not good at the business of it all.

I did years of weird, shitty, bad like super off-off-off-off [Broadway] that I would ask people to not come and see. I just, was getting really depressed about that. A friend of mine from college did theater too, but he took in a lot of puppetry and circus and he went and studied at whatever that circus school is on the west coast for a little bit and he was like "this guy that was in my program is in a show at some place downtown, we should go see it." And it was great. It turned out it was this place called The Slipper Room. And that show was, I actually don't remember who his friend was, but it was like Julie Atlas Muz and Harvest Moon and Doctor Lucky, and I think Tigger! might have even been in the show. We were sitting there and I remember it wasn't super crowded, and we were up front at a table. I was mostly pissed off because I had done four years of Ivy League theater school and nobody told me about this.

[Laughter]

N: I was like "Why didn't …? What, really? Like really?" He was watching me watch the show. Then six months later, the original Galapagos[17] had auditions for their floating vaudeville show. [My friend] was, like, "I want to bring a puppet thing to this, you should put together a burlesque act and go." So I auditioned, *because we had auditions for things* back then. Clearly, somebody cancelled last minute, and they were like: "Can you come in and do three numbers tomorrow?" And I was like "I don't have three numbers, I have one, but sure." I met Veronica Sweet at that show. She said: "You're great! Here's some other people you should call, and wouldn't it be funny if we ever did a show together. We could call it Sweet and Nasty."[18] I just went from there. Eventually, over a couple years, I realized I wasn't going to auditions for theater anymore and I was doing more

burlesque. That just took over, and ended up being more what I wanted to do.

CS: Well, it's more fun.

N: It is. It's way more fun. I'm transitioning a little more, although spaces are closing their doors, into full theatre-burlesque productions. I like that after a decade and a half it came together and in a way that makes sense now.

CS: Well, because you're making it happen after all that experience. How do you think the scene has changed during your burlesque career? And how has costuming changed?

N: Well, the scene. The first bunch of years when I did this I was just in New York. I don't know what was happening anywhere else, but the sense that I've gotten from everyone that has been around for that long is that there *wasn't* a huge scene everywhere like there is now.

CS: Yes

N: I know there were people in Seattle and people in LA. And you know, I, and as far as I know—That's it. That's clearly not true but …

I don't want to be one of those—"it was so much more fun back in the day" because I don't think that. There were days where you were like, you know, [sick of] shitty clubs and not getting paid and whatever. I was 15 years younger, so it was fine. It was fun and I had a day job, and so you just kind of did it for the drinks and the hangout and whatever and the 20 bucks was great.

This is my job now, so the fact that rates are higher is very important to me. And so many shows don't start until somewhere between 10 and 2. I want to be home by 10 now. And it's weird to say this, but I think it's more commercial now in a way that is both good and bad. I know the opportunity still exists and the shows still exist that you can just put stuff on stage and try stuff out, and it can be more performance arty and I love that. It's been the case in other places a lot, but I love that here there's a lot more drag coming back into the scene because it was very separate other than very specific people for a long time. I actually don't think it's a bad thing that there is some sort of structure too. You know, more people are making this their job, either from the production side or the performance side or both. I like that there are more performing producers or people who came through performance rather than just club and venue owners hiring people. Some of that is wonderful, but I think that, ultimately, I'd rather have someone who has been naked on stage themselves, rather than "Hey can you get some girls and do a show or whatever you do, and here's a drink ticket."

CS: Me too.

N: There being a little more organization and structure means that it is a little safer and cleaner. Possibly as I'm getting a little older that is just getting easier for me. You know, the downside to that is I think there are fewer high-profile opportunities for people to try stuff out on stage. I think there is a little bit of a, especially outside of New York and especially now that there's this pageant circuit and things, I think that's led to a little bit of uniformity.

CS: I agree.

N: I don't want to say that, because I don't really want it to be true. There are plenty of people who make a living and don't worry about that. I've gone through a little bit of the festivals and pageant and community at large, which is a very different non-defined thing now. Now it's fun to go to a festival and see people from Canada that I never get to see or from Chicago I never get to see or whatever, but it's less important personally. I think the difficulty now, or what I try to navigate and what I try to tell newer people to navigate is that I think people look at the scene and they're like "I have to start with: a $9000 costume that's covered in rhinestones that was made by insert-name-of-high-profile-costumer-here." I mean, I've been doing this for 14½ years and I don't do $9000 rhinestone costumes, so.

CS: You think that's a new mentality, though?

N: I really think it is. I think when I started there were a lot of people who were coming out of drag and performance arts that were inherently amazing performers, you know? That could get on stage and stand there, and you were just like "Oh my god, this is incredible." I don't think people looked like crap back then, it was just that wasn't the first thought for most people. It seems. And I know that everyone approaches it differently too.

CS: Yes they do.

N: People are like "I really want a costume that does this" or "I want to be a butterfly, how do I make that costume?" I just think that the shift was really subtle and then I realized "Oh everybody's really fucking shiny now." I get that. Also people who do corporate gigs or traveling shows, casino shows, that kind of thing, you have to have that kind of [costume]. I just worry that it discourages the more unique impulses and things.

CS: Yes.

N: Frankly, you know, if this is your job, and you are getting paid X amount of money and you're spending ten times X amount of money on all of this stuff; you can't live like that.

CS: It's not a job at that point.

N: Right, right. At the same time there have been some incredible innovations in not just design—in culture, in shapes … people do amazing things with costuming, props, and puppetry, and that's incredible to see. I absolutely love that.

CS: Yes.

N: That's been a great thing.

CS: When do you think you saw the sparkles …

N: Take over?

CS: Yes, because they have.

N: Right?

CS: I think it's been a really obvious shift, but I don't know if it's—is it just Dita [Von Teese]? When Dita got more mainstream popularity?

N: I think it's when Exotic World became the Burlesque Hall of Fame. I never got to the goat farm.[19]

CS: Me neither.

N: I did the first year in Vegas. I did that show with my Sesame Street number. I got in with a Sesame Street number that did not have a single rhinestone on it. I remember the theater was really fun. It was a weird little off-Fremont Street theater space. And I remember thinking "this is really cool." There was some big shiny stuff but I just remember it like awesome weird shit from all over the country and a little bit all over the world. Then ten years later it was two-story props covered in rhinestones. So somewhere in there [was a shift]. I don't blame BHOF, but I most specifically saw the shift happening there, and radiating out from that. I know, you go to something like that for a week and think: "I'm going to have to update my costuming." I get that. I also like, that people like Boo Bess and Jenny C'est Quoi just brought a sleek number that brought the house down from what I hear.[20] I've seen the number and I love it. It is so visually simple. I think it is really important that it was there and recognized, to see—

CS: There's a variety, it's possible.

N: Exactly, exactly. I love excess. I love that. That's why we get to do this. But, if it's just excess, excess, excess, then nothing registers.

CS: Right.

N: In fact, I'm sure people had two-story sequin props and giant gowns and stuff. But what people remember is "these two people in this number who blew my mind; they were sitting in chairs." (Referring to Jenny C'est Quoi and Boo Bess' recent BHOF duet.) But like *Poof* [makes brain exploding gesture].

CS: Exactly.

N: I think, I'm not a Dita person. I admire her as a business lady, and as a producer, but other than that I don't really care. It's not my jam. I ain't mad. It's fine. I think that [Dita's aesthetic] is probably part of it, but other than the people who work with her, we don't have access to that.

CS: No, it's just a permeating visual.

N: Yeah.

CS: And the visual is becoming more accessible. Those costumes were the first ones I saw awhile after I started performing where there were these encrusted garments.

N: Mhmm.

CS: I think you are right about BHOF too because you would see this stuff on the competitors.

N: Yeah!

CS: And you would think, "Oh I need more rhinestones."

N: That's obviously the stuff people bring to BHOF.

CS: Of course.

N: In New York we don't have rooms to store it, and our rents are too high here, so. You know. I think here we build up. So people have [a new costume] and they're like: "I have the shape, I have the thing. I'm gonna use it five times, and get paid for it. And *then* add stuff to it."

CS: Yes

N: And I think that in other places, my sense is—it's "I'm going to debut my rhinestone-encrusted costume."

CS: "I've been working on this for …

N: "Three years." Or whatever.

CS: Exactly, it's different in other places.

CS: Who do you think has been the biggest influence on your burlesque—on your performance style and how you decide your aesthetic?

N: I think that has shifted. It changes and is added on to over the years. The people that influenced me the most from the very beginning were Julie Atlas Muz, Tigger! and Lady Ace, who I think retired and moved to Europe, and Miss Tickle. These people who it was less about the costuming and more about the—well Tickle not so much.[21] Although her stage presence *is* astonishing.

CS: Yes.

N: They were a huge influence in me starting. Little Brooklyn was a huge influence, just thematically, as a consummate comedienne. And getting to work with her for years, was great. Because you know we didn't have nerdlesque, really.

CS: Right.

N: People were doing stuff, absolutely. People were like "Look I'm Batman." Great, but it wasn't like a *thing* so much. I remember getting upset and I hadn't seen Ed

Figure 6.57 Even while living in a spacious residence for New York City, Nasty is still creative and space-conscious in her home sewing studio, and uses the closet for costumes, shoes and notions. (Photo by Coleen Scott)

Wood when it came out. I rented it, and I thought "This is amazing—what if we did a number with it, and there were little space ships, etc." And the idea that things pop culture could be a part of this started blowing my own mind. So a lot of those [pop culture influenced acts] became nerdlesque. That was a big influence on me.

CS: When did you first do a pop culture number?

N: I think my first, what you could call nerdlesque was probably 2005 or 2006. That was really early on. I covered myself in Christmas lights, and plugged myself into a wall socket, and called that Tron.

   [Laughter]

N: That was real early shit.

CS: That's funny.

N: It was fun. Oh god that number was real stupid. It was before the next Tron movie came out so ... I think it's pretty obvious to people watching me [what inspires me], but it's more subconscious now. I also try very hard to not be like "I like that, I'm going to do it because [it's nerdy]." I know that there are people, I love to watch, that don't do what I do. And I don't do what they do. I love watching dancers and people who are more acrobatic or more physical on stage. And I don't know how that influences me, but I know it does. I know Penny Wren is a huge influence also because she's a moron genius brilliant idiot, but I just like watching, and I'm never going to do physically on stage what she has trained her whole life to do. Somehow, those influences are in there somewhere for me, but what that specifically translates to …?

CS: That leads into the next question. What are your thoughts on the term nerdlesque and the fact that you are credited as one of the pioneers of it?

N: I mean, labels help to sell things and define things. So I think it's fine. I don't hate it. I think though in such a short time it became, I don't know, you call something something, and somebody's going to have a problem with it. People had a problem with boylesque too.

It's interesting, of course, because it's one of the other things that I fight against. I was in a dressing room a year ago or so, and somebody was talking and they asked [another performer] "how was the festival you were at?" and the performer said "it was great, it was really cool, but all of a sudden they stopped the actual show and there was like a five number 'nerdlesque thing' in the middle where everyone was doing Star Wars things and I don't know, and then they got back to the actual show." I was like "umm, OK, I'm going to step outside for a minute." You know it's funny—there's a parallel for every sort of artistic complaint, thought, problem that you have with " regular burlesque" as there is with nerdlesque, you know?

CS: Yes.

N: Where I have a problem with the idea of nerdlesque is you just get applause because you are dressed like wonder woman, cool. But you also just get applause because your corset's really sparkly if you're doing classic burlesque. And there are plenty of numbers that are not particularly skilled but the costume is great. That like people are like, "oh my god she's so shiny." And I'm like, yup. "Oh my god she's so wonder woman," like yup. There you go. I'm not talking about any one specific act in mind or anything. But I try to use it a little bit

advisedly. I think there's enough people who get turned off by nerdlesque, because they're either, like, "I saw a nerdlesque thing and it was just a girl dressed like a whatever," but it think there are people who have the same complaints, about burlesque.

CS: Right.

N: "I saw burlesque, it was like a couple of girls in fishnets. And they weren't very good dancers." We did a show in Chicago and, you know, we booked it like a New York show—people were doing solo acts, and there was one host. I hosted and I did a couple acts, and a girl came up after. She was a local, and she was like "this is really good, and this is the first show I've been to. This was really fun, but what I really want to see is like, when there's like a lot of people on stage and they're all dressed the same and they're doing stuff." And I said "did you by any chance see that movie [*Burlesque*]?" And she said "Yeah, like that!" I said "Yeah, that's not so much what most people do. But I can give you some troupe names, since you're here." So, it's funny—I know people have whatever that version of nerdlesque is in their brain too.

CS: Expectations.

N: I think nerdlesque fosters as much innovation as regular burlesque. I have seen nerdlesque numbers that are transcendent. I think it has as much potential as other forms of striptease. I also think because the nerdlesque community is so open to performers of all genders and backgrounds; not that burlesque isn't, but I think that because corporate shows are not so much on the table. I know a con show can be higher profile, but I still think there's a little more like "fuck it we can do what we want" [in nerdlesque].

CS: Probably true. I think it goes both ways because you can get pigeon-holed easily in any category as a performer.

N: Absolutely.

CS: . I think a good thing a lot of burlesque performers do is break out of one pigeon hole, and show "No, I can do this too!"

N: I just did a show that was a combo of nerds and secret nerds. It was [classic] people like Qualms Galore and Angie Pontani doing numbers that are nerdlesque. I mean, Qualms Galore did a Geordi La Forge[22] number, and it was great. I love when somebody like that, she doesn't do "nerdlesque" [regularly]. It was lovely. I think it's fun. I also encourage people who say "I just do nerdlesque." I'm like cool—try another one, you might like it.

CS: Just for fun.

Figure 6.58 A promotional image from the 2010 film Burlesque, *starring Christina Aguilera, Cher, and Stanley Tucci.*
*(*Burlesque, *Christina Aguilera, 2010. Photo by Stephen Vaughan /©Screen Gems/Courtesy Everett Collection)*

N: Just for fun.

CS: This is a silly question in some ways because I don't know if anyone else has made pieces for you, but the question is who designs and makes your costumes? And when you're thinking about a whole ensemble for yourself how do you go about putting that together?

N: I have never had anybody else do a whole costume for me. Umm. Mostly because a) I'm a control freak, and b) I can't really afford to pay people what they're worth. I have one costume that I very specifically wanted a lot of people to make pieces of. So I had Dangrrr Doll do the headdress and Evelyn Vinyl do the cape for it, and Magdalena Fox did some gloves and some pieces.[23] Bb Heart rhinestoned it, because I hate doing that. And that was really fun. I still love wearing that because it's pieces from a lot people. Mostly these days I have Evelyn [Vinyl] make things that I can't. I'm shit with spandex; I'm still learning. I actually made Qualms' Geordi La Forge costume. I learned some **spandex** [technique] for her. She was very forgiving with that too. Usually, I have

Evelyn make that stuff for me because she is a genius with it. She either makes stuff for me, or she's like my "oh god what did I do wrong?" consultant.

CS: Your advisor.

N: Yes. For my own stuff … I don't really know where I always start. You know every number is different. Every act is different. So sometimes, if it's something really specific like "I want to be a sandwich,"[24] then it's more of a construction thing. I don't do a lot of just, a gown. I don't mean that like "just a gown" but every once in a while I have a couple numbers … I have some real specific guidelines: I don't do prints. I will for real clothes but for costumes I always go for bright, solid colors, and poly satins at $4.99 a yard.

CS: Cost effective.

N: And now, because I'm getting older and my body is changing, I think of a shape and then have to spend a month being like "you can't wear that anymore. It's not going to fit on your body anymore." So that's been a weird thing for me.

Figure 6.59 In Nasty's sewing room: A shelf of custom headdresses and her many Golden Pastie Awards from the New York Burlesque Festivals over the years.
(Photo by Coleen Scott)

CS: It's a shift.

N: Yes, it's strange. It's a physical shift.

CS: It's an adjustment.

N: From here to *here*. (Gestures downward)

> *[Laughter]*

CS: I know.

N: Then [design wise] I do my whole dollar store thing. When I do headdresses I hit dollar stores and, again because of my sort of OCD and type A-ness, I figure out absolutely every bit of it and make a giant list, and get everything and have one bin where I put all things that I could possibly need for this, and then just like dig in to it. I do very start to finish, like all at once. And when I try to make an act, where I'm like "I'm not going to do sketches; I'm not going to make a list; I don't have a due date. I have the music and I have the idea, I'm just going to work on pieces as it happens." It's been sitting in a bag in my workroom for a year and a half now. It's not done. I do have all the pieces for it. I just haven't done it. This summer I'm going to have to give myself a due date on that.

CS: Maybe this month.

N: This month, ah, maybe next month.

> *[Laughter]*

CS: How did you learn to sew? What's your training in costumes and construction?

N: So my grandmother, who was not a sewer, she was a knitter, she had a sewing machine. I don't know why she owned it, I don't think she ever used it.

CS: Because everybody owned one.

N: Because everybody owned one! My family being what it was, when she gave it to me in like '92, it still had the receipt in it box from 1970. In case she had to return it.

CS: Just in case.

N: Which I framed in my room. So I used that machine. I think I like bought, I mean it was the 90s, a mod dress pattern. Simplicity. And I was like "I'm just gonna learn how to do this." I've always been like "there's got to be a book about this somewhere." And I had home-ec class, they didn't call it that—whatever they were calling it in the late 80s—where we learned how to thread a sewing machine. And we made a pillow shaped like a pizza or whatever.

> *[Laughter]*

N: So I know how to thread a machine, and that sort of thing, so I just bought a pattern and figured it out. And then did a little bit more with that and library books.

And then in college I kind of did everything, I did set design, and costuming and all that. And then it was mostly after college I think I just, or during college outside of school. I just kept at it and figured it out, and started doing more stuff for myself. Before I was a burlesque performer I would just make costumes, and I didn't wear them. I just made them. I don't really know why. Like, to see if I could.

CS: Or it's just like an artist doing a sketch, you did that instead.

N: Yeah, I did that instead.

CS: Hmm.

N: Then a couple years ago a woman who used to be a performer, her performer name was Fleur de Lis, she has retired from performing. She had been an independent tailor and then she was hired to be the alterations manager at a bridal shop. And she brought me in as her assistant. And it ended up being a bad situation for her and it was tough for both of us, so I left shortly after she left, and she opened up her own shop. I worked with her about a year, actually as she was opening up. We were in some studio space, and then we were two studios and then we were three studios, and then we were in a store front and then two store fronts. So she's down in Gowanus and it just became too much time for me. We were the only ones, and we had people come in and do some piece work and stuff too. But, she was amazing. She was the most skilled tailor I have ever [met]. It was incredible. She was so skilled and she brought me in, and I was like "You know I don't really know what I'm doing right?" And she was like "You know how to sew. I've seen the stuff you've made. I can teach you everything else." So the, the speed and the volume that we were working at just to pay the rent on these places, I mean. She took in way more work than we could handle really, but we did it. She did it, and I helped. I learned so much real tailoring from her.

CS: That's great.

N: I still make stuff for myself and—you fake stuff. I'm the only one who's going to know, who the fuck cares? Doing costuming for other people, that I'm like "Oh I actually like have to make this look good." But we're talking (bridal)—we did some $5000 gowns, and some bridezillas. You've got to make this shit for real. So I learned the techniques and I learned the speed from her, and that was absolutely amazing. Now, it's funny, every once in a while I'll be working on stuff and come out and my partner will be sitting here and I'll be like

"I just need to say I'm really impressed with myself, cause I just made a thing that the one I made four years ago looks like crap and the one I made now looks really good, so ..." It's just nice to see as I'm basically self-taught and then working with her was the only sort of formal training I had. I'm still progressing and I'm actually really proud of myself and really impressed when I'm like "oh this looks great, and I know what I'm doing."

CS: That's awesome, and you keep working at it. So you work with **commercial patterns**?

N: Yes I do.

CS: You've made suits, for a lot of people.

N: Mhmm.

CS: More tailored-looking things.

N: I haven't done it in years. I haven't made a full suit. And I'm actually curious [to do it again]. I absolutely started with commercial patterns. It's still my go to for stuff.

CS: It's mine too. Because it often takes less time to get started.

N: It is less time. And I obviously never learned patterning. So I've been trying to figure out if there's like a class I can take or something.

CS: There are a lot of classes, you've just got to see which ones aren't $5000. Mood Fabrics has them.

N: Exactly. Maybe that's a thing.

CS: I don't think that they are that expensive. They might be free and you buy the supplies, something like that.

N: Oh. That might be great. Because I also don't want the ones where it's "we teach you how to make a skirt with an elastic waistband." I get that, I know that. So what I've what I've gotten better at, and what I know, and what I'm still working on is altering patterns to suit my needs.

CS: Yes, sometimes the shapes are so odd for things.

N: Exactly.

CS: That if you can just get the right first shape you can do whatever you need. And it saves so much more time. I feel like. You know. I do both. I don't do the really complicated ones, I just get the shape I want because it exists out there in a pattern.

N: Yes. Exactly.

CS: You can get a paper pattern. On eBay for whatever for five bucks and its going to save me four hours of my time.

N: Exactly, and then when I'm sewing for other people. That means you know less money for them too. So.

CS: Exactly.

Figure 6.60 Nasty wears her Coney Island costume at The Coney Island sideshow theater, August 21, 2009. (Photo by Norman Blake)

CS: Alright so that's your sewing background. Now, what acts do you think are your most well-known acts? And then maybe give a little description of your costumes for them.

N: Oddly enough, those ones are not …

CS: Not very costume-y.

N: Not very costume-y yeah.

[Laughter]

N: My fan dance is … my fan dance is to car alarms and I'm literally wearing—when I can get away with it—a merkin, or when I have to—underwear, and big white fans that Rose Wood made for me 15 years ago. Another act, Unknown Stripper, which is a very classic number with Groucho Marx glasses and that dress. It's a black sequin cocktail dress that Creamy Stevens bought in a box lot of dresses on eBay or something. That one didn't fit her and she's like "do you want this, I think it will fit you." And 15 years later, 13 years later whatever, that's the dress for that.

[Laughter]

CS: What do you think one of your most intricate costumes is? Even if it's not a well-known act.

N: My Coney Island act is probably one of the more intricate ones. And it's funny because I've built that one twice. I retired it then somebody asked me to donate the costume to the Coney Island Museum and then somebody asked me to bring it to Vegas for a show and I was like "I will rebuild it if you fly me to Vegas, sure."

[Laughter]

N: That one has all sorts of pieces. I mean it's got a mask, and a lot of painting. There's a fake sideshow banner, and all sorts of stuff. So that one's really in depth, and I do that rarely because I don't think it reads much outside of really even Brooklyn.

CS: Do you have photos of that?

N: I do, or there are Norman Blake photos.

CS: I'll ask Norman then.

N: Actually, a lot of the really intricate costume ones [are] the ones that have come and gone.

CS: Hmm.

N: I did one a couple years ago, that I loved actually, but it was when Diane Nagle passed. I inherited a lot of her supplies. She had a lot of leather scraps and feathered things, and there were a lot of organic things. So I just had this bag of those things, and another friend of mine is a sort of fashion-y person. She inspired me and I was looking at some Thierry Mugler stuff from the 90s. Then I also brought in some Coney Island stuff. Fiji mermaid. So I did a number that was, basically, I wanted it to be transformative. It went from reptile to bird to mammal. And I really loved it. There were 18 layers to this frickin' costume. The sort of tail was made out of these leather pieces. And there was a **harness** with feathers with wings. And just this giant hair piece. I had to sew stuff into my hair. I think I did it three times cause it was a lot of work.

CS: I get it.

N: Again, another one of those costumes that weighed 40 pounds.

CS: It's just an event to do the act.

N: It took up space; it was an event. And then people would either ask me to do Unknown Stripper or I was like "I don't want to carry this frickin thing right now." So that just kinda came and went.

CS: Are there pictures of that one?

N: Some really bad ones.

        [Laughter]

N: I can dig some up.

CS: Do you have it? Do you have pieces still?

N: No I gave it away, well I have one piece left. I kept one of the corsets, that I now use for something else. Everything else I sort of reuse. God, I was adding trim to something the other day and was like "this is the fourth costume I've used this fringe on."

        [Laughter]

CS: That's good. You recycle so you're not rebuying, and it is was expensive in the first place, use it for everything you can. Right?

N: That's the dollar store manifesto, man.

CS: What came first for you—costume or performance?

N: Performance in general. Because I started in theater and all that, but with specific numbers it's always different now I think. There is stuff where I'm like oh my god I should do a ...

CS: When you're thinking of something new, you mean?

N: Yes, I think it's very specific to the act.

Figure 6.61 A teacup filled with rogue rhinestones that await a new home adorns Nasty's pattern shelf.
(Photo by Coleen Scott)

CS: It's nice when you know how to do costumes, cause it can be organic either way.

N: Right, absolutely. I'm super fortunate in that way. I mean, I horde enough in that tiny room that when I have an idea I can probably make pieces anyway.

CS: Yes.

N: I can't always do the performance that's in my head, but you know. "And then there's cartwheels and then ..." No.

CS: No.

        [Laughter]

N: No, I can't do that.

CS: Do you have a favorite costume-making tip? Or costume reveals that you like the best in burlesque? Or both?

N: I am butt-obsessed. So I put an ass reveal in everything.

        [Laughter]

N: I also do a lot of stuff with my butt crack, so it's why I get very frustrated down south where they have their ABC laws where you can't show butt crack. And I'm like "I don't have an act, it's not even showing. I can't do half of the stuff I do, because I need to use my butt."

CS: I can't hold things!

N: I can't hold things.

        [Laughter]

N: That's for my own stuff. I love transformations in costumes. I love that you can literally just go from a cocktail gown to a samba outfit. I'm not super great at that. Medianoche has got some pieces like that. And Miss Tickle builds stuff like that. I want to crawl around in her brain some day.

CS: Me too. Do you have thoughts about cultural appropriation in burlesque specifically? And do you have thought about your former character that was Japanese anime inspired? [referring to Kobayashi Maru]

N: I don't do her anymore because I don't think it's OK.

CS: OK.

N: That was an evolution on my own.

CS: All of us have those.

N: Yeah, absolutely. When it comes down to it. I'm a White lady. So I'm going to shut up and listen to what people have to say about this.

CS: That's kinda where I'm at.

N: There are things, in general. There's one act that was not based on anything. Literally. Was not based on anything. And an audience member was like, "oh, oh I don't know if that's really OK." Oh, you know what? I'm gonna stop doing it then." It was not like, is it appropriate for somebody to be doing a samba act? And I'm, like, it's not a samba act. But if it reads like that, OK not going to do it. In general, I think there are other choices, other options. I don't know. I think where I want people to put the brakes on is you know, listening goes both ways. There's a very knee jerk reaction—I know on *Ru Paul's Drag Race*, Ruth or Dare is an amazing performer, she's a native performer—she's Canadian. She does not "look native" she looks like a white lady with blonde hair. So when she did a performance that was very rooted in her personal traditions and her family traditions. There was initially a lot of outcry about that, and she was like "woah woah woah." So … you know at the same time, if a French girl wears blackface for a fucking number[25]… like let's not fucking do that. Let's just, come ooonnnnn.

CS: Boundaries.

N: I would love people to … and I know, I am a White lady. My family is Italian. I have a very strong connection to them. I'm second generation American.

CS: Yes.

N: Italian American. I also find I'm more Italian-American than Italian. There's stuff with that I work with on stage all the (time). I was raised Catholic. And I'm like, that's still in there. I'm still working through a lot of stuff. A lot of that iconography a lot of that. So, for me, I think I

would love people, instead of "but I wanna do a Mexican hat dance."

CS: Use your own experience.

N: Look at some of your own stuff. Use it as an opportunity to explore your own background. If there's nothing in there that speaks to you, then that's fine. But I don't know. The are other ways, other stories to be told. It's interesting, [I was] talking to somebody backstage the other day [saying] that they had seen a very traditional male and a female burlesque duet. One male and one female performer. And the dynamic was very much, the male was the aggressor, the female was threatened. And because of whatever this threat was her clothes came off, I don't know (I didn't see the number) if he also stripped. I think it was based on a fairy tale or something … Didn't see the number. I don't know the number. Didn't look at a video. Don't know the performers.

CS: I think it was BHOF. A little red riding hood act. I haven't seen it either. But it won best duet.

N: Yes, and just talking about this, and hearing about it, I'm always a little disappointed when that is the narrative. It's a perfectly valid narrative, if that's the story you want to tell. I just think there are more interesting stories to tell. That story has been told a lot of times.

CS: It has.

N: I try to look at it like … that is your story to tell if you want to tell it. There are stories that aren't mine to tell. So where I have a (problem), and this is not an anger thing, this is not a "but I should be able to." This is my question, or my sort of thought—costuming, clothing, the things we wear on our bodies in 2018 in the United States are so influenced by other things. I know like to literally put a native headdress on my head is absolutely inappropriate.

CS: Right.

N: That's not my story to tell. Like at what point—is that where wearing feathers on a hat comes from? So now whatever the progression of that history is—is any feather on a hat, whatever the hat, is *that* then appropriation? I don't know. Language evolves, clothing evolves, and nobody is in a vacuum. So I'm interested in at what point it becomes OK, not so I can finally do it, but I'm just interested in at what point like—who invented pants? should we all be wearing pants? Like what would we do?

CS: Right.

N: it's interesting

CS: Where the lines are.

N: Yeah. I think there are a lot of lines that are absolutely clear.

CS: Yes, there are. There are many clear ones.

N: And then there are a lot of lines that as a White lady, I'm like "it's fine." And somebody else might say "umm not fine." And I think OK. Let's …

CS: … have a conversation about it. And learn things. Cultural appreciation vs appropriation.

N: Yes.

CS: Yeah. OK, last question.

N: Mhmm (affirmative).

CS: What is burlesque? And what does it mean to you? But, really, what is your definition of burlesque?

N: When random drunk people in bars ask "what do you do? What even is that?" I basically say the most encompassing version of it too. That it is theatrical striptease.

CS: That's good.

N: That's your two-word definition. Can there be variety numbers in a burlesque show? Yes. At its heart, it is theatrical striptease, and that is what it is for me too. Actually, it is interesting—in a "why do you do the art you do?" class that I teach sometimes, I ask people to define what they do.

CS: Interesting.

N: I know at one point, I don't know if this is still true, Gal Friday described herself as a burlesque stripper. Other people describe themselves as burlesque dancers, I don't say burlesque dancer, because I don't dance. Like, I move without falling over if I'm lucky. But I'm not a dancer, because I'm an asshole. I tend to say neo-ecdysiast because I think that encompasses both denotatively and connotatively what it is that I do. But I think that it's an interesting thing, when you ask people that. I think more dancers do say "I'm a burlesque dancer." When I can't use words like ecdysiast because I'm too drunk or they're too drunk, I will say burlesque performer.

CS: Most people can't … they're like "what is that …?"

N: And it's not a real word actually. I think at its heart there is an element of stripping. I know you don't have to strip. But I think that, that at its heart. And for me, it is story telling with butts.

            [Laughter]

CS: Good. And what does it mean to you?

N: for me it continues to be the culmination of all the artistic things that I have either learned, studied, absorbed, fallen into. Because even if you're not writing and producing scripted shows, I mean you're still writing a (narrative). It's all you.

CS: Yes.

N: If you want to work that way, and the way that most of us work. You can pick the song, you can create the song or soundscape if you want. Then everything that you put on stage comes from you, there's not a director and a writer and a costumer and stage manager and a this and a that telling you how to do.

CS: That's what I like about it.

N: Yes me too.

NERDLESQUE

Nerdlesque has become its own category and style of burlesque. The first festival specifically celebrating nerdlesque was started by a group of New York City performers in 2014[26], and since then, other nerdlesque festivals have been organized in cities like New Orleans and Kansas City. Nerdlesque acts are regularly seen in non-specific burlesque festivals as well, but nerd-centric festivals tend to include some of the more "inside" and specifically referenced acts that a broader audience would be less likely to recognize.

Figure 6.62
Nasty Canasta in a
Dr. Who themed
costume.
(Photo by Ben Trivett)

Figure 6.63
Clockwise from top left: Miss Mary Cyn as The Joker, Poison Ivory as Lana from Archer, Lux LaCroix as Rocket Racoon from Guardians of the Galaxy, Hazel Honeysuckle as an Ent from Lord of the Rings, Fem Appeal as Blade, Elsa Riot as Pikachu from Pokeman. (Photos by Ben Trivett)

COSPLAY WITH STELLA CHUU

Nerdlesque lends itself to the world of **cosplay**, where people dress up as their favorite anime, cartoon, superhero, or other popular culture characters and attend special **cons**, where they can meet their favorite cosplayers, buy merch, socialize, and exchange tips on costuming. Many cons hire burlesque performers to put on nerdlesque shows. For example, Stella Chuu and her co producer Dangrrr Doll have been putting on the Comicon Vixens show during New York Comicon for years. Stella Chuu is a New York City (and now Southern California-based) burlesque performer who transitioned almost completely into a career in cosplay. Like many cosplay stars, she has a massive social media following and makes a living through sponsorships, online gaming and photo sales of her portraits in costume. Stella has become a fantastic costume maker, and has a YouTube channel where she posts tutorials on how she creates her intricate costumes. One of her materials of choice is **Worbla**—a non-toxic **thermoplastic** that comes in multiple colors and formulas making it easy to create rigid costume shapes. This material has become a cosplay staple, and is one of the reasons Worbla has gotten so much attention in the costume and prop building world.

Figure 6.64 *Burlesque dancer turned cosplayer Stella Chuu in her self-made breakfast burlesque costume.* *(Photo by Ben Trivett)*

From Stella regarding her thoughts about the differences
between cosplay and burlesque[27]:

*Burlesque helped open me up to a world of body positivity that I think the
cosplay community is still struggling to find. I was able to overcome a lot of
my own issues and it allowed me to go further with my cosplays. I wasn't held
back by low self-confidence or embarrassment. If more people learned to love
their own bodies and everyone else's bodies, we could grow a lot more as a
community.*

*Figure 6.65 Stella Chuu in her self-made Pharah from Overwatch cosplay costume.
(Photo by Sorairo-Days. Instagram: @sorairo_days and FB: sorairodayscosplay)*

MODERN DRAG

The art forms of drag and burlesque developed separately in the U.S., and for different audiences, but elements of both have intertwined over the years. Over the last decade of neo burlesque especially, drag has become a popular mode of performance, and a number of modern drag queens have been using striptease technique and costuming in their acts.

Sasha Velour is a Brooklyn, New York drag queen and winner of *RuPaul's Drag Race* Season 9. Sasha's winning lip sync act included a very neo-burlesque wig reveal and glove peel and triggered this author's realization about the influence modern burlesque and drag are having on each other. Sasha is a graphic designer, and has created an incredible fashion aesthetic in gowns and costumes by Diego Montoya 3-D. Sasha is an admired spokesperson for the modern drag world, and has a clear belief in acceptance and inclusion, popular topics of discussion in the United States burlesque community.

A hopeful note about Sasha's artistic inspirations and goals:

I look to people who made a huge cultural impact. The one who's really a huge inspiration is Keith Haring because the political message was so simple and empowering, of love and brotherhood and sisterhood throughout our community, across communities, and especially in urban spaces. But it was conveyed through the most recognizable, accessible, beautiful and simple artwork. And it's joyful. I intuitively understood it even as a kid, even if I didn't understand the context of what was going on with AIDS at the time. That's the kind of art that I'd like to create, art that's a part of pop culture connected with political ideas.[28]

Figure 6.66 *Sasha Velour in Diego Montoya 3D. IslyNY earrings (Photo by Mettie Ostrowski)*

Figure 6.67 *From left to right: The first King of Boylesque, Tigger! by Atticus Stevenson; Boys Night Cirquelesque by Ben Trivett; Chicago's Stage Door Johnnies by Kaylin Idora; 2017 King of Boylesque, Lou Henry Hoover by Ben Trivett.*

BOYLESQUE

I've never been interested in breaking burlesque down into categories. Boylesque—Nerdlesque—Queerlesque etc. ... I'm more focused on coming up with new ways to look like a professional idiot while taking off my clothes. Much like my performances I believe putting too much structure, clarification or titles on live art limits the chance for something brilliantly tragic to take place. Sometimes just throwing your g-string against the wall and seeing what sticks is most satisfying ... well ... woops ... I guess that sounds kinda gross ... but ya know what I mean.

(Mr. Gorgeous, New York City, NY)[29]

Boylesque is male-presenting burlesque, or burlesque performed by men. Boylesque performers can be cis men, trans men, or women in drag. The costumes of boylesque have similar elements as burlesque costumes, although there are more tearaway pants and shirts and significantly fewer gowns. For obvious reasons, the g-string for male dancers is shaped slightly differently than a woman's to accommodate for male genitals. This version is lovingly referred to as a **banana hammock**, and there are thong styles that are a more substantial garment, worn as the final underlayer, or over a g-string. Some performers wear merkins adhered to the pelvic area with pouches that then cup the testicles and penis, and some performers, like Tigger! are known for wearing a sock-like cover or going nude when allowed.

The establishment of a "boylesque" category of burlesque competition in the United States occurred semi-officially in 2006 when Tigger! won the first "King of Boylesque" trophy at the Exotic World Competition, but before that, men who did burlesque, **drag kings**, or male exotic dancers were just that, and did not self-identify as "boylesquers." In a society that drives to categorize everything, burlesque had been roped in. In 2017, cis- female and drag king Lou Henry Hoover won the title of King of Boylesque at The Burlesque Hall of Fame Weekender,[30] and set an example and a precedent that performers should not have to choose the category of their cis gender when they apply to for the annual event. Because of the community acceptance of performers who choose to present in multiple ways on the burlesque stage, the lines of categorization of boylesque, queerlesque and burlesque are blurring for the better.

Even now, as the burlesque revival evolves in an international environment, women, men, non-binary, trans, or however a person identifies and then chooses to present on stage, it is authenticity, creativity, self-possession, and self-love that entices people to enter the world of burlesque performance. Looking to the future, it is this author's hope that the burlesque community continues to grow and celebrate diversity, acceptance, and self-expression through our mutual love of costume.

Notes

1   Patreon is a web-based platform specifically geared toward performers and artists being able to generate sustainable income. See: www.Patreon.com.

2   This list of companies and designers was compiled from individual submissions to a Facebook poll by the author of 2,500 burlesque performers in January 2018.

3   This email interview transcript is from April 2018.

4   This email interview transcript is from April 2018.

5   The Atomic Bombshells is a troupe started by Kitten La Rue and Fanny N Flames in Seattle, 2003.

6   Quotes included in this showcase on Gin Minsky are from a brief interview with the author during a photo shoot with Ben Trivett on March 24, 2018.

7   *Ru Paul's Drag Race* is a reality competition television show that started on the Logo TV network in 2009 and moved to VH1 in its ninth season in 2017. The mission of the show each season is to crown drag's next superstar.

8   Previously published on thepastieproject.com, October 17, 2017.

9   Bella's pasties can be found at www.bellastchotchkis.com.

10 These examples of modern burlesque pasties were published previously in the book *The Pastie Project*, written by the author under the pen name Rosey La Rouge in 2017. The book provides information on many more pastie makers worldwide and a detailed history of the pastie and its construction.

11 *21st Century Burlesque* is a publication and website that features prominent burlesque personalities. It was founded by editor Holli Mae Johnson in 2008, and it's annual "Burlesque Top 50" lists are voted on by the global burlesque community, and are highly regarded ratings for who's who in burlesque.

12 This quote is from a conversation between Darlinda Just Darlinda and the author during a photo shoot with Ben Trivett on March 10, 2018.

13 For more about Darlinda Just Darlinda's *Year in Rainbow*. www.youtube.com/watch?v=cR0TuncVs2s

14 This quote is from a conversation between Cheeky Lane and the author during a photo shoot with Ben Trivett on March 10, 2018

15 Quotes from Gin Minsky are from a brief interview with the author during a photo shoot with Ben Trivett on March 24, 2018

16 Interview date: June 9, 2018.

17 Galapagos was a Williamsburg, Brooklyn, event venue that hosted live entertainment, including burlesque, in the late 1990s and early 2000s. It moved to a newer event venue in DUMBO, Brooklyn, in 2008, and closed in 2014 with the intention to move to Detroit where costs were lower and would make it easier to continue with its mission as an incubator for young artists. www.galapagosdetroit.com and more info on the move: http://gothamist.com/2014/12/08/galapagos_detroit.php

18 Nasty and Veronica produced a series of burlesque shows in New York under the "Sweet N Nasty" name.

19 The original Exotic World Museum was on a goat farm in Helendale, California. It was run by burlesque legend Jennie Lee, and her friend Dixie Evans took operations over after Jennie died in 1991 from breast cancer. The annual Miss Exotic World competitions were held on the farm, but in the early 2000s, the event was relocated to a venue in downtown Las Vegas.

20 Boo Bess and Jenny C'est Quoi are New York City burlesque performers who won the award for Most Innovative at The Burlesque Hall of Fame Competition in 2018 for their act "The Passenger".

21 Miss Tickle is known for her fantastic costumes and original, surprising performances.

22 Geordi La Forge is a *Star Trek: The Next Generation* character played by LeVar Burton.

23 Dangrrr Doll is in Raleigh, North Carolina, and specializes in cosplay and burlesque. Evelyn Vinyl is a performer and costumer based in Nashville with the costume company Blue Lawless, and Magdalena Fox owns Booty and the Geek out of Brooklyn, New York.

24 Nasty has a well-known act where she wears a large sandwich-in-a-plastic-baggie costume and strips out of it.

25 In March of 2017, Eight cast members of the Toulouse Burlesque Festival quit in protest of Fafa Bulleuse's Nina Simone tribute act, which involved her using blackface. More info: http://21stcenturyburlesque.com/toulouse-burlesque-festival-blackface-racist-cast-walkout/

26 In 2014 the first Nerdlesque Festival was started by Nelson Lugo and produced by Lefty Lucy, Anja Keister, Iris Explosion, Magdalena Fox, Stella Chuu, and Dangrrr Doll in New York City. (Info from Lefty Lucy)

27 This quote from Stella Chuu is from an email conversation with the author in September, 2018.

28 https://observer.com/2017/03/sasha-velour-rupauls-drag-race-interview-logo/

29 Quote from Mr. Gorgeous is from an email exchange with the author on September 28, 2018

30 The Exotic World Competition has become the Burlesque Hall of Fame Weekender, as the museum moved to Las Vegas in 2010 and is now called The Burlesque Hall of Fame Museum.

Figure 6.68 The Atomic Bombshells promo, 2016. From left: Mr. Gorgeous, Lou Henry Hoover,
Kitten LaRue, The Maine Attraction, and Victoria DeVille.
(Photo by Ben Trivett)

ACKNOWLEDGEMENTS

Thanks to all those who made this book possible—the museums, libraries, photographers, photo collections, collectors, mentors, and cheerleaders. Special thanks to Stacy Walker and Lucia Accorsi at Routledge, Taylor & Francis for your encouragement, support, and advice. Kris Siosyte and Ting Baker, thanks for stellar production and copy edits. To Harriet Reed and Helen Gush and the Victoria and Albert Cloth Workers Centre, The Bath Fashion Museum, The Museum of the City of New York, Michelle McVicker and The Museum at FIT, The J. Paul Getty Museum, The Metropolitan Museum, and the Smithsonian Institution, thank you for viewing appointments, for answering questions and sending approvals, and for keeping burlesque costume history alive in your collections.

To the Library of Congress, New York Public Library, and Everett Collection, thanks for droves of images. Unending gratitude to Rebecca Jewett at the Jerome Lawrence and Robert E. Lee Theater Research Institute at The Ohio State University for helping so much in my research of the invaluable McCaghy Collection. To Mark Schmitt at Illinois State University and the Ueckert Collection of circus memorabilia—thank you for your fast and thorough work. To the Textbook and Academic Authors Association—thank you for a whirlwind education in this specialized area of writing, and for being so welcoming.

To the United States Institute for Theater Technology thanks for being a petri dish for ideas like this one, and a platform for new authors in technical theater and academics to find a publisher. Thanks to Miss Indigo Blue and BurlyCon for being the best source for burlesque education in the universe, and for allowing me to present my research with kind and constructive feedback. Thanks to Ed Barnas and Dr. Lucky PhD for advising me through the proposal process, and to Margaret Raywood at NYU for reading it. Thank you to all the photographers, friends, and new acquaintances who contributed to this book in any way—especially Angie Pontani, April March, Bella La Blanc, Bic Carroll, Billie Madley, Bridget's Closet, Camille 2000, Catherine D'Lish, Cheeky Lane, Danielle Colby, Darlinda Just Darlinda, David Byrd,, Dirty Martini, Dita Von Teese, Don Spiro, Fatema Gharzai, Garo Sparo, Gin Minsky, Jajas Garden, James Andrew Ridley, Jamie Von Stratton, Jian Bastille, Judith Stein, Kitten Natividad, Laura Byrnes, Lauren Stevens, Leslie Zemeckis, Lorelei Fuller, Luke Littell, Michelle Carr, Mr. Gorgeous, Nasty Canasta, Olena Sullivan, Ronald Seymour, Ronnie Magri, Satan's Angel, Stella Chuu, Stephanie Blake, Sydni Devereaux, Tiffany Carter, Tigger!, Tony Morando, Vicky Butterfly, and everyone who contributed to The Pastie Project. To my New York City burlesque family—I love you; thank you for including me since 2008.

Thanks to Dustin Wax and the Burlesque Hall of Fame Museum in Las Vegas for your help, and for keeping the dream of Dixie Evans and Jennie Lee alive and growing. To Jo Weldon—thank you for your friendship, mentorship and for modeling how to pursue your dreams and make them reality. To Neil "Nez" Kendall, Janelle Smith, and my husband, Ben Trivett—there really would be no book without you, your generosity, and your passion for burlesque history.

GLOSSARY

Act—a performance that is usually one part of a larger show or presentation. It can be a group or solo presentation.

Aerial—a performance style that involves using suspended apparatus like silks, lyra, or pole. Performances include dance and gymnastic movement and require strength and flexibility.

Aggressive Art—A term coined by burlesque legend Camille 2000 to describe her avant-garde approach to burlesque in the late 1960s and 1970s.

Animal act—a burlesque or variety act that employs a live animal.

Appliqué—A decorative accent applied to a garment or fabric; often a piece that is attached around its perimeter. A patch is a type of appliqué.

Art Deco—a decorative style that began in the 1920s and 1930s. Geometric shapes and strong colors are part of this style that can be seen in architecture, furniture and textiles.

Assels—pasties that are applied on the buttocks, most often with tassels for twirling.

Avant garde burlesque—A conceptual style that developed in the neo-burlesque movement. Avant garde burlesque is closer to performance art while still involving striptease.

Balloon dance—A burlesque or variety act where a performer wears an outfit made of balloons and through the course of the act, pops them or has the audience do so to reveal more of what's underneath. This was popular in the 1960s, but an altered version is seen as early as the 19-teens in Ziegfeld's Midnight Frolic.

Banana hammock—a men's g-string style that has thin straps and a fabric pouch to contain male genitalia. This term can also apply to a men's thong.

Barker—a travelling carnival or circus sideshow employee with the job of describing attractions to passers-by with the goal of filling seats and selling tickets.

Bellydance—known first as the "hoochie-coochie" dance, this dance style involves fluid pelvic undulations and arm movements, as well as strong muscle control for isolations of the ribcage and hips.

Bias—in garment making: 45 degrees diagonal from the straight of grain. Using this diagonal line as the straight grain with woven fabrics creates stretch. Bias draping was used in the 1930s to achieve close fitting shapes without using stretch knit.

Bloomers—an undergarment similar in structure to shorts with waist and sometimes leg openings gathered to control volume. Length can range from waist to upper thigh, all the way to the mid-calf.

Body double—a person who stands in for a leading actor in a film especially common in scenes with nudity.

Bodysuit—a fitted garment that closely follows the line of the body. A full bodysuit covers the arms and legs, but there are partial versions that are sleeveless and pants-less, or with cropped legs.

Boylesque—a style of burlesque performed by men or male-presenting performers.

Breastplate bra—a bra made of two circular metal plates with ornate decoration including relief designs and colored stones in settings. The plates are joined by chain or links in the center front and attach to the body with chains or straps around the neck and ribcage. These bras are commonly seen at the turn of the twentieth century in stage productions of *Salome* or in non-descript oriental production designs.

British Blondes—the name for Lydia Thompson's burlesque troupe as advertised in the 1860s. The women bleached their hair or wore blonde wigs on stage, which generated the moniker.

Bubble dance—a burlesque or variety performance where a dancer uses a giant balloon prop. The balloon is tossed in the air and, while it floats, the performer can dance or remove clothing. In modern translations, performers like Julie Atlas Muz have worked with bubbles large enough to get inside as part of the act.

Buckram—A stiff, mesh material used for making hats. It is the most common base for pasties.

Bugle bead—a bead that is shaped like a long hollow tube. They come in varying lengths.

Bullet bra—a bra developed in the 1950s that has conical cups shaped to a point. The silhouette created by the bra is pointy like the tops of bullets or torpedoes. Also known as a "torpedo bra."

Bump—see also **Bump and grind**—a dance move that consists of quickly thrusting the pelvis forward, or side to side, usually on a strong beat of the music. Often used in a combination with a "grind."

Bump and grind—a sensual burlesque dancing style popular in the 1950s and later that includes circular hip gyrations called the "grind" and fast thrusting in forward or side to side direction called a "bump." This combination of movements is done in coordination to music that emphasizes both styles.

Burlesque—post 1920: striptease performance that includes theatricality, narrative, and/or the illusion of ultimate glamour.

Burlesques—satirical performances of a popular play or storyline, sometimes with all-female casts.

Burlesque circuit—a number of collaborative or member theaters in multiple cities and states that constitute stops on a burlesque tour.

Burlesque theater—a theater that specializes in burlesque performance, specifically solo performers doing burlesque acts. Before the 1970s, burlesque theaters hosted burlesque shows that involved solo performers, comics and group numbers.

Busk—The center front, boned closure on a corset made up of two sides—one with evenly spaced small knobs and the other with round, flat hooks to fit over the knobs for a secure and rigid structure.

Bustle—a gathered flounce of fabric added to the back of a costume or belt that adds volume, and alters the silhouette. In the late 1800s, the bustle was formed by a cage shape worn over the buttocks and under the skirts creating an extended rear silhouette.

C-string—a wired, c-shaped undergarment worn by strippers and burlesque performers that covers the front pubic area and curves between the buttocks, holding it in place.

Cabinet card—from the Victorian era: a collectible card with a portrait or image that was saved in albums (and stored in cabinets), which were then shown to guests as a popular pastime.

Camp—exaggerated, over the top and farcical humor in performance.

Can-can—a French chorus girl dance that includes very high kicks and voluminous skirts lined in ruffles or with layered petticoats.

Canned music—recorded music.

Carte de viste—from the mid-late 1800s and turn of the twentieth century, collectible postcards. Subject matter could range from landscape to portraits of performers of the stage, circus and sideshow.

Chainette fringe—fringe made of rayon or other synthetic fiber that is held together with a chainstitch.

Chair work—in burlesque, using movement on a chair as part of the choreography in an act.

Chaps—leggings without a seat and joined at the waistband. Often in leather. Chaps are worn over other pants as protection for cowboys, but in burlesque, they are usually worn with a thong or g-string.

Cheesecake—another term for pin-up photos or magazines.

Chiffon-a sheer, flowing fabric that drapes softly. Chiffon can be made from silk or synthetic fibers like polyester.

Chippendales—a group of male exotic dancers that were organized in New York in 1979.

Chorus girl—a member of the chorus in a stage show or musical.

Classic burlesque—burlesque style that evokes the "classic" style of the golden age of burlesque, including a glamorous ensemble and no narrative.

Clubs—in the 1940s and later, venues that might feature burlesque, but also require dancers to mingle with the audience members to sell drinks. In the mid-1960s and beyond, clubs were also referred to as strip clubs.

Columbia Wheel—one branch of the burlesque circuit functioning from 1902 to 1927 including New York, and extending east of the Missouri river, north of the Ohio, and into the Canadian cities of Toronto and Montreal.

Commercial pattern—a printed, graded sewing pattern produced by a company to be used for the home sewer or costumer.

Conjoined twins—twin siblings who are adjoined, sharing a body part and/or organs.

Cons—short for conferences, usually related to a common interest or hobby.

Cooch dancer—an early bellydancer or striptease performer in the cooch tent in a circus sideshow or midway.

Cooch tent—the tent that housed dancing women in a circus sideshow or midway

Cornely sequin machine—A specialized sewing machine that stitches slung sequins onto fabric in intricate patterns from the bottom, so that the operator can draw patterns as they sew.

Corset cover—a cotton or silk sleeveless undershirt that is worn over a corset and under the outer garments.

Corset—a structured undergarment common in the mid-1800s through the turn of the twentieth century that is tightly laced around the bust, torso and high hip to create a desired silhouette. The structure is created with "boning," rigid vertical strips sewn into casings along the garment's seams that were made of whale bone and, later, steel.

Cosplay—an activity that involves dressing in costume like a favorite pop culture or mythical character and sometimes taking on their persona in person or on camera.

Costume jewelry—jewelry that looks like real precious stones and metals, but is made of synthetic versions.

Craft foam-thin (1/16–1/8") EVA foam that is made in numerous colors and is sold by the sheet or roll. A popular material for pasties and cosplay costume pieces.

Crinoline—the material crinoline is a stiff mesh used to create volume under garments. The garment crinoline is a skirt made of ruffles of net that creates volume under a short, mid-length or long full skirt.

"Dance of the Seven Veils"—the dance mentioned in the Old Testament and other religious documents that was used by a female character to free a lover from hell, or in the tale of Salome, to persuade a ruler to kill and enemy. The dance involves the removal of veils, one at a time.

"Danse Sauvage"—the name for Josephine Baker's famous banana dance.

Deviant—in the twentieth century, people who strayed from the accepted social norm were all considered deviants with more or less extremity. This included strippers, punks, fetishists, homosexuals, and members of the trans and queer community. The term is used in relation to these groups in formal psychology and sociology texts late into the twentieth century.

DIY—An acronym for "Do It Yourself"; also a word meaning self-made.

Dominatrix—a female or feminine-presenting person who dominates self-identified submissives, often in a sexual situation, as a profession.

Drag— 1. To dress in a costume that is either for the opposite gender that a person identifies with, or to dress in a costume that is an exaggerated representation of a gender. 2. The makeup worn by drag queens or burlesque performers.

Drag king—traditionally a cis-woman or trans man dressed in an exaggerated, hyper-masculinized or satirical costume who performs comedy, lip sync or dance, including burlesque.

Drag queen—traditionally, a cis-man dressed in an exaggerated, hyper-feminized costume who performs comedy, lip sync or dance, including burlesque.

Draped—see **draping**.

Draping—a way to design and construct clothing that entails organically sculpting garment and pattern shapes directly on a dress form.

Dressing gowns—similar to a robe, but, in modern day, implying more fabric volume, embellishment or detail, and frequently made in chiffon or satin. See: Duster.

Duster—similar to a dressing gown. An embellished or voluminous robe or coat. In burlesque, a duster is frequently made of organza and embellished with ruffles or feathers.

E6000—a strong adhesive used by theatrical craftspeople and burlesque costumers to add rhinestones to garments (a newer version specifically for fabric is called E6000 Fabric Fuse).

E6000 Fabri-Fuse—see E6000.

Ecdysiast—a word devised by linguist and writer H.L. Mencken synonymous with stripper, or one who takes off their clothes.

Embellishment—decoration.

Exotic dance—another term for stripping or striptease.

Exotic dancer—another term for stripper, ecdysiast or burlesque dancer.

Exotic—1. Of an ethnicity other than Caucasian (in relation to burlesque pre-1960s). 2. Sensual or sexual (in relation to burlesque and stripping post 1960s)

Exploitation films—films that explore controversial or sensational subjects to attract an audience.

Falsies—1. A term for false eyelashes. 2. A term for breast accessories that are inserted into a bra.

Fan dance—in burlesque, a dance that uses large feather, silk or original fans to cover a nude (or the illusion of a nude) body

Fan dancer—a dancer who specializes in the fan dance, e.g. Sally Rand and Jean Idell.

Fan work—in burlesque, using fans as part of an act.

Female impersonator—traditionally, a cis-male dressing and acting like a woman in performance, sometimes impersonating celebrities.

Femme fatale—a beautiful woman who can inflict violence or puts men in danger when they are distracted by her beauty.

Fetish—an obsession with or desire for something outside the social norm that is often sexual in nature.

Fetish model—a model demonstrating fetishized qualities, clothing or behavior, e.g. latex clothing, dominatrix attire and dungeon environment, shibari.

Fetish scene—a counter-culture movement of people who are interested in fetish activities, dress and lifestyle.

Filament—for 3D printing—coiled plastic (or other materials including metal and organic matter) strip that is inserted into 3D printers and melted to construct 3D designs.

Fire tassel—pasties with tassels that can be lit on fire and twirled.

Firebrand—a revolutionary pioneer.

Fishnet—in clothing—a stretch mesh fabric that is most commonly used for tights and shirts. The holes in the mesh can range in size, and the color of fishnet ranges, but popular colors are black and fleshtone.

Fishtail gown—see Mermaid gown. A fitted gown that widens from the knee down creating a triangular silhouette from knee to hem.

Flapper—a 1920s woman who lived a free spirited lifestyle and shed the conservative views and social constraints of the Victorian era.

Flasher—in burlesque, an accessory that is worn over the front pubic area, suspended on an elastic or band around the hips, and is not secured between the legs to allow for a "flash" of flesh when a dancer does bumps and grinds. The flasher is decorative and often has fringe applied to accentuate movement.

Floor work—in burlesque—performing movement or choreography on the stage floor.

Folies Bergerè—The long-running French follies show that Ziegfeld based his revues on.

Follies—as in Ziegfeld Follies, a live show that includes large group dance and musical numbers including choruses of women in ornate costumes, sometimes revealing partial nudity.

Full-nude nightclubs—strip clubs that require dancers to get completely nude at the end of their act, or when dancing a set.

G-string—an undergarment that has a triangular panel to cover the pubic area and between the legs joined with an elastic band that goes between the buttocks and attaches to an elastic waistband.

Garter belt—an elastic belt or wider band that has garters attached front and back to clip onto tall stockings and keep them from rolling down the leg. Garter belts traditionally have two clips for each leg, but some have additional clips on the sides.

Garter clip— a metal clip with a rubber tab used to hold stockings up when attached to a garter. The tab is placed under the stocking and the metal loop goes over the stocking and around the rubber tab. (See p. 000 corselet garter clip, Chapter 3.)

Garter— An elasticized band or loop with a metal clasp to attach to a stocking or sock, which helps keep it up on the leg. Garters can be bands worn around the calf, or attached to corselets or belts for longer stockings that reach the thigh. A decorative garter is an elastic band that has lace or embellishment and is worn around the thigh without any stocking-controlling function.

Gauntlet—in burlesque—a fingerless glove that covers the arm up to mid-bicep, or a fingerless glove that has a flange or flare from the wrist outward. (See pp. 000–000, Chapter 3.)

Gender fluidity—allowance for all genders; a concept of undefined gender.

Gig—a booking or job. A gig can be a long-term job in one location, or a one night booking.

Girdle—an undergarment that covers the waist to below the buttocks and is very fitted to help create a smooth silhouette. Often has garters attached.

Glitter glove—a burlesque convention when a handful of glitter or confetti is hidden in the interior palm of a glove, which enables the performer to throw a shower of glitter into the air when the glove is removed.

Glove peel—sensual removal of a glove in a burlesque act.

Go-go dancing—dancing on a stage, bar, in a cage or other performative area to live or recorded music, sometimes tips are collected. Go-go can be solo or with several dancers, who help add to the atmosphere of a disco, dance club, or music venue.

Grind—see also **Bump and grind**—a dance move that consists of slowly rotating the pelvis in a circular motion. Often used in combination with a "bump."

Grinder act—in burlesque or sideshow—an act that employs a metal grinder used against a special steel plate that is attached to one or more parts of a performer's costume. The grinder contact with the plate throws an arc of sparks.

Grommet—a round metal ring and a second ring with a collar that are hammered together with a setting tool to create a bound hole in fabric or leather. Grommets come in multiple sizes. Commonly seen on shoes or on the back of corsets.

Grosgrain—a type of ribbon that has horizontal ribbing across the width of the ribbon and a subtle scalloped edge because of the weave. Commonly used for hat bands and waistbands on undergarments like petticoats.

Guarantee—an agreed-upon fee for payment between a producer and performer.

Half and half act—an act where a performer portrays two characters at once, often with a costume that divides the body in half.

Harness—in burlesque—a garment made of straps that span the area of a bodysuit, or an accessory of straps that centers on the chest and upper back area.

Headliner—a performer that received top billing in a show.

High-brow—a classist term to describe activities implying an air of wealth or upper class.

High glam—the pinnacle of feminine glamour to the point of exaggeration.

Hoochie-coochie dance—also hootchy-kootchy—an early name for bellydance.

Hook and eye—a closure that employs a metal hook and a separate metal bar or loop. The pieces are sewn to opposite sides of an opening on a garment, and hook closed.

Hook—a gimmick.

Horsehair —a stiff wide-weave mesh trim made in varying widths. Now made of plastic, it used to be made of horsehair. Used to shape and stiffen hemlines on gowns and as loops in hats for securing to hair.

Hot pants—very short shorts that resemble a high-waisted brief.

Hula skirt—a skirt made of dried grass or raffia worn by hula dancers.

Hula—a style of dance created by the Hawaiian people.

Ice capades—travelling shows featuring ice skating performances within a theme. Former Olympic and US National Champion figure skaters who had retired from formal competition were featured. It began in 1940 and continued for 50 years.

Illusion pasties —a style of pastie that is built with a fine tulle or mesh border with rhinestones concentrated in the center and gradually decreasing toward the mesh. The wearing of illusion pasties gives the visual "illusion" that the pastie is blending into the skin.

In drag—in drag or burlesque—wearing makeup and clothing for performance.

Independent Wheel—one of the burlesque circuits known for being more risqué.

Isis wings—a bellydance accessory made with two half circles of pleated organza, joined to a neck band with dowels or rods at the ends of the outer edges so that the performer can extend their reach when dancing. Isis wings give a similar effect in motion to the butterfly dance of Loîe Fuller.

Jazz Age —a time in the 1920s and 1930s that jazz became a national phenomenon in the United States.

Jazz—a style of music originating in the Black American communities of New Orleans in the late nineteenth and early twentieth century with roots in the blues and ragtime genres.

Kinetoscope —an early film viewing device that allowed a series of still images to move rapidly over a light source.

Las Vegas Strip —the area of Las Vegas where hotels and casinos are concentrated.

Leg shows—in the late 1800s/early 1900s— any stage shows that displayed choruses of women dancing and flashing a bit of leg.

Leg-o-mutton sleeve —a sleeve shape of the late 1800s with a tremendous amount of volume at the cap of the sleeve and a slender fit from the elbow to wrist, resembling the shape of a leg of lamb.

Legitimate theater—mainstream theater, ballet and opera productions with higher ticket prices. A term of classist separation from burlesque and vaudeville performances attended by the common person.

Leotard—a long, short or sleeveless bodysuit ending around the top of the leg that is primarily worn in dance and gymnastics.

Lip sync —the act of realistically mouthing the words to a song, usually in performance.

Low-brow—a classist term to describe activities implying lower class or lack of taste.

Lyra—an aerial apparatus in the form of a hoop that spins, hung from the ceiling or rigged from the top.

Merkin—1. A pubic wig. 2. A decorative pubic cover that is adhered to the area, avoiding the straps of a g-string.

Mermaid gown—see Fishtail gown. A fitted gown that widens from the knee down creating a triangular silhouette from knee to hem.

Mermaid skirt—a skirt that widens from the knee down creating a triangular silhouette from knee to hem. See Mermaid gown and Fishtail gown.

Monokini—1. A topless bathing suit designed by Rudi Gernreich. 2. A bathing suit that covers the breasts and lower region of the body like a bikini, but that is connected in some way so that it is a one piece garment.

Mother of burlesque—a woman credited with some facet of the birth and/or endurance of burlesque.

Museum—a collection of artifacts and live displays that served as a form of public entertainment and education.

Music hall—a venue for live performances and socializing popular in the Victorian era.

Mutual Wheel —one of the burlesque circuits. It became the first where women bared their breasts.

Negligee—see **Duster**. A voluminous robe, sometimes with a matching nightgown and often made of sheer fabric.

Neo-burlesque—burlesque performance that began in the 1990s and continues to evolve today. It includes a multitude of styles including classic, boylesque, nerdlesque, and performance art.

Nerdlesque—a style of neo-burlesque that incorporates popular culture references including movies, TV, comics, and trends.

Net bra—a triangle-shaped bra that is made of tulle or stretch mesh. It is often embellished with beading or rhinestones.

Nickelodeon—a Victorian era venue where patrons paid a nickel to watch short films on kinetoscope or other early film devices.

Nightclub—in the 1940s and 1950s—a venue where couples could have a "night out" with dinner, dancing and entertainment.

Nuclear family—The "ideal" modern family of the 1950s. The nuclear family includes a mother and father, one sister and brother, and a pet.

Obscenity regulations—rules generated by obscenity and censorship groups in cities and towns that regulated social and leisure activities by defining what is inappropriate. These rules included dress codes, alcohol regulations and performance limitations. The obscenity regulations in New York City and Boston led to the first related legislation in the United States.

Organza—a stiff, sheer fabric made of silk or synthetic fibers popular for ruffled or voluminous garments.

Orientalism—a stereotyped representation of Asian style or traits that expresses a colonialist point of view.

Paillettes—metal or plastic disks similar in style to sequins, but larger in size and with a hole near one side instead of the center.

Panel skirt—a classic burlesque costume piece consisting of a waistband and individual pieces of fabric that commonly detach from the waistband for striptease reveals.

Papier mâché—a sculpting technique that involves shredded paper or paper pulp and paste smoothed over a mold that forms a hard layer when dry.

Parade and pose—an act or number where a performer walks the length of the stage and pauses intermittently to hold a still position.

Pasties—decorative costume accessories to cover the areola and nipple on a breast used most commonly on stage or anywhere a woman cannot legally be topless.

Performance art—a combination of dramatic live performance and visual art.

Petticoat—see **Crinoline**—a long underskirt worn to create volume or silhouette under a dress or outer skirt. Length ranges from short to floor length.

Pigeon-breasted—in the Victorian era—this desirable women's silhouette created a smooth rounded chest that narrowed at the waist, looking similar to the puffed breast of a bird.

Pin-up—1. A female presenting model that poses seductively, often in lingerie or a bathing suit. 2. An image or magazine tear of a female presenting model that can be hung on the wall.

Pinked seams—Raw seam edges that are cut with pinking shears to create a zig-zag shape. This is done to prevent fraying at the seams.

Pole dancing—a style of dance and fitness that uses a tall metal pole as a tool for gymnastic and sensual dance moves.

Pornography—print material and film that is overtly sexual in nature.

Porn theaters—theaters that screen pornographic films

Post-feminist—a person who was born after the second wave of feminism

Presentation of gender—the way one chooses to demonstrate their character or person. This can include feminine, masculine and non-binary qualities.

Pusty—see **Merkin**—a decorative pubic cover that is adhered to the area, avoiding the straps of a g-string.

Quiver dance—a style of dance that involves making parts of the body vibrate or shake subtly while standing relatively still.

Rave—an all-night dance party at a private space, festival location or nightclub that involves DJ curated music, special performances and attendees in original fashions that coincide with the party theme.

Resin stones—rhinestones or decorative stones made from resin, a moldable polymer.

Retro—from the past.

Reveal—a moment in an act where a performer removes an article of clothing or costume to show a surprise element or a part of the body.

Reverse strip—a burlesque act where a performer begins nude or in very little clothing and gets dressed.

Rhinestone—a glass or crystal faceted stone that is intended to look like a precious stones.

Rhinestoning—decorating or encrusting something with rhinestones by sewing or gluing them on.

Rise—the curved seam of trunks, pants or briefs that runs from the center front waist between the legs to the center back waist.

Rolled hem—a finishing technique where the raw edge of the fabric is turned twice to the inside of the garment and stitched down.

S-curve corset—a Victorian style corset that creates an "S" shape with a full bust, a nipped in waist, and a protruding back hip and buttocks.

Salomania—a period of time at the end of the nineteenth century when the Biblical character of Salome was a popular character featured in the Western arts, including fine art, theater, opera and dance. The term is mentioned by Nancy Pressly in her essay "Salome: La belle dame sans merci."

Second wave feminist movement—the feminist movement of the 1960s.

Seed bead—a typically glass bead that is a very small round ball with a hole in the center, typically 2–3 mm in size.

Self fabric—the same fabric used on the outside of a garment. This term is most often applied to lining.

Sequin—a small, flat, metal or plastic disc with a hole in the middle used for decoration. Typically 5–10mm, but varying in size. They can be sewn on individually, but are also sold "slung" on chain stitch strips.

Sexploitation films—films that explore controversial or outlandish sexual themes to attract an audience.

Shake dancing—see Shimmy dance, a dance style that involves isolating different body parts and shaking them, usually in a costume that is accented with fringe to accentuate the movement.

Shimmy—to move the body or parts of the body back and forth rhythmically.

Shimmy belt—a fringe belt worn at the hips to accentuate shake and shimmy dancing.

Shimmy dance—see Shake dancing, a dance style that involves isolating different body parts and shaking them, usually in a costume that is accented with fringe to accentuate the movement.

Shirtwaist—a Victorian blouse. Frequently with buttons or closures in the back and a decorative placket or yoke on the front.

Show—in burlesque, sideshow or stripping: an act.

Showgirl—a female presenting dancer that is in a follies style chorus or production, known for wearing extravagant, though often scant, costumes.

Sideshow—the secondary exhibits or performances accompanying a circus, museum or carnival.

Silent film—early film that had title cards for narration with background music and no vocalization from actors.

Silhouette—the shape of a garment or ensemble on a body.

Slung sequins—sequins that are strung with a chain stitch and can be sewn into lines and shapes.

Soubrette—1. A female character in an operetta that causes mischief or is sexual. Often a maid or servant. 2. A solo female or female presenting singer in a music hall.

Sourcing fabric—shopping and swatching fabric for a costume design or fashion collection.

Soutache— a fine trim that resembles a braid or flat cord commonly seen on uniforms in decorative flourishes.

Spandex—1. A polyester fabric that has four-way stretch 2. A stretch fiber that can be blended with others to create stretch in fabric.

Speakeasy— an illegal or underground bar or club.

Spinners—rotating metal fasteners that fishing lures are attached to so that they spin in the water.

Spirit gum—a cosmetic adhesive originally made of resin and ether.

Steel hooping—flat steel bands that can be cut to form circular hoops and inserted into tunnels on a skirt to create a voluminous shape without many layers.

Stiletto—a very slim heeled shoe that can range in height.

Stockings—thin socks that vary in color and in length from calf to thigh high. Worn with garters. Can be silk or synthetic.

Strip club—a dance club where women strip to varying degrees of nudity on stage for their audience.

Strip club style—see **Stripper-wear**—specific body-conscious fashion expected of dancers working in a strip club. Some examples include lingerie, slingshot bikinis, and string bikinis.

Stripper-wear—specific body-conscious fashion expected of dancers working in a strip club. Some examples include lingerie, slingshot bikinis, and string bikinis.

Striptease—removing clothing or the suggestion of removing clothing in a prolonged performance.

Strongwoman—the female version of a strong man in a circus or sideshow.

Suffrage—women's civil rights, especially the right to vote.

Swim club dancer—a dancer that wears a bathing suit and performs in a club with a pool. Swim clubs were popular in San Francisco in the 1960s.

Swing dance—the 1940s and 1950s style of fast-paced couples dancing. It has 6 count and 8 count styles including East Coast, West Coast, and the Lindy Hop. Swing dancing was re-popularized in the 1990s in Los Angeles.

Swing flags—large weighted silk pieces of varying shapes that are used in dance.

Swinger—in the 1990s—a person who frequents swing clubs and likes to swing dance.

Swinger clubs—In the 1990s, particularly in Los Angeles, clubs that featured swing dancing and live bands specializing in the same style of music. The clubs catered to a growing population of people interested in mid-century style and culture, also associated with the 1990s rockabilly and pinup movements.

Tableaux vivants—living pictures. Large-scale recreations of famous paintings and sculpture using live models.

Taffeta—a lightweight fabric that can be made of silk or synthetic fiber. It has a stiffness that holds sculptural shapes, and when layered, it makes a distinct noise as it moves against itself.

Talkies—early films with voice tracks.

Tap pants—high-waisted shorts worn by tap dancers with full leg openings to allow for free movement.

Tassel twirling—in burlesque—performing dance movements that make tassels on pasties twirl.

Tassels—a bundle of fringe, string or strung beads that is bound at the top

Tasticle—a tassel attached to the front of a man's g-string or thong that can be twirled when the performer thrusts his hips forward or in circles.

Tear-away—a garment that easily opens or is easily removed because of seams rigged with snap tape or Velcro.

Tease —in burlesque: to delay or simply suggest the removal of a garment while titillating the audience.

The Black Crook—the first American musical.

The New Look—Christian Dior's luxurious late 1940s clothing designs for women that included slim waists and voluminous skirts immediately after fabric rationing during WWII kept garments slim fitting.

Thermoplastic—a plastic material molded with heat.

Thong—an undergarment worn by either gender that covers the genitals in front and reveals the buttocks with only a fabric strip between them; joined by a waistband.

Transgender—a person born as one gender, but living and presenting as the opposite gender.

Trunks—briefs. A bottom undergarment or in the case of Victorian dancers, acrobats or circus performers, an outer costume garment worn over tights.

Tulle—a mesh fabric that can be made from synthetic or natural fibers available in varying degrees of stiffness.

Twerking—a dance style that involves vigorous thrusting of the buttocks while in a squatting position.

Underpinnings—undergarments.

Underwire—the stiff wire in the bottom of a bra cup used for support.

Variety Show—a presentation of different types of acts usually led by a host. Act styles can include dance, comedy, singing, animal acts, and more.

Vaudeville—a performance art form that developed alongside burlesque and included various styles of acts including burlesque.

Velcro—a fastener developed commercially in the 1970s that uses two opposing textured strips that stick together firmly but easily pull apart when desired. It can be sewn to garments or glued onto surfaces.

Vintage revival—in the 1990s in the US, mid-century style, fashion, cars, and furnishings became popular again.

Whopper popper—a very large snap in metal or plastic.

Worbla— a moldable thermoplastic sheeting or pebble that comes in multiple colors with two heat requirements.

Zig-zag stitch—a sewing machine stitch that moves side to side creating v shapes. The stitch is useful for stretch fabrics to help prevent thread breakage along seams.

BIBLIOGRAPHY

Abbott, Karen. *American Rose: A Nation Laid Bare: The Life and Times of Gypsy Rose Lee*. New York: Random House Trade Paperbacks, 2010.

Adams, Rachel. *Sideshow U.S.A.: Freaks and the American Cultural Imagination*. Chicago: University of Chicago Press, 2001.

Adams, Samuel Hopkins. "The Indecent Stage." *American Magazine* LXVIII (May, 1909): 41–47.

Allen, Robert C. *Horrible Prettiness: Burlesque and American Culture (Cultural Studies of the United States)*. Chapel Hill: University of North Carolina Press, 1991.

Allyn, David. *Make Love, Not War: The Sexual Revolution—An Unfettered History by David Allyn*. London: Little, Brown & Company, 2001.

Baker, Roger. *Drag: A History of Female Impersonation in the Performing Arts*. New York: NYU Press, 1995.

Barthes, Roland. "Striptease." In *Mythologies*, 84–87. New York: Hill and Wang, 1972.

Bentley, Toni. *Sisters of Salome*. Lincoln: University of Nebraska, 2005.

Bizot, Richard. "The Turn-of-the-Century Salome Era: High- and Pop-culture Variations on the Dance of the Seven Veils." In *Choreography and Dance*, Part 3. Vol. 2, 71–87. United Kingdom: Harwood Academic Publishers GmbH, 1992.

Borgdan, Robert. *Freak Show: Presenting Human Oddities for Amusement and Profit*. Reprint 2009 ed. Chicago: University of Chicago Press, 1990.

Bosse, Katharina. *New Burlesque*. Paperback ed. Chicago, IL: Distributed Art Publishers Inc., 2004.

Briggeman, Jane. *Burlesque: A Living History*. Albany, GA: BearManor Media, 2009.

Brown, Julie K. *Contesting Images: Photography and the World's Columbian Exposition*. Tucson: University of Arizona, 1994.

Bryk, Nancy V. *American Dress Pattern Catalogs*. Mineola, NY: Dover Publications, 1909.

Buszek, Maria Elena. *Pin-Up Grrrls: Feminism, Sexuality, Popular Culture*. Durham, NC: Duke University Press, 2006.

Carlton, Donna. *Looking for Little Egypt*. Bloomington, IN: IDD Books, 2002.

Carr, Michelle and Klanten, Robert. *The Velvet Hammer Burlesque*. Berlin: Die-Gestalten-Verl, 2008.

Castle, Charles. *The Folies Bergère*. London: Methuen Publishing Ltd, 1984.

Cherniavsky, Felix. *The Salome Dancer: The Life and Times of Maud Allan*. Toronto: McClelland & Stewart, 1991.

Churchill, Allen. *The Theatrical 20s*. New York: McGraw-Hill, 1975.

Corio, Ann and DiMona, Joseph. *This was Burlesque: A Rollicking, Colorfully Illustrated History of Burlesque as Seen through the Eyes of its First Lady*. New York: Castle Books, 1968.

Cox, Caroline. *Lingerie: A Lexicon of Style*. 1st ed. New York: Thomas Dunne Books, 2001.

Davis, Nanette J. and Jone M. Keith, eds. *Women and Deviance: Issues in Social Conflict and Change: An Annotated Bibliography*. Routledge Library Editions: Women and Crime (Book 1). 1st ed. Vol. 5. New York: Routledge, 2015.

DeCaro, Frank, 1962 and Gideon Lewin. *Unmistakably Mackie*. New York: Universe Pub., 1999.

Denuet, Richard. *Inside Hollywood: 60 Years of Globe Photos*, edited by Konemann Inc. 1st US ed. New York: Konemann, 2001.

Derval, Paul. *The Folies Bergère*. 1st British ed. London: Methuen & Co. Ltd, 1955.

Dinardo, Kelly. *Gilded Lili: Lili St. Cyr and the striptease mystique*. 1st ed. New York: Back Stage Books, 2007.

Donahue, Matthew A. *I'll Take You There: An Oral and Photographic History of the Hines Farm Blues Club*. Toledo: Jive Bomb Press, 1999.

Edwards, Holly, Brian T. Allen, and Francine Clark Art Institute. *Noble Dreams, Wicked Pleasures: Orientalism in America, 1870–1930*. Princeton, NJ: Princeton University Press, 2000.

Ellmann, Richard. *Oscar Wilde*. New York: Alfred A Knopf, 1988.

Emery, Lynne Fauley. *Black Dance in the United States from 1619 to 1970*. London: National Press Books, 1972.

Farnell, Gary. "The Enigma of 'La Belle Dame Sans Merci.'" *Romanticism* 17, no. 2 (2011): 195–208, http://proxy.library.nyu.edu/login?url=http://search.ebscohost.com.proxy.

library.nyu.edu/login.aspx?direct=true&db=a9h&AN=63287
224&site=eds-live (accessed February 2018).

Farnsworth, Marjorie. *The Ziegfeld Follies: A History in Text and
Pictures.* New York: P. Davies, 1957.

Fliotsos, Anne. "Gotta Get a Gimmick: The Burlesque Career of
Millie De Leon." *Journal of American Culture* 21, no. 4: 1–8,
Winter 1998.

Friedman, Andrea. *Prurient Interests: Gender, Democracy, and
Obscenity in New York City, 1909-1945.* New York: Columbia
University Press, 2000.

Garelick, Rhonda. *Electric Salome.* 1st ed. New Jersey: Princeton
University Press, 2009.

Goldstein, Laurence. *The Female Body: Figures, Styles, Speculations.*
1st ed. Ann Arbor: University of Michigan Press, 1991.

Goldwyn, Liz. *Pretty Things: The Last Generation of American
Burlesque Queens.* Vol. 103 Chicago: American Library
Association, 2006.

Govey, Geoffrey. *Hot Strip Tease.* London: Cresset Press, 1934.

Granfield, Linda and Dominique Jando, eds. *The Circus Book,
1870s–1950s. The Greatest Show on Earth: The History and
Legacy of the Circus,* edited by Noel Daniel. Cologne,
Germany: TASCHEN, 2010.

Green, William. "Strippers and Coochers—the Quintessence of
American Burlesque." In *Western Popular Theatre,* edited by
David Mayer and Kenneth Richards, 167–169. London:
Methuen & Co. Ltd, 1977.

Hanna, Judith Lynne. *Dance, Sex, and Gender: Signs of Identity,
Dominance, Defiance, and Desire.* 2nd ed. Chicago, IL:
University of Chicago Press, 1988.

Hansen, Chadwick. "Jenny's Toe: Negro Shaking Dances in
America." *American Quarterly* 19, no. 3 (1967): 554–
563, www.jstor.org.proxy.library.nyu.edu/stable/2711072
(accessed July 2018).

Hart, Avril and Susan North. *Fashion in Detail: From the 17th and
18th Centuries.* New York: Rizzoli, 1998.

Hartzman, Marc. *American Sideshow: An Encyclopedia of History's
Most Wondrous and Curiously Strange Performers.* Reprint ed.
New York: TarcherPerigee, 2006.

Immerso, Michael. *Coney Island: The People's Playground.*
Piscataway, NJ: Rutgers University Press, 2002.

Ives, Halsey C. *The Dream City. A Portfolio of Photographic Views of
the World's Columbian Exposition.* 1st ed. St. Louis, MO: N.D.
Thompson Publishing Co., 1893.

Janes, Brian C. *It's all that Glitters: Portraits of Burlesque Performers
in their Homes.* Atglen, PA: Schiffer Publishing Ltd, 2012.

Kasson, John F. *Amusing the Million: Coney Island at the Turn of the
Century.* American Century. 1st ed. New York: Hill & Wang,
1978.

Kendall, Elizabeth. *Where She Danced.* 1st ed. New York: Knopf,
1979.

La Rouge, Rosey. *The Pastie Project.* New York: Blurb Books, 2017.

Landis, Deborah Nadoolman. *Dressed: A Century of Hollywood
Costume Design.* Limited ed. New York: Harper Design,
2007.

Langum, David J. *Crossing Over the Line: Legislating Morality and
the Mann Act.* Chicago Series on Sexuality, History, and
Society. 1st ed. Chicago, IL: University of Chicago Press,
2007.

Latham, Angela J. *Posing a Threat: Flappers, Chorus Girls, and Other
Brazen Performers of the American 1920s.* 1st ed. Hanover,
NH: Wesleyan University Press, 2000.

Leinwand, Gerald. *1927: High Tide of The Twenties.* New York:
Four Walls Eight Windows, 2001.

Mankowitz, Wolf. *Mazeppa, the Lives, Loves, and Legends of Adah
Isaacs Menken: A Biographical Quest.* 1st ed. New York: Stein
& Day Publishing, 1982.

March, April and Sue Baird. *Reflections of My Life—April March:
The First Lady of Burlesque.* Manchester, VT: Shirespress,
2016.

Matlaw, Myron, ed. *American Popular Entertainment.* Papers and
Proceedings of the Conference on the History of American
Popular Entertainment. Westport, CT: Greenwood Press,
1977.

Minsky, Morton and Milt Machlin. *Minsky's Burlesque: A Fast and
Funny Look at America's Bawdiest Era.* 1st ed. Gettysburg, PA:
Arbor House, 1986.

Morrison, Denton E. and Carlin Paige Holden. *The Burning Bra:
The American Breast Fetish and Women's Liberation: A
Scholarly Analysis of Fashion, Status, and Sex* Okemos, Mich: A.
Brown Printing and Typing Service, 1970.

Murray, Ken. *The Body Merchant: The Story of Earl Carroll.* 1st ed.
Pasadena, CA: Ward Ritchie Press, 1976.

Newquist, Roy. *Showcase.* New York: William Morrow & Co.,
1966.

Newton, Esther. *Mother Camp: Female Impersonators in America.*
Chicago, IL: University of Chicago Press, 1979.

Olian, JoAnne. *Everyday Fashions of the Fifties as Pictured in Sears
Catalogs (Dover Fashion and Costumes).* Dover Fashion and
Costumes. Mineola, NY: Dover Publications, 2002.

Prewitt, Terry J. "Like a Virgin: The Semiotics of Illusion in Erotic
Performance." *American Journal of Semiotics* 6, no. 4 (1989):
137–152.

Raffe, Walter George. *Dictionary of the Dance.* New York: Barnes;
Yoseloff, 1964.

Redniss, Lauren. *Century Girl: 100 Years in the Life of Doris Eaton
Travis, Last Living Star of the Ziegfeld Follies.* Reprint ed. New
York: It Books, HarperCollins Publishers, 2012.

Regehr, Kaitlyn and Matilda Temperley. *The League of Exotic Dancers: Legends from Americans Burlesque*. 1st ed. New York: Oxford University Press Inc., 2017.

Robertson, Pamela. *Guilty Pleasures: Feminist Camp from Mae West to Madonna*. London, UK: Duke University Press Books, 1996.

Ross, Becki. *Burlesque West: Showgirls, Sex, and Sin in Postwar Vancouver*. 1st ed. Vancouver, Toronto: University of Toronto Press, 2009.

Rothe, Len. *The Queens of Burlesque: Vintage Photographs from the 1940s and 1950s*. Schiffer Pictorial Essay. 1st ed. Atglen, PA: Schiffer Publishing, 1997.

Saffle, Michael and James R. Heintze, eds. *Music and Culture in America, 1861–1918 (Essays in American Music)*. Essays in American Music (Book 2). 1st ed. New York: Garland Publishing Inc., 1998.

Salen, Jill. *Corsets: Historical Patterns; Technique*. Hollywood, CA: Costume and Fashion Press, 2007.

Seidel, Linda. *Salome and the Canons*. Vol. 11:1–2, 29–66. London/New York: Taylor and Francis, 1984.

Senelick, Laurence, ed. *Gender in Performance: The Presentation of Difference in the Performing Arts*, essays by Jill Dolan, Adrian Kiernander, John Emigh, Judith Lynne Hanna, Ann Daly, Karl Toepfer, Megan Terry, et al. Hanover, NH: University Press of New England, 1992.

Shteir, Rachel. *Striptease: The Untold History of the Girlie Show*. Oxford: Oxford University Press, 2005.

Shteir, Rachel and Mark Crispin Miller. *Gypsy: The Art of the Tease (Icons of America)*. New Haven, CT: Yale University Press, 2009.

Sobel, Bernard. *Burleycue: An Underground History of Burlesque Days*. Reprint ed. New York: B. Franklin, 1975.

———. *A Pictorial History of Burlesque*. New York: Putnam, 1956.

Sochen, June. *Enduring Values: Women in Popular Culture*. Media and Society Series. Santa Barbara, CA: Praeger, 1987.

Starr, Blaze and Huey Perry. *Blaze Starr: My Life as Told by Huey Perry*. 1st ed. Santa Barbara, CA: Praeger Publishers, 1974.

Teese, Dita Von. *Burlesque and the Art of the Teese/ Fetish and the Art of the Teese*. New York: It Books, Harpers Bazaar, 2006.

Thorpe, Edward. *Black Dance*. Woodstock, NY: The Overlook Press, 1995.

Toll, Robert C. *The Entertainment Machine: American Show Business in the Twentieth Century*. New York: Oxford University Press, 1982.

Ullman, Sharon R. *Sex Seen: The Emergence of Modern Sexuality in America*. 1st ed. Oakland, CA: University of California Press, 1998.

Urish, Ben. "Narrative Striptease in the Nightclub Era." *The Journal of American Culture* 27, no. 2 (June, 2004): 157–165, https://onlinelibrary-wiley-com.proxy.library.nyu.edu/doi/abs/10.1111/j.1537-4726.2004.00126.x (accessed February 2018).

Watts, Jill. *Mae West, an Icon in Black and White*. Oxford: Oxford University Press: 2001.

Weinraub, Bernard. "Obscenity or Art? A Stubborn Issue" *New York Times*, July 7, 1969, https://search-proquest.com.proxy.library.nyu.edu/cv_525234/docview/118632949/A7EEA8A2F0C84CCAPQ/1?accountid=12768 (accessed October 2, 2017).

Weldon, Jo. *The Burlesque Handbook*. New York: Harper Collins, 2010.

Wesely, Jennifer K. "'Where Am I Going to Stop?': Exotic Dancing, Fluid Body Boundaries, and Effects on Identity." *Deviant Behavior* 24, no. 5 (September, 2003): 483–503. New York: Taylor and Francis, 2003

West, Mae. *The Constant Sinner, Babe Gordon*. 1st ed. New York: Macaulay Co., 1930.

Wilde, Brandy. *Tease*. 1st ed. Ventura, CA: Purple Distinctions, 2015.

Willett, C. and Phillis Cunnington. *The History of Underclothes*. Dover Fashion and Costumes. New York: Dover Publications, 1992.

Willson, Jacki. *The Happy Stripper*. 1st ed. London: IB Tauris & Co. Ltd, 2008.

Zeidman, Irving. *The American Burlesque Show*. 1st ed. New York: Hawthorn Books, 1967. Zemeckis, Leslie Harter and Blaze Starr. *Behind the Burly Q: The Story of Burlesque in America*. New York: Skyhorse Publishing, 2013.

Zemeckis, Leslie Harter. *Feuding Fan Dancers: Faith Bacon, Sally Rand, and the Golden Age of the Showgirl*. 1st ed. Berkeley, CA: Counterpoint, 2018

Zemeckis, Leslie Harter. *Goddess of Love Incarnate: The Life of Stripteuse Lili St. Cyr*. Reprint ed. Berkeley, CA: Counterpoint, 2016.

Ziegfeld, Richard and Paulette Ziegfeld. *The Ziegfeld Touch: The Life and Times of Florenz Ziegfeld, Jr.* 1st ed. Harry N Abrams Inc, 1993.

FILMOGRAPHY

A Wink and A Smile. Directed by Deirdre Allen Timmons. Starring: Miss Indigo Blue, Diane Bruch. United States: Doc Club, 2009. Streaming online—Amazon Prime.

Behind the Burly Q—The Story of Burlesque in America. Directed by Leslie Zemeckis. Featuring: Alan Alda, Dixie Evans. United States: Mistress Inc., 2011. DVD.

Bound by Flesh. Directed by Leslie Harter Zemeckis. United States: Mistress Inc, 2012. Streaming online—Amazon Prime.

Exotic World and The Burlesque Revival. Directed by Red Tremmel. Starring: Dixie Evans, Margaret Cho. United States: Unavailable, 2012. Streaming online—Netflix.

Getting Naked: A Burlesque Story. Directed by James Lester. Starring: Hazel Honeysuckle, Darlinda Just Darlinda, Gal Friday, Jezebel Express. United States: Scott Rayow Productions, 2017. Streaming online—Netflix.

Stripped. Directed by Jill Morley. Starring: Billie Madley. United States: A Jill Morley Production, 2001. Private request online access August 27, 2018.

Stripper. Directed by Jerome Gary. Starring: Janette Boyd, Sara Costa, Kimberly Holcomb. United States: Embassy International Pictures, Twentieth Century Fox, Visionaire Communications Inc., 1985. Streaming online—Amazon Prime.

INDEX

Note: page numbers in italic refer to figures or captions.

T - #0225 - 091120 - C320 - 279/216/19 - PB - 9781138742260 - Gloss Lamination